GIDEON'S PROMISE

GIDEON'S PROMISE

A

PUBLIC DEFENDER MOVEMENT

TO TRANSFORM

CRIMINAL JUSTICE

JONATHAN RAPPING

BEACON PRESS · BOSTON

BEACON PRESS
Boston, Massachusetts
www.beacon.org

Beacon Press books
are published under the auspices of
the Unitarian Universalist Association of Congregations.

23 22 21 20   8 7 6 5 4 3 2 1

This book is printed on acid-free paper that meets the uncoated paper
ANSI/NISO specifications for permanence as revised in 1992.

Text design and composition by Kim Arney

Library of Congress Cataloging-in-Publication Data

Names: Rapping, Jonathan, author.
Title: Gideon's promise : a public defender movement to transform
criminal justice / Jonathan Rapping.
Description: Boston : Beacon Press, 2020. | Includes bibliographical
references and index.
Identifiers: LCCN 2019059060 (print) | LCCN 2019059061 (ebook) |
ISBN 9780807064627 (hardcover) | ISBN 9780807064986 (ebook)
Subjects: LCSH: Public defenders—United States. | Legal assistance to the
poor—United States. | Rapping, Jonathan. | Public defenders—United
States—Biography. | Gideon's Promise (Organization)
Classification: LCC KF9646 . R37 2020 (print) | LCC KF9646 (ebook) |
DDC 345.73/0126—dc23
LC record available at https://lccn.loc.gov/2019059060
LC ebook record available at https://lccn.loc.gov/2019059061

AUTHOR'S NOTE

This book is a collection of experiences that have clarified for me what
drives our modern approach to criminal justice and helped me to see a
path forward. There are conversations I recount for which I cannot recall
the wording verbatim. But I have tried to be as accurate in my recollec-
tion as possible. Discussions are in quotation marks to illustrate dialogue
between participants. Any quotes that are precise are cited. Those that are
not cited are based on my memory. In all cases, the spirit and messaging
of every conversation presented here is true.

To my parents, Leonard and Elayne, for giving me guidance.
To my life partner, Ilham, for giving me support.
And mostly to my children, Aaliyah and Lucas,
for giving me boundless hope for the future.

[The assistance of counsel] is one of the safeguards of the Sixth Amendment deemed necessary to insure fundamental human rights of life and liberty. . . . The Sixth Amendment stands as a constant admonition that, if the constitutional safeguards it provides be lost, justice will not "still be done."

—*Gideon v. Wainwright*, 372 U.S. 335 (1963),
citing *Johnson v. Zerbst*, 304 U.S. 458, 304 U.S. 462 (1938)

CONTENTS

A SHARED VISION

I DECIDED I WANTED TO BE A LAWYER the first time I walked into a courtroom. I could not have been more than six years old. My parents were activists in Pittsburgh, Pennsylvania. As Jews, they both embraced the concept of Tikkun Olam: that we all have a duty to help repair the world. My sister and I were taught that we had an obligation to stand up to oppression. We would frequently accompany our parents to various demonstrations.

On this occasion, several friends had been arrested protesting the Vietnam War. I went to court with my mother to show support. Even at this young age, I had been taught to have a healthy dose of skepticism of authority. True to these teachings, I went to court with my toy water gun tucked in my pants.

I remember the courtroom being packed with protestors, and a heavy police presence lining the walls. The audience was vocal in its support of the accused, and the police appeared ready for confrontation. Amid the chaos, our friends stood at counsel table. Their lawyers were by their sides. To me, these defenders were like superheroes, ready to protect our friends from whatever the law enforcement machine was trying to do to them. I wanted to run up to the defense table and stand with the lawyers. It seemed safer up there.

All of a sudden, the lights in the courtroom went out. I heard yelling. I felt myself get bumped. I held my mother's hand tightly and waited for the lights to come back on. When they did, some of our friends in the audience had been roughed up. A few were being arrested. I looked over and saw the sleeve of my mother's coat was ripped. At that moment, I understood courtrooms as places where it was possible for injustice to happen. I knew that I wanted to be on the side of those arrested. I decided then that I wanted to defend people.

At about the same time I first stepped into a courtroom, a man named Donald Brown was robbing people in Buffalo, New York. Until that point, he had spent his adulthood surviving outside the law. But he was on the cusp of making a transition in life. Within a few years, Brown would convert to Islam, take the name Shakir Askia, invest in a fish market, marry an intelligent and hardworking girl from downtown Buffalo, and begin to raise a family. Ilham—"Illy," as I would come to call her—would be their first child together. By the time Illy was five years old she would have two younger sisters and her mother would be pregnant with her baby brother. But to Illy, she may as well have been her father's only child. He was Illy's world, and she felt like nothing in life competed for his attention. He assured her that she was beautiful, smart, and capable. He was her everything.

And then her world shattered. Shakir was arrested for crimes he had committed years earlier. He was given a public defender who did not seem to care. The defender did not fight for Illy's father. He never offered a counternarrative to the picture of "Donald Brown" painted by the state. Without a voice committed to telling Shakir's story, he was convicted and sent to Attica state prison for ten years.

In the early years, Illy maintained a relationship through visits to the prison. But over time, the strain of trying to stay connected to Shakir, who became increasingly institutionalized, took its toll. He began to fade from her life.

As Illy grew up in Buffalo, she would watch almost every man in her family get caught up in the criminal justice system. She helped raise her baby brother, even bringing him to live with her when she attended Cornell University. But without any male role models in his life who were not involved with the system, he too spent time incarcerated.

As difficult as it was being separated from the men Illy loved, the greatest toll the experience took was leaving her with the understanding that the lives of the people in her black community have less value than the lives of other people in our society. She learned at the tender age of five that some lives do not matter.

Illy and I both had our first experiences with the criminal legal system very early in life. We both learned that the system is not fair. We each had very different reactions to that experience. I saw lawyers as valiant defenders of justice in an unjust world. That experience shaped my ultimate career path. I would go on to become a public defender, an advocate devoted to fighting for the most marginalized members of society in our nation's criminal courtrooms.

Illy's experience taught her that the system was hostile to the people she loved. It viewed her community as subhuman. It destroyed families and left children scarred, without a shred of empathy for the people harmed along the way. In her experience, the lawyer was not a hero at all. He was the medium through which her family came to understand that their lives did not matter. It was through the public defender that the callousness and indifference of the criminal justice system was so clearly conveyed.

Unlike me, Illy decided she wanted nothing to do with the criminal justice system. She decided to become a schoolteacher. She would dedicate her life to helping children like herself escape the cradle-to-prison pipeline that claimed so many people she knew and loved.

Illy and I met in Washington, DC, where she began her career as a first-grade teacher in a community similar to the one that raised her—low-income, predominantly African American, presumed dangerous. She understood it was a neighborhood filled with wonderful people, with incredible potential and little opportunity. I was a few years into my career as a public defender in the same city. My work frequently brought me to the neighborhood where she taught. I learned that to be effective, public defenders had to be committed to learning and telling the stories of impacted people. They had to listen to those they served. They truly had to value their voices.

Illy and I would soon fall in love and eventually marry. As our relationship blossomed, she got to know the many passionate public defenders I worked with. They were a very different type of public defender than those she'd experienced growing up in Buffalo. She saw that public defenders could be incredibly important allies to the communities she cared about. She began to believe that a public defender office that truly respected the people it served could be a powerful vehicle against the demands of a callous system.

Illy quickly came to understand the inevitable intersection of the criminal justice system and urban education. Every child in her classroom was experiencing some degree of trauma from living in the wake of mass incarceration. She realized that, left unaddressed, the problems within the criminal justice system that she sought to distance herself from would make it impossible for educators to give children the help they need. She began to understand that a dedicated public defender could be the vehicle through which families like hers could attain justice.

AFTER NEARLY A DECADE IN DC, I moved to Atlanta to work on indigent defense reform in the South. Over the next three years, I helped establish a statewide public defender system in Georgia, and I joined the effort to rebuild a public defender office in New Orleans in the wake of Hurricane Katrina. I also did some indigent defense work in Alabama and Mississippi. It was my introduction to criminal justice systems that had come to accept an embarrassingly low standard of justice for poor people. The systems pressured everyone within them to aim for this low standard. The only realistic way to survive in these systems was to adapt. It was simply too hard to continue to care in such an unfeeling environment. I came to understand that nothing determined the quality of criminal justice more than culture.

Meanwhile, as a teacher, Illy saw the same challenges from her childhood plaguing the communities she taught in southwest Atlanta. The families she worked with often felt helpless when a person they cared about was pulled into the system. They frequently felt like the public defender was part of the very system that was swallowing their loved one. Through my work, Illy knew that many of the public defenders cared very much. But they were often resigned to a system that treated vulnerable populations as though they did not matter. She understood that public defenders had become part of the problem. She also realized public defenders were a critical piece of the solution.

So in 2007, when I decided to launch an organization that would transform public defense in the South, Illy agreed to take time away from teaching to help me. She was convinced cultural forces made it impossible for good public defenders to become the lawyers their clients deserved, and I was convinced that we could provide these advocates with the supportive community they needed to resist the pressures. Illy had come to believe that with the proper training and support, public defenders could ensure that poor communities have a voice in the system. This was a voice the men she loved never had. She believed this was critical for the psychological well-being of children with loved ones in the system. She understood this effort as more than criminal justice reform work; for her it was about healing communities.

Our experiences were critical to our shared understanding of the criminal justice challenge facing us. We imagined public defenders who embraced their roles as agents and advocates for vulnerable populations. We dreamed of communities that saw public defenders as trusted allies in their ongoing struggle for racial and economic justice. Informed by the convergence of these two journeys, Illy and I started the Southern Public Defender Training Center as a program to groom young defenders into change agents who could begin to raise the standard of justice immediately while preparing to become tomorrow's criminal justice leaders. Within six years, the initiative blossomed into a much more comprehensive model for reform, with a significantly more ambitious mission, and a new name: Gideon's Promise.

IN 1963, THE SUPREME COURT decided the case of *Gideon v. Wainwright*, guaranteeing the right to a lawyer for all people accused of crimes if they could not afford one. In this sense, it birthed public defense. *Gideon* reminded the nation of the American promise of equal justice and emphasized that this ideal could be realized only through a committed and capable lawyer.

This book is the story of Gideon's Promise—the organization. But it is also a clarion call to all of us to recognize the critical role that public defenders must play in the ongoing struggle to fulfill the promise of equal justice. This book urges us to reenvision our criminal justice challenge as a cultural dilemma, and it warns that policy fixes alone will not get us where we need to go. It presses us to recognize the power of a public defender movement, in alliance with impacted communities, to drive this cultural transformation. And, unlike so many other books that discuss the problems with the current approach to criminal justice, it provides a blueprint to accomplish this task.

This story will be told in three parts. In the first part, I look at the role of culture in shaping our criminal legal system—how it is impacted by our perception of marginalized communities and how those communities deserve to be treated—and the role of public defenders in challenging this narrative and reminding us of what justice demands. It challenges us to imagine what it would take to truly value and protect the dignity and freedom of all people the way the men who drafted our Constitution imagined for the privileged few. The second part introduces a model to drive culture change and examines the work of Gideon's Promise in applying these lessons to the field of public defense. The third part proposes a strategy to transform criminal justice culture more broadly.

Before getting started, I want to make clear that culture is powerful. Systems shaped by corrupted value sets can mold anyone into a professional they never meant to become. In this book, you will meet a number of people who have come to perpetuate injustice. I do not mean to criticize any individual or to suggest that they are the problem. This is a story about how even the noblest of public defenders—the legal professionals I most admire—cannot last in this system for too long unscathed. Some of the lawyers you will meet in the book never deserved the title "public defender." Some have been shaped into uncaring lawyers over time. Some have been heroic advocates for years, despite the constant barrage of pressure to perpetuate the status quo. However, I believe public defenders are our best hope to transform the narrative that drives our criminal legal system. But it will require that we mobilize them into a collective force with the resources and support to do so.

The work Illy and I have committed ourselves to urges us all to look deeper; to tackle the powerful forces that have long kept us from realizing our democratic aspirations. And it proposes a comprehensive strategy to begin this process. It is a strategy that requires our collective will. It requires a long-term commitment to real justice. But if we fail to tackle the cultural challenge laid out in this book, and continue to offer surface-level policy fixes, we will ensure that another generation will have to grapple with the next manifestation of America's corrupted value system.

So come with me. Let's try another way.

PART I

VALUES

CHAPTER 1

VOICE FOR THE VOICELESS

THIS IS AMERICA!

"Baseball, hot dogs, apple pie, and Chevrolet."

It was 1974 when that jingle first echoed from television sets across the nation. Chevrolet had just launched a new campaign to reinvent itself. It was wildly successful.

The most popular commercial of my childhood masterfully positioned a car brand among the most iconic symbols of America. It is an association I still make forty years later.

What none of us could have known was that at the time the nation was also beginning a new campaign to reinvent itself. It was the dawn of a newly launched crusade against crime. The idea was to increase popular demand for a new commodity—protection from bad people—so that politicians could appeal to the public by providing it. This campaign required that we first invent a whole new population of criminals. We would then build the systems needed to capture them. Finally, we would invest in the cages to warehouse them. It was the beginning of mass incarceration.

In 2015, Chevrolet remade its classic commercial.[1] That familiar jingle played once again, desperately trying to convince the audience that these same symbols still captured the essence of American life. But, forty years later, a new, quintessentially American symbol had emerged.

It was the prison. In the four decades since the Chevrolet commercial debuted, no institution had become more a part of who we are as a nation. It had surpassed any sport, food, or automobile as representative of our country.

Since 1970, when America's jails and prisons housed fewer than two hundred thousand people, our incarcerated population has increased by 700 percent.[2] Today, the American penal system cages roughly 2.3 million people in its prisons and jails.[3] Another 4.5 million are on probation or parole, bringing the total number of Americans under correctional control to nearly seven million.

While one in twenty people worldwide live in America, 25 percent of all people incarcerated globally are locked up in our country. Thirty-one of our fifty states have higher incarceration rates than any country other than America. Only nine countries have incarceration rates higher than Massachusetts, the state with the lowest rate of incarceration.[4]

This data alone is staggering. But as we dig deeper, it is clear that our approach to criminal justice shatters another myth: that the quality of justice a person receives is independent of their income or race.

Not true.

Not only is America's penal system the largest in the world, it is also one of the few systems to which a person has greater access the less income they have. Roughly 80 percent of people accused of crimes cannot afford a lawyer, increasing the likelihood that they will end up convicted. A boy raised by a family in the bottom 10 percent of the income distribution is twenty times more likely to be incarcerated as an adult than is a boy raised by a family in the top 10 percent.[5] One study found that less than half of all incarcerated people were employed for two full years before being incarcerated. It also found that of those who were, the median income was only $6,250.[6] Indeed, our criminal justice system has been created for the most economically disadvantaged.

It is also a system to which one's access increases with one's skin color. Sixty percent of the people in our jails and prisons are racial and ethnic minorities.[7] Since roughly 75 percent of Americans are white,[8] this figure should be alarming. While 0.4 percent of white Americans are among those incarcerated, the figure for black Americans is 2.2 percent.[9] In short, African Americans are nearly six times as likely to be incarcerated as are their white counterparts. For African American men in their thirties, one in every ten is in prison or jail at any given time.[10] In fact, soon after I began my career as a public defender in Washington, DC, a study revealed that, in that city, nearly 50 percent of all black men between the ages of eighteen and thirty-five were under the supervision of the criminal justice system.[11] This is not surprising when one learns that a black male born today has a one-in-three chance of being incarcerated at some time in his life.[12]

But perhaps the biggest misconception about our criminal justice system is that we are all presumed innocent, and that this presumption is really hard for the government to overcome. One may offer justifications for why our criminal justice system is so large. One may have theories about why certain populations are disproportionately impacted. Nevertheless, we believe that no person ends up convicted of a crime, and locked behind bars, without going through a process that ensures a just result. The presumption of innocence is at the heart of our democracy, as are the constitutional protections that force the government to prove that a person no longer deserves that presumption.

The reality is, our system could not be further from that ideal. People are not protected when they are charged with a crime. Instead, they are deposited onto a legal assembly line that whisks them from accusation to conviction. Rather than taking the time to understand the individual and tailoring a just outcome to the circumstances at hand, the criminal justice system views people as case files to be quickly processed and disposed of.

Criminal justice in America is a long, vast conveyor belt. Vulnerable people are dumped onto it at the beginning. By the time they reach the other end, their lives are shattered beyond recognition. The general public is taught that there are rules that govern how a person proceeds through the process. These rules are designed to slow the conveyor belt down. They create opportunities for people to get off the conveyor belt. They ensure that no one reaches the end of the conveyor belt who did not belong on it in the first place.

In reality, the rules are ignored. Rather than presuming innocence, we assume everyone on the conveyor belt deserves to be there. We resent having to use any more resources than are absolutely necessary to get them to the other end. The goal is to do so as quickly as possible, and the rules get in the way. So we figure out how to get around them. If this gets the accused through the conveyor belt more quickly, the ends justify the means.

Why do so many criminal justice professionals go along with this? How have the men and women who are tasked with administering justice in our courts come to participate in a practice that is so inconsistent with this ideal? Until we answer this question, we cannot begin to truly transform our criminal justice system. The answer is "culture."

Rather than embracing the presumption of innocence, America's criminal justice culture assumes the criminality of those accused. It dehumanizes them, driving those who administer justice to devalue the dignity of the people their decisions impact. Safeguards designed to protect the individual are therefore devalued. Speedy convictions and harsh punishments are prioritized. This culture shapes those in it until they act in ways contrary to the ideals and principles at the heart of our democracy.

Due to the pressures to get through cases quickly, to appear tough on crime, and to adhere to our nation's increasingly punitive culture, many prosecutors come to see their role solely as protecting society from the lawbreakers they charge—even if they have to ignore the rules, cut corners, or ignore exculpatory evidence to do so. With increasing frequency, the public is becoming aware of cases where prosecutors saw constitutional safeguards as pesky obstacles to be circumvented, so they doggedly worked to engineer convictions. It has been estimated that between 2 and 10 percent of people in prison were wrongfully convicted, meaning America has between 46,000 and 230,000 innocent people behind bars.[13] Countless others were over-punished for mistakes they made. Prosecutors frequently pressure defendants to give up their constitutional rights and plead guilty, to avoid the risk that the defendant will be treated substantially more harshly. As prosecutors are acculturated to believe that the accused is a villain and the punishment is deserved, they come to see hallowed principles of procedure as irritating technicalities. They lose little sleep if they have to disregard the appropriate process to ensure the desired result is achieved.

Judges face their own pressures to keep the conveyor belt moving along. They have to manage heavy caseloads without allowing a backlog to develop. Litigation is time-consuming and expensive. So judges face subtle—or not-so-subtle—pressure to be efficient. They are also often sensitive to strained court budgets. These pressures frequently cause judges to prioritize processing cases over providing individualized justice. There is little time to get a full picture of a person and really understand the context of a case. As a result, it is not uncommon for judges to aid the machinery of injustice in an effort to continue operating smoothly.

Lawyers who cut corners are rarely chastised, while those who are too litigious are often met with scorn.

But it was neither my experience with prosecutors nor with judges that inspired me to study culture as the primary culprit in shaping America's criminal legal system. It was watching what happened to men and women who were tasked with defending the accused in some of our nation's most dysfunctional court systems. The defense attorney is the advocate who is supposed to zealously fight for the accused. The person facing a loss of liberty should be their only concern. The defender must ferret out violations of the process and correct them. They must challenge abusive prosecutors and judges. They are the last line of defense for the individual who is facing the power of the state. They are the force that is expected to ensure the conveyor belt encounters friction. And plenty of it.

However, this is a vision of the defender that the current legal system finds pesky and does not tolerate. Defense lawyers face tremendous pressure to go along with the status quo. They are expected to help with the processing of cases. The system encourages them to join forces with prosecutors and judges in the effort to grease the wheels of the machine. They are under-resourced and overwhelmed. Early in their careers, even the most passionate defenders will get beaten down. It is not possible for a person to withstand an entire culture by themselves.

You could walk into any courthouse in America and find a roomful of criminal justice professionals who have become resigned to a system that would shock those who are untainted by this culture. For the most part, these are well-intentioned people. They got into criminal justice because they wanted to make a positive impact on the world. But they were unprepared for the culture that awaited them.

This lesson could not have been more strongly reinforced than when I brought my children to the Superior Court for the District of Columbia, where I began my legal career. We had just spent the morning visiting the National Museum of African American History and Culture. We began our tour at the bottom level and journeyed from the early days of the transatlantic slave trade to the emancipation of enslaved people in America. We were emotionally drained and decided to return the next day to see the rest of the museum. After lunch, I decided to take the kids to see one of the courtrooms where I used to practice as a public defender.

We walked into courtroom C-10, where "first appearance hearings" take place. I knew many of the people working in the courtroom that day. I knew the judge. I knew most of the clerks who were handling the paperwork. I knew the defense lawyers. While I did not know the prosecutors working that day, I was sure I had known many just like them. These were all well-intentioned people. None harbored any conscious animosity toward the men who would be brought before the judge that afternoon.

Soon the clerk started calling cases. One by one, men were brought before the judge. All of them were black. They each had their hands cuffed together and attached to a chain around their waists. Each case was resolved fairly quickly. All were relatively minor charges. After about half a dozen cases were called, Lucas, my ten-year-old son, turned to me and said, "Daddy, this is just like the museum."

A room full of criminal justice professionals had become used to something that a ten-year-old child understood was more akin to slavery than to justice. Lucas was troubled. He was confused. He understood the scene unfolding in that courtroom belonged in a museum documenting our tragic history of racial oppression. Not in a sanctuary of justice. No one else was troubled. An accepted narrative that casts those accused of crimes as subhuman is the only explanation for how judges, lawyers, and courtroom administrators could become desensitized to injustices that even children can recognize.

THE POWER OF CULTURE

Lucas's question made me think of an example from a Spalding County, Georgia, courtroom where sixteen people lined up in dark-green jail uniforms, some in shackles, prepared to admit guilt and forgo a trial.[14] The presiding judge was Johnnie L. Caldwell Jr. He was eager to dispense with this lot of cases. There were more waiting to be churned through. He quickly had them acknowledge the rights they were giving up and pronounced sentence on each. He then dismissed the group and moved on to the next batch of inmates. Americans may believe that every person is entitled to their day in court. But, in Judge Caldwell's courtroom, every person is entitled only to a mere moment in court. And even that time is shared with fifteen others.

Judges are responsible for ensuring that every person in the court-room has been afforded the rights they are due. Judge Caldwell clearly did not take the time to do that. Prosecutors have a duty to tailor the outcome they seek to the unique facts of each case and the qualities of each person accused. The prosecutor who stood by and witnessed this judicial fire sale certainly did not fulfill this role. These actors were clearly products of a culture that places little value on the lives of the people dressed in green.

But there was also a defense attorney in the courtroom at the time. This is the person charged with speaking for those sixteen human beings. Defense attorneys are tasked with challenging anything happening in the courtroom that falls short of what their clients deserve. They are to serve as the system's conscience, reminding judges and prosecutors when they are not doing their jobs. When defense counsel fails to live up to this ob-ligation, the system is allowed to cut corners. Without the defender, there is no protection for the person abused by the system. Johnny Mostiler was the attorney assigned to represent people who could not afford a lawyer in Caldwell's courtroom. He had no objection to what unfolded before his eyes. In fact, he facilitated the process.

There was no individualized justice that day. Judge Caldwell knew nothing about the human beings inside those green uniforms. Their law-yer did not take the time to enlighten the judge. Their stories did not matter. That day they were like widgets. Caldwell's courtroom was a brief stop along a well-oiled assembly line. The prevailing criminal justice cul-ture taught these professionals how to do their jobs. Their mechanical and inhumane approach to justice was valued in it. But it came with a cost.

The price was borne by people like fifteen-year-old Melishia Renee Gosha. Melishia was accused of shooting her aunt to death following an argument when she was just fourteen. Johnny Mostiler was appointed to represent her. Her "day in court" lasted ten minutes. That was how long it took for Judge Paschal English to hear the prosecution's summary of the case, obtain Melishia's waiver of her right to trial, and sentence her to a term of life in prison.[15] Mostiler never challenged the prosecution's deci-sion to try Melishia as an adult for a crime she committed as a child. He did not retain an expert who might be able to convince a jury to spare her such a harsh sentence due to her immaturity, emotional development, or abu-sive childhood.[16] Mostiler believed a life sentence is what his young client deserved. Rather than challenge the prosecution's evidence or fight for a less severe punishment, he acquiesced to the sentence the state wanted. Without an advocate, young Melishia became resigned to her fate.

Despite the obvious lack of energy put into Melishia's defense, there was no complaint from the prosecutor who decided to charge her as an adult and offer a plea that carried a life sentence, nor from the judge who presided over the ten-minute hearing that sealed the child's fate. In fact, Judge English felt confident that Mostiler gave poor folks like Melishia all the justice to which they were entitled. When asked, English said, "I've seen high-profile lawyers come through here at $25,000 and $50,000 per client who do half the job of Johnny Mostiler. I don't think anyone gives better representation than Mr. Mostiler."[17]

Judges like Caldwell and English preferred lawyers who did not put up a fight. They understood their role as clearing dockets cheaply and quickly, by any means necessary. They wanted lawyers who would partner with them in this endeavor. Such judicial attitudes are perhaps the best barometer of what the system expects of its lawyers. In Spalding County, the answer was "not much."

PUBLIC DEFENDERS: THE KEY TO EQUAL JUSTICE

I learned about Johnny Mostiler when I first began working on public defender reform in Georgia. In fact, I learned about many lawyers who provided their clients a similar level of representation. The people who relied on these lawyers never had a chance. The lawyers did not take the time to investigate the facts of the case. They did not look into critical legal issues. They never took the time to learn about the person accused and the circumstances that brought them into contact with the system. Without an advocate, these people were at the mercy of prosecutors and judges who could never know the critical information only the defense attorney could bring to the case. It was obvious that the defense lawyer was the key to making sure justice was done. Without a good defense attorney, the accused would find their humanity remained invisible.

In a system that devalued the lives of society's most vulnerable members, the greatest threat was to those who had little means. These people relied on public defenders, advocates appointed to represent people who had been accused of crimes but who could not afford to hire a lawyer.

Roughly 80 percent of all people brought into the criminal legal system fell into this category. Public defenders were essential to transforming the system. There could be no criminal justice reform without healthy public defender offices. I was excited to help transform public defense in Georgia.

I began studying the problems facing public defense in America. There were some common themes that were obvious. The challenges generally seemed to fall into one of two categories. The first was financial challenges. Public defenders were routinely forced to take on far more cases than they could competently handle. They were deprived of the resources needed to adequately represent their clients. They were paid meager salaries, and many of them carried crushing educational debt from law school, making it very hard for them to make ends meet.

The second category included structural challenges that created a disincentive for public defenders to be loyal to the people they represented. Many defenders relied on the very judges they appeared before for resources, creating pressure to get along rather than fight for their clients. Some were incentivized to take on paying clients as well, to make ends meet, creating a disincentive to invest too much time in their appointed cases.

Heartbreaking stories about what these challenges meant for the people who depended on public defenders were everywhere. They included stories like those of Judy Haney and Gary Nelson. Haney was sentenced to death in Talladega County, Alabama, for arranging to have her abusive husband killed. She was appointed an alcoholic lawyer who was so drunk during trial that the proceedings had to be stopped as he was held in contempt and sent to jail. The next morning the lawyer was brought to court from the jail, along with Haney, so the trial could resume. Several days later, Haney was sentenced to die. Her lawyer never presented hospital records showing injuries received by Haney and her daughter that would have corroborated her testimony. He did not bring their expert witness on domestic abuse to visit Haney until eight o'clock the night before he testified at trial.[18] Haney never had a chance.

Gary Nelson was convicted and sentenced to death in Georgia after being forced to rely on a lawyer who had never tried a capital case. The lawyer, who was struggling financially and going through a divorce, was paid only fifteen to twenty dollars per hour. The lawyer's request for co-counsel was denied as was his request for an investigator. Despite the fact that the case against Nelson was based on questionable scientific evidence, including testimony by a prosecution expert connecting a hair found on the victim's body to the accused, the lawyer never requested his own expert. Clearly defeated, the lawyer delivered a closing argument that was only 255 words long.[19] It took eleven years for post-conviction lawyers to demonstrate that the forensic evidence was unreliable and for Nelson to be released.[20] More than a decade of a man's life was lost because of a lousy lawyer.

As the pressure to move cases efficiently mounts, states have forced poor people to rely on lawyers like Mark Straughn. Straughn, a lawyer from Dodge County, Georgia, agreed to handle cases for roughly $50 each.[21] When he testified before a commission investigating problems with the way Georgia provides representation to the poor, he said when clients insist they are innocent, he assumes they are lying. Rather than investigate his clients' versions of events, Straughn embraced a presumption that they committed the crime and told them to plead guilty.[22]

Robert Surrency held the contract to represent poor people in Greene County, Georgia. Surrency willingly gave in to judges' demands that he process cases quickly, agreeing to represent hundreds of people each year. Almost none went to trial, and Surrency often spent only minutes with clients before pleading them guilty. He assumed the police reports to be an accurate reflection of what actually happened and therefore did not request investigative or expert services. Instead he saw his high-volume, plea-bargain practice as "a uniquely productive way to do business." When clients complained about the insufficient time he spent talking to them, Surrency chalked it up to "their need for attention," rather than their need for a lawyer.[23]

Robert Surrency was considered a part-time public defender, yet his annual caseload was twice the number deemed manageable by the American Bar Association.[24] But Surrency had grown quite efficient at helping the court process cases. He would resolve more than 99 percent of his cases through guilty pleas. Some days he would plead dozens of clients in a single court session, with little time to get the details necessary to negotiate on their behalf.

Johnny Mostiler made Robert Surrency's situation seem reasonable. Mostiler's contract with Spalding County required him to handle as many as nine hundred felonies per year.[25] Despite this overwhelming workload, his contract allowed him to supplement his income with outside work, resulting in Mostiler spending only about 60 percent of his time on his court-appointed work.[26] In one two-week trial calendar, Mostiler had 150 cases scheduled. Nearly every one was resolved with a plea. As Mostiler bragged, "We'll enter pleas all week, at a rate of about 10 to 12 every 45 minutes."[27]

Public defenders with barely enough time to push cases through the criminal justice pipeline are a common feature in American courtrooms. Judges and prosecutors, often less concerned about the human beings behind each case than they are about getting them through the system, rarely protest. Studies have shown that, in some places, public defenders have only minutes to work on each case.[28] One study found that in Atlanta, public defenders spent only fifty-nine minutes per case; in Detroit, the average was thirty-two, and in New Orleans, only seven.[29]

If the criminal defense lawyer was the key to realizing justice, poor people across the nation were locked out. It was obvious that ensuring those most impacted by our criminal legal system had good lawyers was at the heart of criminal justice reform. This is what brought me to the South.

SYMPTOMS VS. DISEASE

As I began my work in Georgia, I studied everything I could find about public defense in America. Experts routinely discussed the various financial and structural problems. However, culture was completely overlooked. I could not help but believe that this was a fatal omission. I was certain that transforming culture was the fundamental challenge facing public defense reformers.

Everyone in the system adopted a mind-set that was inconsistent with what justice demanded. They valued efficiency and cost savings over all else. This mind-set was fueled by a narrative that saw the accused as less valuable. All of the problems identified by experts—the financial and structural challenges facing public defenders—were symptoms of a culture in which people charged with crimes were less human. These people were not worthy of justice. Therefore they were undeserving of the kind of lawyer we would demand for ourselves.

Crushing caseloads, a lack of resources, and judicial expectations of public defenders that ran afoul of defenders' duties to their clients, as well as the fact that public defenders were incentivized to handle private cases to supplement their public defender salaries, were all symptoms of this cultural disease.

The stories above were perfect examples of the challenges. Like Robert Surrency and Johnny Mostiler, lawyers across the nation often agreed to take on far more cases than they could responsibly handle. As in Gary Nelson's case, lawyers for the poor were frequently denied access to the resources they needed to mount a competent defense. There was simply not enough money allocated to public defense to give poor people the lawyers and resources they needed to be adequately protected. Efforts to keep spending on public defense low depended on lawyers willing to accommodate this burden.

Structurally, many jurisdictions used low-bid contracts to identify lawyers like Surrency and Mostiler who agreed to handle all cases for a flat fee. Others paid lawyers a set fee per case, promising a specified amount of money and no more. Defenders often had no incentive to do more than the bare minimum. In fact, they were frequently discouraged from doing too much on any given case because they needed to take on so many cases to simply make a living. To compound the structural problems, in some places judges selected the lawyers who would get the work. This encouraged defenders to move cases quickly to appease judges, rather than to truly defend those they represented. Making a living required a willingness to process many cases and remain in good grace with the judge.

This combination of inadequate resources and a system designed to facilitate the efficient processing of cases leads to what is known as the "meet 'em, greet 'em, and plead 'em" process.[30]

Stories about lawyers like Surrency, Straughn, and Mostiler litter systems across the country. Any law student who studied the procedures designed to protect against injustice would be deeply troubled by these accounts. The lawyers at the heart of the stories appear to be the poster children for financial and structural reform. Logically, reformers focus on these fixes. In doing so, they overlook culture.

It is a culture that places the life of a man like Curtis Osborne in the hands of a lawyer who does not think he deserves to live. On June 5, 2008, the State of Georgia executed Osborne. Several years earlier, Johnny Mostiler was appointed to represent him in a capital murder case. After

Osborne was sentenced to die, it was reported that Mostiler allegedly refused to convey a plea deal to Osborne that would have spared his life. It was further reported that the lawyer said of Osborne, "That little n****r deserves the chair."[31]

This culture, which I was introduced to in Georgia, is one in which respect for a client is not required to be appointed to a case. All that is needed is for the lawyer to agree to move cases along the conveyor belt without any friction. This culture teaches public defenders to become lawyers who contribute to injustice rather than combat it. Robert Surrency spent fourteen years handling the contract for Greene County. His tenure there shaped him into such a lawyer. He came to understand his role as helping to clear many cases cheaply. His fear of getting people "riled up about spending the county's money"[32] led him to forgo using investigative or expert services. In order to handle the crushing volume of cases assigned to him, he spent virtually no time talking to his clients. Instead, he relied largely on the prosecution's version of events.

As this practice became habit, he lost the ability to question the allegations against his clients. He came to see his cases as "open and shut."[33] When clients complained about the insufficient time Surrency spent talking to them, he became dismissive, believing their demands were unreasonable.[34] In this environment, legal research, investigation, and communication with clients became a waste of time. While any outsider could understand that justice was not being served, Surrency actually believed that he "achieved good results" for his clients.[35] He believed he was the lawyer his clients deserved. In fact, he was a necessary cog in a machinery of injustice. So was Johnny Mostiler.

Of course this mind-set was born out of a system that struggled to process far more cases that it was resourced to handle. As prosecutors sought quick convictions on the cases they poured into the system, and judges prioritized efficiently clearing dockets, defense lawyers were praised for their willingness to cooperate. In smaller counties, public defenders dealt with the same judges and prosecutors day in and day out, compounding the pressure to get along. They did not appreciate how "going along to get along" reinforced a low standard of justice system-wide. The best virtue of a good lawyer was maintaining good relationships. No one considered that they were trading the interests of their current clients for the speculative value these relationships would have for future clients. No one discussed how this was a concern that no competent private lawyer, whose allegiance lay solely with the person who paid them, would ever entertain.

These defenders truly believed they were good lawyers. They could be paid more money, given fewer cases, or provided access to more resources. It would not matter. They did not believe there were improvements to be made to their practice. Even if they did not feel pressure to cater to the judges, they had come to understand that doing so was their role. Policies that addressed these symptoms would not ensure justice to low-income people. These lawyers believed they were giving their clients what they deserved.

This worldview easily created tension with the people the lawyers represented, who had little interest in the lawyers' efforts to maintain good relationships with judges. They were singularly focused on their cases and expected their lawyers would be as well. As lawyers tried to adapt to the pressures of the system, their clients were not always cooperative. Clients might ask lawyers to provide information, follow investigative leads, or look into legal issues. Often the requests were not unreasonable. But to the overwhelmed public defender focused on getting cases through the system, such requests were irritating. Defenders often prided themselves on being able to look at a police report and know the appropriate resolution. Being able to quickly determine which cases should result in pleas was a sign of good lawyering instincts. Taking shortcuts was seen as "experience," and clients who asked lawyers to do more were seen as problematic. The defender would come to expect the client to simply remain invisible while the lawyer engineered the best result. When clients refused, they would become the butt of demeaning jokes and disparaging comments. Far too often, jaded public defenders came to resent the people they represented. Not surprisingly, the people who had to rely on public defenders also harbored disdain for the lawyers.

PUBLIC DEFENDERS—THE KEY TO JUSTICE AND DIGNITY

As I poured myself into reform work in the South, I often thought of my wife Illy's words when she discussed her experience with her father. As hard as it was growing up with her dad behind bars, she would say, it was even harder realizing that the lives of those she loved did not matter. It struck me even harder, given what I had seen in my work with public defense systems, that she primarily came to understand that fact through the lawyer who represented her father. He was the medium through which that message was delivered—not by anything the lawyer said but by his indifference. He conveyed the message that her father was not worthy of dignity, an experience that negatively effected her own sense of worth.

I do not know much about Illy's father's case. I do not know anything about the evidence against him. It is certainly possible that he would have received a significant prison sentence even with the best lawyer in the country. However, what a compassionate lawyer could have done was to give him dignity. They could have assured Illy that her father mattered. They could have shown that someone in the system cared. The lawyer failed to do that. This is the lesson that stuck most with that five-year-old girl.

To be clear, I met some wonderful public defenders in Georgia. But it was also where I first learned about lawyers who were not only incapable of providing their clients justice; they were incapable of giving them dignity. As I continued to expand my work in the South, this realization crystallized in my mind. Public defenders are the key to giving justice to the people the system disregards, and they are key to bringing them dignity.

I thought about the many amazing public defenders I knew. They were some of the best lawyers in the country. I understood that even these lawyers could not walk into incredibly dysfunctional systems and guarantee justice for their clients. The systems had become far too accepting of oppressive practices. Change would require time. However, what they could do was to immediately give the people they represent dignity. They could listen to their stories and hear their concerns. They could learn their clients' goals for the representation and work hand in hand to achieve them. They might not overcome all the injustice in the short run, but they could choose to loudly object to it rather than to passively accept it. This matters.

CLIENT-CENTERED DEFENSE

Treating the people I represented this way had been an expected practice in Washington, DC. There was plenty of injustice there. Prosecutors routinely overcharged. Sentences were far too draconian. There were still some judges who were too willing to overlook constitutional violations.

But the public defenders' office was adequately resourced. The defenders had manageable caseloads. Respecting the people we represented was an expectation. Communicating with clients, meeting with their families, doing a thorough investigation, and engaging in vigorous litigation were the norm. In any court proceeding, there was no question whose side the public defenders were on. They were fiercely loyal to the men, women, and children they represented. Public defenders in DC raised the standard of justice throughout the entire court system. I witnessed plenty of injustice in Washington. But you could be sure the public defenders were always resisting. You could be equally sure they had as much respect for the people they represented as they did for anyone else in the courtroom.

I went to Georgia with a commitment to develop a community of client-centered public defenders. Marginalized communities had come to see every professional in the system as the enemy. To them, judges, prosecutors, and public defenders worked together to mechanically push their loved ones through the system. In their eyes, none of these professionals cared about them.

The communities had never been treated with dignity in the system. Their voices were always ignored. To become the advocates the clients needed, public defenders had to begin the difficult work of repairing relationships. It would not be enough to know the law. It would not be enough to excel at courtroom advocacy. The public defender had to make the system see people whom it had become accustomed to rendering invisible. Defenders would have to force the system to hear voices it had previously only silenced. They would need to transform from professionals who facilitate the status quo to warriors who resist it. This would require a special kind of advocate.

The public defenders would need the skill, passion, and inclination to learn the complete experience of those they serve, to understand the stories behind every person accused, and to bring that narrative to life in a system that will otherwise disregard the humanity of the accused. Once a person is charged, the defense lawyer is the vehicle through which this voice is amplified. Making sure that they are faithful to this voice is essential if the dignity of each person is to be respected.

Client-centered lawyering is at the heart of a system that respects the dignity of those most impacted. Lawyers may not substitute their priorities for those of the person they represent. They must use their expertise to advise and counsel. But ultimately, they must serve as the representatives. To trump the desires of the person who is accused is to further strip that person of dignity.

If my doctor believes I need heart surgery, she may advise me to have it. She may counsel me about the risks of not having surgery and the benefits of going through with the procedure. She may urge me to follow her advice. However, she cannot perform the surgery if I do not agree. Similarly, a lawyer should be equally respectful of the wishes of a well-advised client. The client may ultimately disagree with the course of action urged by the lawyer, and may do so for reasons the lawyer cannot comprehend. But the client must have that right in a system that has historically silenced those deemed criminal if we are to ever achieve a more dignified system of justice.

Several years ago, a former colleague forwarded me an email thread. He was irritated with the content. I had trained and supervised this lawyer. He had since left to practice elsewhere and was a member of a listserv that included many accomplished private criminal defense lawyers. I helped to teach him that client-centered lawyering must be at the heart of our work as public defenders. So he saw me as an obvious person to vent his frustration to.

In the thread, a novice lawyer asked for advice. The lawyer thought one course of action was best. The client desired another. The young lawyer wanted help figuring out how to resolve the dilemma. My former colleague was disheartened by the responses. Several prominent lawyers argued strenuously that the lawyer must make the call. The theme of the responses was similar. Lawyers have legal training and experience. They certainly have a better sense of the best course of action to take. They used metaphors like "You are the captain of the ship" to emphasize their point.

While my colleague understood that the lawyers' advice might be the better strategy to accomplish the client's goals, the concern was that the discussion seemed to discount the importance of ensuring the client's voice was heard. The exchange focused solely on who had the authority to make the decision, as if that answered the question.

The responders never seemed to consider the need to gain a better understanding of why the client felt so strongly about his position. The lawyers focused solely on the legal dilemma in front of them and considered approaching the problem only through the lens of their own experiences—experiences almost surely different from the client's. Were there other issues of concern to the client? Were the client's reasons worthy of any weight? Even if the lawyer's recommendation is objectively the correct one with respect to the legal dilemma, should we be troubled by so easily dismissing clients' input about decisions that impact their lives?

My colleague weighed in with a suggestion that the client deserved significant autonomy over decisions that impacted his case. He argued that, while the lawyer must ensure the client has been sufficiently advised to ensure that the client's decisions are informed and that the risks have been appropriately conveyed, the lawyer must respect the client's priorities. He found no support in this view.

It is significant that the conversation was conducted among lawyers who charge quite a bit for their services.

When a person can afford to pay a lawyer, they can fire that lawyer and choose another. That person can find a lawyer who is willing to act as their agent. People given public defenders almost never have any say in who represents them. It is very unlikely that they will be able to successfully request a new lawyer. Should people who rely on public defenders lose the agency that wealthier counterparts have? Have they forfeited their rights to control important decisions because they are poor? Arguably, public defenders have an even greater obligation to respect the voices of their clients who have been deprived of the ability to turn elsewhere for help.

Furthermore, when it comes to the rare criminal defendant who is powerful, and who has means, that person's dignity is already respected. Such a person likely has not lived a life in which his or her humanity was ignored. Wealthier criminal defendants may be looking only for justice. That they deserve to be treated with dignity is assumed. They may vest in their lawyers the authority to make any decisions the lawyers deem important. The fact that they paid top dollar likely means they already trust their lawyers. The public defender cannot make this assumption. Respect must be earned. Dignity must be afforded.

Client-centered representation sees the role of the public defender as taking the time to learn clients' desires and, after advising them of all of the ramifications of their actions, working to fulfill those desires. It requires that lawyers use their education, experience, and talent to arm clients with the advice necessary for those clients to control the representation consistent with the clients' desires. In this way, it empowers a client to receive the same quality of representation as would a person who has more choice based on education and income.

Client-centered representation values the dignity of the client. It ultimately prioritizes the client's right to make important decisions that can impact all aspects of the person's life. And, because the consequences in any criminal case are so much broader than the potential sentence, this approach is even more necessary.

A conviction for even the most minor offenses can result in the loss of a job or housing. A person may become ineligible for educational loans, healthcare, or public assistance. For noncitizens, it could result in deportation. There are many considerations beyond the criminal sanction that the accused must weigh personally.[36]

A client may be concerned about how certain courses of action could reveal embarrassing or sensitive information, and how they might impact the client's reputation or safety in the community. Clients may never have had anyone respect their voice or their opinion and may simply want their lawyer to help them have some control in a system that devalues their humanity. Some of these issues may be more important to the client than the conviction itself.

Taking the time to learn the issues that matter to the client and respecting how the person prioritizes each is critical for client-centered representation. Effectively developing the relationship with the client to learn personal information and to discuss what matters to the client requires that the lawyer actually care about the client. Under a client-centered model, the client is not simply the vehicle through which the lawyer gets to try cases; the client is the entire reason for everything the lawyer does.

While many defense lawyers practice client-centered lawyering, it is certainly not universally embraced throughout the profession. Many see cases as legal problems to be resolved. As the "experts," they are best positioned to figure out the resolution. This mind-set can cause the lawyer to focus on the case, and not on the client. The person behind the case becomes invisible. The busier the defender becomes, the more frustrated they can get with the person who wants the lawyer to take time to listen. Overwhelmed public defenders can come to resent their clients.

This resentment explains one particular email thread that was shared among some public defender leaders in Georgia shortly after the new statewide system was launched. One sent an email to colleagues titled "You won't believe this . . ." that relayed the story of a client who stole the defender's office mail and forged some of his checks. A second described how he structured his office to make sure employees could keep an eye on clients, concluding, "This will be an extremely unpopular statement with [the] true believers but our clients are our clients for a reason. Don't trust them. Don't believe them. Don't turn your back on them and you will never have to say 'you won't believe this.'" A third chimed in about the lengths his office went through to monitor clients, adding, "These folks are who they are."

The sentiment was clear. Rather than being the very reason we do this work, the clients were seen by many of the emailers as being among the challenges we face as public defenders. One would not have been surprised if the next response in the thread was, "This would be a great job if it weren't for those damned clients."

The attitude is born of the mistaken idea the one can be a successful public defender without respecting the people represented. It sees justice and dignity as disconnected. It could not be more wrong.

When we disregard a group's humanity, and therefore its members' dignity, it is easy to see them as unworthy of justice. In this sense, dignity and justice are inextricably linked. Public defenders are at the heart of both. Defenders are the key to forcing the system to treat the accused with dignity and to therefore accept real justice in courtrooms.

This is a cultural challenge. A public defender movement, with a renewed vision for public defense, will be critical to transforming the culture. It starts with a client-centered vision of public defense leading to a defender-driven movement to transform systemic assumptions. That is what this book is about.

But first we must understand what justice demands in our courts, so we can push systems to live up to this ideal. We must also understand how we got to a place where justice is so easily disregarded. We cannot reform our justice system as long as we see those impacted as others. Changing our collective mind-set about impacted people must go hand in hand with efforts to make our courts live up to our democratic ideals.

CHAPTER 2

THE EVOLVING
NARRATIVE OF JUSTICE

ON SEPTEMBER 19, 2017, forty-eight-year-old Sean Ramsey stood steps away from the Atlanta municipal courthouse pleading for help. Ramsey, homeless and hungry, desperately needed mercy. It turns out, the Atlanta city courthouse was the wrong place to seek it.

He was arrested as he stood on the corner holding a handmade cardboard sign that read "Homeless, please help." The next day, without even expending the energy it would take to bring him into the courtroom, Judge Terrinee Gundy ordered him detained at the local jail. To the judge, Ramsey was invisible. He was a case number, not a human being. She never even saw his face. For more than two months, he remained locked away. He was never given access to a lawyer. He was never afforded any judicial process. He was whisked from arrest to indefinite confinement. Seventy-two days later, he was finally released, but only after civil rights lawyers found him and petitioned the Superior Court. For two and a half months he had no chance to share his story.

Ramsey's crime was that he was undesirable; he was one of the thousands of homeless men, women, and children living on the streets of Atlanta. He was also black, which further contributed to the narrative that he was the "other," among that population of people from whom the rest of us must be protected. Ramsey was the quintessential minority our justice system is designed to protect from the approbation of the majority. That protection was nonexistent.

Ramsey's story is the definition of injustice. The government targets an unpopular population and outlaws behavior that is disproportionately associated with it. Police then arrest a member of that group when he inevitably violates the law. A judge then sends the violator to jail with no opportunity to defend himself. This was precisely the tyranny that our constitutional forefathers sought to eliminate.

American democracy was founded on the belief that while government is necessary, it cannot be trusted. Nothing was more precious to the colonists than individual liberty, and our society was designed to jealously guard it against an inherently abusive government. The men who fought the American Revolution understood that a government unchecked morphs into tyranny. They knew that there would always be populations who are marginalized and oppressed. By definition, equal justice cannot survive tyranny. Tyranny is justice's greatest enemy.

So it was with the dangers of an unchecked government in mind that the men who drafted our Constitution painstakingly laid out a set of protections deemed essential to democracy. They understood that those with the power to accuse and prosecute would trample individual liberties in an effort achieve their desired outcomes. So, it was necessary to have a system of checks and balances on those who would execute our criminal laws. These protections define justice in America.

Of course, some behavior had to be criminalized, and it would fall upon government actors to identify and punish wrongdoers. To ensure that those with the authority to arrest and prosecute could not single out disfavored members of a minority group, the framers established a legislative branch of government, tasked with the authority to define the conduct that would be outlawed. By narrowly proscribing those actions that would be criminalized, this branch would help to contain the ability of the executive branch to abuse its power. The executive could only enforce those laws promulgated by the legislature.

But the framers recognized that additional checks would be needed. An executive branch that was hell-bent on going after a citizen would look for ways to get around the limitations placed upon it. It might cheat to win or seek a punishment that was overly severe. So the judicial branch was established to ensure law enforcement abided by the law and to determine the appropriate punishment, should any violation be established. While the legislature determined the rules of engagement, the judiciary functioned as the referee. It ensured the executive played by the rules and pronounced the appropriate penalty should the accused be found guilty.

These checks on the government when it had a citizen in its cross-hairs were an essential component of the justice system envisioned by the colonists. But they were not nearly enough. The framers recognized that even with the checks in place, mistakes could be made. A person could be wrongly accused, convicted, and punished. The men who drafted our Constitution saw the wrongful conviction of the innocent as the greatest danger in any system of criminal justice.

The English jurist William Blackstone famously wrote: "It is better that ten guilty persons escape than that one innocent suffer."[1] This principle of English jurisprudence was adopted as the bedrock of our justice system by the men who designed our democracy. They firmly believed that before the government could deprive one of liberty, it would have to overcome a set of obstacles that tilted the playing field heavily in favor of the accused. First, any person alleged to have committed a crime must be presumed innocent. In other words, it is critical that at the outset of any criminal case the finder of fact be convinced that the prosecution's allegations are false.

Second, the prosecution bears the burden of convincing the finder of fact of the accused's guilt. The prosecution alone is required to produce evidence sufficient to overcome the presumption of innocence. The accused need not do a thing to prove his innocence. He need not explain his whereabouts, offer an alibi, or address the allegations or evidence against him in any way. He has the right to sit back and force the government to prove its allegations against him.

Third, the burden of proof that the prosecution must overcome is the highest burden possible: proof beyond a reasonable doubt. Should the finder of fact have a reasonable doubt—a legitimate question—about the prosecution's case, it is duty-bound to find the accused not guilty. This means that in our system of justice, we are required to acquit people accused of crimes who we believe are probably guilty, are likely guilty, even who are almost certainly guilty, as long as we have a single doubt about their guilt. In other words, American justice demands that many factually guilty people will never be convicted, because this balance is required to sufficiently protect the innocent from wrongful conviction. Factually guilty people being acquitted is perfectly consistent with justice in America. We have chosen to err on the side of under-punishing as opposed to risking wrongful punishment. That is the American tradition.

This brings me to the next protection so necessary to our system of justice: the jury. Our founders understood that the executive was tasked with ferreting out crime. As the branch that leveled accusations and presented evidence to prove a person's guilt, it could not also impartially presume the allegations incorrect and without bias evaluate the kinks in a case. Therefore, for the bedrock principles discussed above—the presumption of innocence, the burden of proof, and the beyond-a-reasonable-doubt standard of proof—to be faithfully applied, the allegations must be presented to a jury. The idea that a trial by jury was required before the government could deprive a citizen of his liberty was as central to our democracy as these core principles themselves.[2] In a world where roughly 95 percent of all convictions are the result of plea bargaining, the centrality of the jury trial to our system of justice can be easily overlooked. But, at the time our democracy was being designed, the concept of plea bargaining did not even exist. It would not be introduced into America's justice system until after the end of the Civil War.

During colonial times, the jury was seen as essential to our democracy. It was the one vehicle ordinary citizens had to block an overzealous government.[3] While the government may have the power to accuse an individual, a jury ultimately must be available to decide whether such allegations are warranted. It serves as a buffer between the accused and a prosecutor focused on securing a conviction: "an inestimable safeguard against the corrupt or overzealous prosecutor," cautioned the Supreme Court.[4]

The right to a jury was so central to the framers' notion of justice that it was not only enshrined in the body of the Constitution but also was guaranteed in the Sixth Amendment to the Bill of Rights. The first ten amendments to the Constitution laid out those rights deemed most fundamental to our core ideals. Collectively, they served to protect the rights of the minority against an oppressive government representing the will of the majority.[5] This was of paramount importance in the criminal justice arena.

The Bill of Rights not only reinforced the right to a trial by jury, it also severely restricted the methods police could use in gathering evidence to attempt to prove a person's guilt. Our constitutional ancestors experienced the dangers of suspicionless searches and seizures, unjust arrests, and coerced confessions. Colonists understood that without clear limitations on the investigative power of the executive, government agents would disregard individual liberties in their zeal to punish the accused. It was through the Bill of Rights that police were prohibited from detaining people without justification, rummaging through people's homes and belongings without cause, and pressuring people to incriminate themselves. The Bill of Rights also guaranteed various protections at trial, such as the right to confront witnesses against the accused, the right to present a defense, and the right to a speedy and public trial. All of these rights were part of a collection of protections designed to guard against the unfair deprivation of individual liberty.

But in the criminal justice context, no right is more significant than the right to counsel. For as important as are all of the other rights set forth in the Bill of Rights, none can be realized without the assistance of a skilled lawyer. It is only through the advocacy of counsel that the jury can appreciate how to apply the presumption of innocence, burden of proof, and standard of proof. It takes the dogged work of a committed lawyer to ferret out and bring to the court's attention constitutional violations in the investigative phase of the process. And without a skilled advocate at trial, the accused is incapable of ensuring that his trial rights are respected and that the rules designed to produce a just outcome are followed.

Fundamental to our system of justice is the notion, which can be traced back to the Magna Carta, that before one may be deprived of his or her liberty by his government, the fight must be fair. The accused must have the opportunity to prepare his defense, to challenge the allegations against him, and to ensure that basic rights are protected in the process. None of these values can be realized without a lawyer "skill[ed] in the science of law."[6] A lawyer must be available to protect each of the rights deemed fundamental to justice. Quite literally, every protection the framers viewed as foundational to our system of justice is at risk without counsel to ensure their enforcement.

So it is absolutely clear that the men who drafted the Constitution measured justice by our fidelity to a process that severely restricts the power of the executive branch. It restricts the evidence available to the government by limiting through the Bill of Rights the ability of police to investigate wrongdoing. It confines the prosecution to charging an individual only with misconduct defined as criminal by the legislature and then presenting evidence of the crime with a judge acting as referee to make sure all rules are followed. It requires that a jury determine guilt after applying the presumption of innocence and demanding the prosecution overcome the highest standard of proof possible. And, most importantly, it recognizes the essential role counsel must play in ensuring the process is faithfully followed and that all protections are respected. Without the presence of these safeguards, any result falls short of justice.

I thought about how critical these safeguards are to any democracy as I listened to a man named Albie Sachs speak at a lunch talk I attended recently. Sachs is a heroic man who literally gave a limb fighting for justice. This was before he would become an inaugural member of South Africa's Constitutional Court in 1995. It was before he would become a chief architect of South Africa's post-apartheid constitution and author landmark decisions interpreting it. And it was before he would be recognized as one of the founding fathers of modern South Africa.

I spent a summer working in South Africa in 1991, and I followed the democracy movement there. But I did not know much about Justice Sachs's life as an activist. As he began to speak to a group of us in the living room of a friend's East Atlanta home, I was immediately pulled into his story.

He described how, in 1952, as a seventeen-year-old law student, he became politically conscious, launching his career as a lawyer defending anti-apartheid freedom fighters. He then fast-forwarded to his experience in solitary confinement for 168 days without trial, a tactic the South African security forces used to break the spirit of those fighting against the system of apartheid. He shared how he would pass the time making up songs and poems as he struggled to maintain his sanity. He was then forced into exile, separated from the country where he was born, eventually landing in Mozambique, where he continued to fight for a free South Africa.

As the room sat riveted by this account of tremendous personal sacrifice for the cause of justice, he brought us to another period in his life. He recounted how there was an explosion, and darkness. He thought he would die. But he was later awakened by a woman's voice. She told him he was in a hospital. She told him he would lose his right arm. He asked what happened. She explained it was a car bomb.

He also lost sight in one eye. But what was so amazing about his telling this story was that he did not seem to have any disappointment that it happened. In fact, he viewed it as a critical turning point in his own consciousness. This tragic incident seemed to bring him hope. He described his healing process and how he felt that, at the same time, his country was healing.

His allies in the struggle promised to avenge him. But he had no interest in vengeance in the retributive sense. He told of how a comrade came to him one day. "Comrade Albie, they caught the person who set off the bomb," he was told. "You will now get vengeance." And then, in his response, he shared the most powerful words of the afternoon. "If they gather all the evidence and present it to a jury, and if there is a reasonable doubt and they acquit the man, that will be my soft vengeance." He went on to say, "Then there will be the rule of law in South Africa."

His country denied him all human contact for nearly half a year, forced him into exile, nearly assassinated him, and left him with only one arm and one seeing eye. Yet, justice had nothing to do with revenge, or with making others suffer. It had to do with a rule of law, equally applied to all who were subjected to it—even applied to those who would want him destroyed. The afternoon made me think about how far our own system of criminal law and procedure is from accomplishing justice. Most of those who run America's justice systems have never stopped to consider what the concept actually means.

But it also made me think of the students I teach as a professor at Atlanta's John Marshall Law School. At the heart of a comprehensive curriculum I designed to help future lawyers think about their role in transforming our criminal justice system is a class called "Criminal Justice Lawyering." We begin the course asking a seemingly obvious, but critical, question: "What is justice?" As lawyers, justice is our business. Yet in law schools across America, students spend three years of study without ever having to consider this question. It is not part of any required course offered in any law school of which I am aware. The extent to which any law student will even consider this question is almost exclusively dependent on whether they have a professor who challenges them to consider it. It's not surprising, then, that legal professionals do not embrace a common definition of justice. Most who administer justice learn to answer the question based on the pressures of the job they find themselves doing.

This explains why so many judges can come to believe that success means disposing of cases quickly. For them, the ability to manage heavy calendars equates to justice. It explains why so many prosecutors understand justice as manipulating the system to get people from arrest to conviction with as little friction as possible. For them, the assumption is that those arrested are guilty, and justice demands that they be held accountable regardless of the process. And it explains why so many public defenders can come to value the ability to assess a case and resolve it quickly. They see their role as working with prosecutors and judges to manage an overwhelmed system as best as possible. Resistance is not necessary under this view of justice.

My students wrestle with the meaning of justice. Through books, articles, documentaries, and speakers they examine our current justice system and contrast it to our democratic ideals. They know the reality falls far short of our aspiration. They then discuss how so many professionals can contribute to a system that is obviously unjust, before being asked to consider how lawyers can help transform the existing system. But the first step is coming to a common understanding of what justice means in the context of our democracy. This is not just an academic exercise. If we are to build a movement to finally realize justice in America, we will have to answer this critical question. We will need a common understanding of the goal we are trying to achieve.

My students come to understand that building a movement to transform this institution is as important as any effort we must undertake. There is no better gauge of the health of American democracy than the way human beings are treated in our criminal justice system. Our fidelity to a process, regardless of whose liberty is at stake, is at the heart of this system of justice. We are not always comfortable with the results. Take O.J., for instance.

The People v. O. J. Simpson was dubbed "the trial of the century" for good reason. Simpson, the sensational NFL running back turned television celebrity, was one of America's biggest stars. He was accused of stabbing to death his wife, Nicole Brown Simpson, and a male acquaintance, Ron Goldman, sixteen months earlier. Since the summer of 1994, the nation had been collectively transfixed by every aspect of the case, from the videotaped police pursuit of Simpson as he fled in his white Ford Bronco, to every televised moment of the nine-month trial, to the around-the-clock, tabloid coverage.

The evidence against Simpson appeared overwhelming, including DNA from a bloody glove allegedly found at Simpson's home that seemed to clearly link him to the crime scene.[7] The State of California spared no expense in proving its case against him. It would call seventy-two witnesses over the course of ninety-nine days[8] and spend roughly $9 million before the trial was over.[9] Most Americans could never hope to mount a defense to counter the firepower the government brought to this prosecution. But Simpson was not "most Americans." On the date of the murders, Simpson was worth an estimated $11 million.[10] He hired a stable of lawyers, dubbed the "dream team," led by the incomparable Johnnie Cochran, which cost him an average of $50,000 a day.[11] Prior to the trial, DNA evidence was believed to be infallible. But Simpson was able to hire defense experts who could show that the blood evidence that was so central to the prosecution's case was likely contaminated and unreliable.[12] And perhaps the biggest factor was the ability of the defense team to uncover evidence that Mark Fuhrman, the ever-so-important detective who found the bloody glove, was racially biased and particularly hostile to interracial relationships, a critical revelation given the fact that Simpson was African American and Nicole Brown Simpson was white.

Simpson was one of the few Americans who could afford to purchase the protections the Constitution guaranteed. Almost anyone else, confronted with this level of prosecutorial muscle, would be forced to plead guilty, unable to afford to fight the allegations in court. Simpson had the means to ensure the case would be scrutinized by a jury. He could afford lawyers who would be able to carefully examine every piece of the state's evidence and investigate each of the state's witnesses in order to raise all pertinent legal issues and confront all of the proof presented against him at trial. And through his legal team, Simpson was assured that all constitutional protections would be realized. Cochran's powerful theme "If the glove doesn't fit, you must acquit" summed up the presumption of innocence, the burden of proof, and the need to be convinced beyond a reasonable doubt. With resources sufficient to match the intensity of the prosecution, Simpson's lawyers brought out reasonable doubt. The jury, true to its duty, found Simpson not guilty.

Twenty-five years later, I use the Simpson case to teach my students. It provides a perfect opportunity to consider what justice means and the role lawyers play in making it a reality.

Each semester, the students raise common themes. Initially, there are always some who express the view that Simpson bought an acquittal, and that it is unfair that a person with money is able to engineer the outcome. Others will invariably point out that California spent millions to prosecute Simpson and that perhaps the unfairness is that not everyone has the resources to match the prosecution's resources.

Through their conversation, the students begin to appreciate the critical role that lawyering plays in making tangible the ideals we will discuss throughout the semester. They see how the defense team methodically challenged each aspect of a seemingly open and shut prosecution case, and how the investment was made to effectively challenge an accusation leveled by an all-powerful government. We call our fidelity to these principles "procedural justice." It ensures fairness in the process. Through the Simpson case, the students see that even for the most privileged Americans, procedural justice can only be realized through the efforts of the defense lawyer.

With four out of five accused Americans forced to rely on public defenders who are overwhelmed and under-resourced, an outcome such as Simpson's seems like a fantasy. The average person's lawyers simply do not have the time to litigate important legal issues or adequately conduct necessary investigations. They do not have the funding to secure expert witnesses, who have become so essential to challenging complex forensic evidence that their testimony is increasingly a staple of even routine prosecutions. The prosecution has developed a formidable arsenal it can use to coerce people into giving up the protections at the heart of our justice system, and now only one in twenty Americans convicted of a crime even experience a trial. Over the semester, the course provides a glimpse into how criminal cases are routinely handled in America's courts.

As the conversation in my class continues, it invariably turns to whether the jury got it right. Many of the students think Simpson was involved, but they all tend to respect the jury's conclusion that there was a reasonable doubt. They struggle with the idea that they agree with a verdict that fails to hold a likely murderer accountable. For many of the students, it is the first time they have been asked to really think about what justice means in our democracy. They have heard of "reasonable doubt" but never considered what it looks like. I think this is true of most Americans.

Simpson's defense team prevailed not because it bamboozled or misled the jury, although those angry about the outcome frequently suggest that is what happened. It prevailed because it helped the jurors understand that it was not their job to solve the crime. In fact, the truth is often unknowable. It was also not their job to figure out which side is more believable. The only question: is there any reason to question the prosecution's evidence?

To further hammer home the stakes in the criminal justice arena, and why we err on the side of extreme caution, I have my students identify one of the hundreds of men and women wrongfully convicted and exonerated through the use of DNA. Each student must research the person they select and, in the voice of that person, share their story with the class. The stories are the counterexample of the price that is paid when we fail to strictly honor the protections in our Constitution. They reveal a litany of errors caused by shortcuts and rushes to judgment by police and prosecutors. The students understand that there is a choice to be made: tolerating the acquittal of a person who may have violated the law or accepting the wrongful conviction of an innocent person. The verdict in the Simpson case is perfectly consistent with a justice system that chooses to prioritize the protection of the innocent.

The Simpson case also reveals an America in which blacks and whites perceive justice very differently. Black people pleased with the "not guilty" verdict saw it as an example of the rule of law finally being applied to a black man. They acknowledged that Simpson got the result only because he was wealthy. But many relished the idea that a black man had the resources to force the system to work for him, led by a bombastic black lawyer named Johnnie Cochran.

Sociology professor Michael Eric Dyson summed it up: "I don't think we should make the mistake of believing that black people who celebrated a) thought O.J. was innocent, or b) were even concerned most about O.J. as opposed to their [own family members] who had been screwed by a system that never paid attention to them." He added, "White people were upset with Johnnie Cochran. Why be upset with Johnnie? He's taking your rules, playing by them, and he won. And that's why black people were so happy."[13]

A *Frontline* documentary about the case supported this view. African Americans who were interviewed acknowledged that Simpson was likely involved but also believed the police broke the rules in their effort to convict him. They were pleased with the verdict.[14]

The reactions of white people interviewed were equally telling when it came to whose perspective they believed should be prioritized. Well-known legal analyst and author Jeffrey Toobin belittled the judgment of the jury. Acknowledging that the case teaches that reasonable doubt means something different for blacks and whites, he opined that the black perspective is wrong. He referred to the jury as the "all-black jury," although the twelve members included one Hispanic and two whites. He denigrated the jury's idea of what constitutes reasonable doubt, suggesting that, while trying their best, the jurors failed to understand the concept. "I believe the jury was sincere; I don't think they were faking, but I think they're just wrong."[15]

Toobin's view is revealing about how we got to this place in our justice system. It suggests not only that what causes black people to doubt the presence of justice in our system is unreasonable but that a jury with a predominately black presence is incapable of understanding what justice demands in America. In his mind, at least when there is a racial dimension to a case, justice seems to demand white juries, who are seen as able to dispassionately assess justice in America in a way that black juries cannot.

Accusing Simpson's defense team of "playing the race card," Toobin suggested that asking the jury to consider race detracts from an honest assessment of the case, rather than helping to illuminate it. He called it a "monstrous" strategy. But the idea that the jury should not consider race, against the backdrop of a system that so disproportionately impacts people of color, cannot sit well with Americans on the losing end of that viewpoint.

What the O. J. Simpson case reveals, as much as anything, is how differently whites and blacks understand justice in America. White Americans are more inclined to believe everyone is on an even playing field and look to a trial to hold the accused accountable. Black Americans are more likely to understand the playing field has never been even. The government has never been forced to follow the rules when it comes to African Americans. Therefore, when a black person is on trial, they may be more enthusiastic about a lawyer holding the government to the standard of justice enshrined in our Constitution—a standard that was never designed to protect them. Two systems emerge: one designed to ensure justice for a segment of Americans and one that doesn't. It is no secret that the founding fathers did not create our system of justice to apply to black people. A completely separate set of laws, known as slave codes, governed the treatment of most black people at the time the Constitution was drafted. White supremacy was part of the accepted fabric of America's legal system.

Post-slavery, in the decades following the Civil War, black codes and Jim Crow laws were used to heavily regulate and criminalize free blacks. As the system of criminal regulation replaced slavery as the mechanism to subjugate black people, our fidelity to these hallowed constitutional protections waned. Accusations of criminal wrongdoing against a black person were frequently justification enough to bypass the process entirely.

While the Fourteenth Amendment purported to give fundamental protections to African Americans, a wave of racial terrorism shaped what justice for blacks looked like practically. African Americans were routinely lynched in the United States, without any pretense of due process. Justice for a black man accused of a crime frequently meant an accusation leveled, a lynch mob assembled, guilt hastily declared, and a sentence pronounced and executed. There was no jury and no trial, and no concern for any evidence of innocence. There was literally no attempt at procedural justice. Thousands of lynchings occurred in the decades following the ratification of the Fourteenth Amendment.[16]

Eventually Americans slowly lost their appetite for such injustice. Courageous civil rights activists stood up to lynch mobs, and organizations like the NAACP led an effort to change American attitudes about lynching. By the 1930s, those attitudes began to shift. There was growing pressure to end a practice that was so antithetical to everything America claimed to stand for. And the Southern criminal justice system got the message.

To adapt to changing attitudes, those responsible for administering justice in the South needed at least the pretense of justice, so they made an implicit bargain with the lynch mobs. If you bring the accused to us, instead of organizing a lynching, we will very quickly try them, convict them, and execute them. These "legal lynchings" began to take the place of the less civilized variety. To further the appearance of complying with the law, defense attorneys were used as window dressing, allowing the public to rest easy that justice had been served. And for a while, this kept the nation at bay.

There was little outrage over the perfunctory "day in court" that John Downer, an accused rapist, received in Elberton, Georgia. One week after his arrest, Downer was tried. He was given a lawyer on the day of trial. No continuance was requested so that the defense could conduct an investigation or interview Downer. Trial began around 11 a.m. and concluded that afternoon. The jury deliberated a mere six minutes before returning a guilty verdict. Downer was sentenced to die. The year was 1931.[17] It was the same year nine black teenagers were on a train passing through Alabama when they prevailed in a fight against a group of white boys on board. Deputies in Scottsboro, Alabama, pulled the nine young black men from the train and charged them with raping two white women. The nine black teenagers were rushed to trial twelve days later. They had been appointed counsel the morning of trial. One of their lawyers was an alcoholic real estate lawyer from Tennessee who had no knowledge of criminal procedure in Alabama. The second was a local lawyer, in his seventies, who hadn't tried a case in thirty years. The two lawyers willingly went to trial that day without conducting any investigation, litigating any motions, or preparing their clients. As expected, the young men were convicted, and eight were sentenced to die. The ninth, only thirteen, was sentenced to life in prison. The Scottsboro Boys, as the group became known, are still widely remembered for the gross miscarriage of justice they endured.

The case of the Scottsboro Boys seemed to further awaken America's need to claim its unrealized ideals. It became a cause célèbre. Across the nation, and the world, voices decried the obvious unfairness of the system that now sought to execute children. The case dramatically tested who we believed ourselves to be as a nation. Forced to look into the mirror and see this reflection, the American public jerked away. The protests that followed seemed to remind us that, at our core, we are a nation that roots for the underdog. We don't like bullies. The Scottsboro Boys brought into focus the fact that the accused is the underdog of the criminal justice system, in need of protection—and the defender is the protector, who symbolizes American ideals.

This was reflected in the popular culture of the times. For a season and a half, beginning in 1954, the CBS television series *The Public Defender* starred Reed Hadley, and for two seasons beginning that same year NBC aired *Justice*, about Legal Aid Society lawyers. From 1956 to 1957, Charlton Comics published a comic book called *Public Defender in Action*, in which the court-appointed lawyer was the hero.

Hollywood also cast the criminal defense lawyer as hero, hiring the era's biggest stars to represent the protectors of the accused. In 1959, James Stewart played defense lawyer Paul Biegler in the movie *Anatomy of a Murder*, about an army lieutenant accused of murder. Three years later, in perhaps the most highly acclaimed criminal justice film of all time, *To Kill a Mockingbird*, Gregory Peck played Atticus Finch. Finch is the proto-typical public defender, whose heroism lies in his willingness to valiantly represent Tom Robinson, a black man accused of raping a white woman in small-town 1930s Alabama, despite the derision and hatred he and his family receive from members of the community.

To Kill a Mockingbird captured the public imagination, presenting a model of what a lawyer should be: a vehicle through which we can realize our most noble ideals, even in the face of great opposition. It inspired a nation to believe in its system of justice and to revere the role of the law-yer at its foundation.

The popular culture narrative that heroized the defender was a clear reaction to an era in which we barely paid lip service to our loftiest consti-tutional ideals. As a nation, we were shamed by the brutality of our crimi-nal justice system and by the fact that we stood by and watched as so many citizens were denied the most basic protections guaranteed all Americans. We longed to redefine ourselves. Through the criminal defense lawyer, we could do just that.

If history reflects a national mind-set that ebbs and flows between aspiring to our highest ideals and sinking to our most wretched instincts, admiration for the defense lawyer served as a proxy for our collective fan-tasy that everyone is treated fairly in our courts, regardless of race or class. There was a sense of shame over the way the US allowed African Ameri-cans to be treated inhumanely. Weaving the laudable defense lawyer into the national narrative was an attempt to absolve ourselves of our guilt.

It is no coincidence that a year after *To Kill a Mockingbird* hit the silver screen, the Supreme Court clarified the critical role the public defender must play if we are to realize our constitutional guarantees. Amid a col-lective, national embrace of the concept of defending the most vulnerable among us against the power of the system, the court decided *Gideon v. Wainwright.*

Clarence Earl Gideon was tried and convicted in a Florida courtroom of breaking into a local pool hall. He could not afford a lawyer and was consequently forced to represent himself. Gideon appealed to the Supreme Court, arguing that the Sixth Amendment requires states that want to prosecute a person criminally to provide that person with a lawyer if one cannot be afforded. The court agreed, making clear for the first time that the right to counsel is fundamental to our system of justice. Gideon was retried, this time with a lawyer. This time he was acquitted.

The year was 1963. As a nation, we were involved in an ongoing struggle to recognize basic civil rights for all people in education, public accommodations, and voting. We had also come to understand that discrimination in the criminal justice system, as much as anywhere, was driving outcomes that were patently inconsistent with who we claimed to be. *Gideon* promised an army of advocates to ensure civil rights were protected in the courts, the arena where the stakes were the highest.

In this sense, lawyers for the poor were civil rights heroes, a critical component of a campaign to address the nation's pervasive abuse of civil and human rights. Proponents of a robust right to counsel celebrated. Protecting the underdog when the stakes are highest was no longer an American fairy tale told on television, in comic books, and in movies. It was a reality. As the nation's courts and legislature continued to build upon the protections afforded historically vulnerable citizens, the defense lawyer was celebrated in our popular culture with more television shows, series like *The Defenders*, featuring a father-son criminal defense team, which ran until 1965, and *Perry Mason*, perhaps the best-known television defender, which ran until 1966 and made a brief revival several years later.

This renewed respect for lawyers who protect individual rights was accompanied by a deeply humane narrative about the outlaw himself. In the decade after *Gideon*, Hollywood repeatedly cast the lawbreaker as hero. In the 1967 film *Cool Hand Luke*, Paul Newman played a Florida prisoner who refused to submit to authority. That same year, Warren Beatty and Faye Dunaway glamorized notorious bank robbers in *Bonnie and Clyde*. Two years later, Paul Newman teamed up with Robert Redford to glorify the lives of notorious train robbers in *Butch Cassidy and the Sundance Kid*. And in 1975, Al Pacino starred as a flawed but lovable bank robber in *Dog Day Afternoon*. These, and numerous other films of this genre, reinforced a narrative in which the protagonist was a deeply humane outlaw pitted against a common antagonist: a faceless and heartless government. Over and over again, the public rallied behind the criminal.

As a young public defender, I decorated my office walls with quotes that inspired me. One of my favorites, attributed to Sister Helen Prejean, served as a constant reminder of the humanity of every person we represent: "The dignity of the human person means that every human being is worth more than the worst thing they've ever done."[18] More recently, this idea is associated with the teachings of famed civil rights lawyer Bryan Stevenson. During this post-*Gideon* era, films reflected this truism, showing outlaws as deeply human and the lawyers who represent them—against a system that strives to reduce them to a label constructed from their worst acts—as heroic. This was a time when we believed in the worth of the individual, we believed in justice tempered by mercy, and we revered the lawyer willing to fight for these values.

For many of us raised on them, these movies instilled a certain set of values about what justice means. They were part of a popular culture that reflected a deep cynicism about government power. It respected individual rights. It spoke to our desire to see the little guy prevail over an all-powerful state. But despite the history that propelled this narrative, it was devoid of any racial analysis. As a nation we had been embarrassed by our history of racial injustice, and it remained too uncomfortable to be constantly reminded of.

Television shows about public defenders that did not deal with race, and movies in which outlaws were portrayed by our most glamorous—and whitest—stars, allowed the viewing public to champion our constitutional values without having to reckon with our complicity in denying them to so many for so long. A narrative in which the lawyer who takes on white supremacy is played by the white actor Gregory Peck, as opposed to a real-life, African American defender-hero like Thurgood Marshall, made it easy for white America to cheer for the triumph of American ideals without feeling defensive. And surely the fact that Clarence Earl Gideon, an older white man, was the face of *Gideon v. Wainwright* made it far easier for America to widely embrace the decision.

Gideon must be understood in the context of our nation's ongoing struggle to realize basic civil and human rights. But our struggle for equal justice in America has always been an ebb and flow, with periods of progress followed by a reactionary response. The renewed commitment to criminal justice, and the accompanying respect for public defenders, was part of an era in which we made a number of civil rights gains. It was a period that saw the dissolution of the formal system of Jim Crow laws. Pushback was inevitable.

As African Americans continued to press for equality, conservative politicians seized the opportunity to galvanize white working-class voters. They painted restless black protesters as a threat to the moral fabric of America. A new tough-on-crime era was ushered in, with criminal courts taking the place of Jim Crow laws to control black communities.

Our commitment to civil rights quickly gave way to a national desire to maintain the prevailing racial order. The criminal justice system would become the next system of control. Black men were portrayed as criminals. We abandoned any hope that we would be faithful to the protections at the heart of our democracy. We could not have both. We chose the former. In the ensuing decades the criminal justice system would morph from a symbol of liberty to one of oppression. A new narrative of the superpredator would emerge. And with it, our respect for the lawyers necessary to protect the accused would wither.

Now in Hollywood the public defender was seen as an incompetent, bumbling fool, symbolized by the comical court-appointed lawyer portrayed by Austin Pendleton in *My Cousin Vinny*. The role of the public defender was also revamped for television, a transformation perhaps best reflected in the introduction to *Law & Order*, the longest-running crime drama in American television history:

> In the criminal justice system, the people are represented by two separate, yet equally important groups: the police who investigate crime and the district attorneys who prosecute the offenders.

In this most revered and influential of TV series, defense attorneys were not worth mentioning in the introduction. They were literally rendered irrelevant in the new criminal justice narrative. When they were portrayed, it was as hopelessly stupid, incompetent, and naive, or slick, sleazy, and corrupt.

And the people they defended began to look less like Paul Newman and more like the young toughs portrayed in movies like *Menace II Society* and *Juice*, young "superpredators" who cared little for human life and posed a threat to our very survival. In this new narrative, the outlaw is no longer worthy of the fundamental constitutional protections guaranteed us all.

This narrative not only shaped how justice was presented through fictional entertainment; it shaped the way news media reported about justice. In a case that has garnered renewed attention thanks to the searing Ava DuVernay series *When They See Us*, on April 19, 1989, a young investment banker named Trisha Meili was beaten and raped as she jogged in New York's Central Park. Almost immediately, five young men—four black and one Hispanic—were arrested. Within forty-eight hours, the *New York Daily News* published a cover story with the headline "Wolf Pack's Prey." The media coined the phrase "wilding" to describe groups of young menaces who were more animal than human. In the media frenzy that ensued, there was little public doubt about the guilt of the teenagers. They were tried and convicted without receiving any benefit of the doubt. It turned out these young men were completely innocent. But in the "lock 'em up first, ask questions later" atmosphere that had a firm grasp on society at the time, they never stood a chance. It was a narrative fueled by crime reporters of every ilk. It was so powerful it drove every decision we made as a nation. And when it introduced us to Willie Horton, it transformed politics and policy in America.

Whole presidential elections have been built on this politics of fear. Republican presidential nominee George H. W. Bush built his campaign against then Massachusetts governor Michael Dukakis around a man named Willie Horton, who was serving a life sentence for murder when he was released as part of a weekend furlough program. Horton used the furlough as an opportunity to escape, and later committed several violent crimes, including rape. Bush made Horton the face of his campaign, painting Dukakis as soft on crime. Horton's image—dark skin, unkempt hair, and bushy beard—perhaps became more widely recognized than Dukakis's.

As this new criminal justice narrative continued to shape our collective assumptions, it held decision makers hostage without regard to party. Conservatives and liberals got in on the action.

Within four years of Bush's Horton campaign, future liberal standard-bearer Bill Clinton left the presidential campaign trail to fly back to Arkansas to personally witness the execution of a mentally challenged man named Ricky Ray Rector. Clinton, then governor of Arkansas, was vying for the Democratic nomination to take on Bush in the 1992 election. But he had a problem. Rector was scheduled to be executed in Arkansas during the primaries. Rector had killed a man, along with a police officer who tried to arrest him, before shooting himself in the head in an attempt to take his own life. While he did not kill himself, he blew away a portion of his brain, rendering him extremely mentally limited. He was so low-functioning he did not understand that his victims were not still alive, nor could he appreciate what death was. Nevertheless, he was convicted and sentenced to die.

A humanitarian push to have Clinton commute the death sentence and spare his life struck many, including Clinton, as reasonable. In an essay in the *New Yorker*, friends of Clinton described how tortured he was over the decision. He knew it was wrong to execute Rector, given his mental condition. But Clinton had lost an election after being labeled soft on crime. He would not make that mistake again. He flew back to Arkansas to preside over the execution. Sparing a human life was not worth the risk of another political defeat.

The night before he was executed, Rector ordered his last meal. It included a piece of pecan pie that he did not eat. He asked the guards to put it away for later. Rector was so limited, he did not understand there would be no later.

The story foreshadowed the way Clinton would govern, as a new kind of Democrat, as well as the direction of a party many viewed as the more compassionate of the two major options. Clinton signed some of the toughest criminal justice legislation, and he is widely regarded as being as responsible as anyone for fueling the era of mass incarceration. His wife, the future Democratic presidential nominee Hillary Clinton, famously made a speech discussing "the kinds of kids that are called superpredators; no conscience, no empathy. We can talk about why they ended up that way, but first we have to bring them to heel."[19] The family most associated with shaping the modern Democratic Party had fully bought into a narrative driven by those who sought to divide the country into the "us" and the "them." This narrative would haunt every political candidate who sought to realize our forefathers' democratic ideals.

Whether explicit (as in the Willie Horton campaign) or implicit (as in Hillary Clinton's pronouncement that we must bring young "superpredators" to heel), the narrative around criminal justice strongly associates race and dangerousness. It explains why, in 1994, *Time* magazine's cover portrayed a darkened image of the face of O. J. Simpson, the former darling of white America, who many believed transcended race. And it explains why even civil rights icon Jesse Jackson famously said, "There is nothing more painful to me at this stage in my life than to walk down the street and hear footsteps and start thinking about robbery . . . then look around and see someone white and feel relieved."[20] Whether this association is intentionally used to fan people's fears or subconsciously embraced in our criminal justice thinking, our perception of race and dangerousness are intertwined in the way we all think about criminal justice in America.

Social scientists today understand how Americans have subconsciously accepted a narrative that sees African Americans as more dangerous. We are more likely to assume criminality when the accused is black. These assumptions entice us to be more accepting of harsh treatment of this population, and less compassionate about the consequences to impacted families and communities.

This implicit racial bias explains how the best-intentioned of us can perpetuate a racially disparate approach to criminal justice while believing we are being fair. As a nation, we have embraced a narrative that sees African Americans as less human, and as more dangerous. It shapes every aspect of our lives, none more than our approach to criminal justice. This narrative is at the heart of a criminal legal culture that has seduced us into accepting a system that looks nothing like the one designed by our democratic forefathers.

Implicit bias is subconscious. Structural changes will not change the assumptions that drive us to engineer disparate racial outcomes. The solution won't lie in policy fixes. Addressing implicit bias requires that we raise consciousness, rewrite narrative, and change values.

Until we truly come to see those accused of wrongdoing as valuable members of our community, we will not be inclined to reimagine a criminal justice system in which the protections at the heart of our democracy are applied with equal force to all.

WHEN AFRICAN AMERICANS CELEBRATED the O. J. Simpson verdict, they were responding to a victory over a system that had always found a way to deny them justice. It was a system that had undergone a series of structural changes since the Civil War, yet had maintained a consistent narrative in which they were unworthy of protection. The criminal justice system was simply its latest incarnation. Johnnie Cochran was a symbol of hope—hope that justice could be extracted from this system. He was a real-life example of the importance of a meaningful right to counsel.

On March 29, 2005, Cochran died. The Reverend Al Sharpton delivered a eulogy at his memorial service. His words served as an exclamation point on the idea that justice can only be extracted from the criminal justice system through the defense lawyer.

"In all due respect to you, Brother Simpson, we didn't clap, when the acquittal of Simpson came, for O. J. We were clapping for Johnny."[21]

PART II

CULTURE

CHAPTER 3

ROUTINE INJUSTICE

TWENTY YEARS AFTER my first experience in a courtroom, as a child with a water gun and a budding antiauthority streak, I went to law school. Determined to become a defense attorney, I took every criminal law course I could find. I understood defense attorneys as the men and women who protected individual rights when the state tried to take one's liberty. They were the last line of defense against a government prone to tyranny if left unchecked. I came to believe deeply in abstract principles of law like *due process* and *equal justice*. What I did not really understand, and what law school did not teach me, is that the law is about people. When you cut through all the theory and doctrine, when you wade past the lofty legal principles, when you push aside the laws and procedure, the measure of our legal system is in how it treats those who depend on it for justice. Illy understood this from her girlhood. I began to understand this fully only after I became a lawyer.

I was five months into my new career as a public defender in Washington, DC, when I was assigned to represent a fifteen-year-old boy named Jacob. He and his best friend, Mark—two curious teenagers—were at Mark's house when they found a gun that belonged to Mark's father. They did not know the gun was loaded. Jacob was playing with the gun when it accidentally fired, killing Mark.

I first met Jacob when he was brought to court the morning after the accident. I spoke with Jacob in his cell; it was not much of a conversation. The young man appeared almost comatose, unable to communicate, and grief-stricken over the role he played in his best friend's death. It was apparent that there was no punishment the juvenile justice system could visit upon this child that was greater than the punishment he was wielding on himself. Far from being a threat to society, he was a young man deep in the throes of remorse and sorrow. Yet he was charged with murder.

As my co-counsel and I prepared for trial, we got to know this young man well. He was smart and compassionate, and so appreciative to have us fighting for him. He had such a promising future ahead of him. He desperately wanted to finish high school and go on to college, something that would be unlikely if the court committed him to Oak Hill, Washington's juvenile detention facility, where kids were more likely to be guided toward crime than higher education.

Jacob grew up in an environment that made it easy for young people to get into trouble. Guns were prevalent and easily accessible. He had successfully navigated this environment without any problems for fifteen years. But none of that mattered to the prosecutor who charged him, or to the judge who handed down the conviction.

The judge sentenced Jacob to detention at Oak Hill until his twenty-first birthday—the most severe sentence available in juvenile court. Jacob's dreams ended at that moment. As he was led through the courtroom's back door toward the cellblock, I was devastated—for Mark's family and for Jacob's future.

I walked back to my office across the street from the courthouse. I closed the door, turned out the lights, sat down, and cried. I was twenty-nine years old at the time. Intellectually, I knew I had done all I could for this young man, but viscerally I felt like I failed. I could not prevent what I clearly believed was a great injustice. I questioned my career choice: "This work is too hard," I told myself. "It is too hard watching terrible things happen to people you come to care about deeply." I knew this was part of the job, and I knew I could not change it. I seriously questioned whether I made the right career choice. I thought about quitting, but I stayed with the work.

THE PUBLIC DEFENDER SERVICE (PDS) for the District of Columbia was built around the concept of "client-centered representation." This requires getting close to a person, working hand in hand to develop a strategy to try to achieve their goals. Inevitably, when you get this close—when you learn the stories that make the person who they are—the relationship becomes personal. The work becomes personal. And when you come to understand how inhumane the justice system is, and how cruelly it treats those thrown into it, the obligation to try to liberate the person you represent from its grasp takes on a sense of urgency.

I felt this sense of urgency when I represented Jacob. Before meeting him, I understood what client-centered representation meant in theory. But through my relationship with Jacob, I learned three important lessons that have since shaped my perspective about public defense. The first lesson is that it is incredibly hard to be a caring lawyer in a system that judges without compassion. The second is that no quality is more important to being a good public defender than caring. The third is that it takes a supportive community to help you continue to care when you work within a system that encourages you not to.

Through my relationship with Jacob I certainly learned that caring comes with a cost. I questioned whether I could continue to invest so much in people I might not be able to save. I was unsure how long I would be able to endure the pain. But one thing I knew for certain was that there was no way I would be able to withstand for long, without support, the systemic pressure to not care.

Fortunately, I worked in a public defender office where I was surrounded by a community of committed, inspired lawyers. They helped me understand that the result had nothing to do with any shortcoming on my part. They pointed out that Jacob benefited from having a lawyer who cared, who treated him as a person, who fought for him. They taught me that we cannot underestimate the importance of giving our clients respect and a sense of their own deep humanity during the most trying time of their lives. I quickly realized public defenders need a community to help sustain their positive work. Even with my great colleagues during a difficult time in the infancy of my career, I still struggled to deal with what I catalogued as "losses." At that stage of my career, I equated guilty verdicts with losing. I viewed the work of the public defender narrowly. I saw the role of the public defender as dealing with a precise problem (an accusation) in a limited forum (the criminal case). Through this narrow lens I understood my experience with Jacob as a failure. I was young. I had much to learn.

It was not until six years later that I began to appreciate that success must be measured in something other than not-guilty verdicts. Elliott

Johns taught me this lesson. As a supervising attorney, I was assigned to represent Mr. Johns, a man accused of committing a series of sexual assaults. His file was left on my desk. It included little more than a police report, accompanied by a note asking me to meet my new client.

As I read the report, I learned this man was accused of attacking several prostitutes he solicited. The violence involved was horrific, leaving the women horribly injured, both physically and psychologically. At first blush, the evidence appeared overwhelming. The report claimed that DNA, hair, and clothing fibers linked Mr. Johns to the crime and linked the victims to the van that he allegedly used to pick them up. The women all identified him and, although he never admitted to the crimes, he made a statement that placed him at the relevant scenes at the relevant times.

At this stage in my career I had represented many people accused of serious felonies, including rape and murder. I had yet to meet a client I did not deeply connect with on a human level. I had come to believe that there was no person you could not come to care about if you took the time to know their story. Yet, as I read about the horrific nature of the assaults on perfect strangers, I wondered who could do these things. As I considered the strength of the evidence pointing to the man I was about to meet, I wondered if this would be the first client I could not connect with on a human level. When I arrived at the jail, my expectations were proven wrong.

I walked into the visiting room and met an African American man in his early forties. He was not the person I was expecting to meet. He was soft-spoken and polite. He asked how I was, he asked about his family, and he asked about the women who were his accusers. He was neither defensive nor hostile. He did not seem capable of doing the things he was accused of. I began to question the evidence as laid out in that police report. But if he did commit the crimes, he proved the message that hung on my office wall. People are complex. They are not the sum total of their worst acts.

I soon met his family: a very concerned mother, three doting sisters, a loving and supportive wife, and two little children who loved their daddy so very much. Through each of them I came to understand Mr. Johns better. I began to form a much more complete picture of the man than the one painted through the assumptions I drew based on the police report. As our trial date approached, we became closer. He never seemed worried about his own fate. He was much more concerned about how this ordeal would impact his family. The trial lasted a couple of weeks and, as expected, the evidence was quite damning. However, our investigation revealed some evidence that suggested someone else may have committed the sexual assault. The jury deliberated for several days, giving the defense team increasing hope. I began to imagine Mr. Johns being reunited with his family. The prospect of his children being able to jump into their daddy's arms began to feel very real. Then the jury reached a decision.

As we stood in the courtroom, awaiting the verdict, I was hopeful. The foreperson was asked to share the jury's findings. The foreperson did: guilty on all counts. My heart dropped. The judge sentenced Mr. Johns to a term of imprisonment that would guarantee he died in prison. As he was led through the back doors and I walked through the front, I had that same feeling that I remembered from six years earlier: "This work is just too hard. It is too hard watching terrible things happen to people you come to care about deeply." That evening I collected myself and went to see Mr. Johns at the jail.

As I entered the visiting room to meet him, I looked at him and said, "I am so sorry."

He interrupted me. "Mr. Rapping . . . thank you."

"Thank you?" I replied. "Maybe you don't understand what happened today . . . but things didn't go so well."

He smiled. "No, you don't understand."

As I recall it, he continued:

All my life I've been in the system. I went to DC public schools and never had a teacher who cared about me. I was in the juvenile system and never had a lawyer care about me. I've had adult charges before and no lawyer ever fought for me. But you, your co-counsel, your investigator, your law clerks . . . you all cared about me. You fought for me. You gave me the kind of representation the Constitution says I deserve. And for that, I thank you. But even more importantly, my family sat through the trial. My mother, sisters, wife, and children heard what they said I did and are convinced that the jury got it wrong. I could easily spend the rest of my life in prison as long as my family does not believe I had anything to do with these awful crimes. For that, I thank you.

I went home that night and had an epiphany. If Jacob taught me the importance of being a caring lawyer and the need to have a supportive community to remain inspired, Mr. Johns taught me a new definition of success, one that felt much more attainable. For the first time in six years, I had an understanding with which I was comfortable of what it meant to be successful as a public defender. It was not simply "not guilty" verdicts, dismissals, and great plea offers. It meant being able to look in the mirror each night and know that today you gave each and every client the representation you would want for your own loved ones. It meant making sure each client knew they had a lawyer who cared intensely, worked tirelessly, and respected their humanity without condition. If you could do that as a public defender, you could go to sleep knowing you had a "good day."

I had spent six years in an organization surrounded by public defenders who could do this each and every day. PDS was nationally recognized as a model public defender agency. The lawyers had manageable caseloads and access to the resources necessary to represent every client well. These were certainly critical ingredients to its success. But what was truly special about the organization was the spirit of the lawyers themselves. They were carefully selected and trained to embrace a client-centered practice.

I was surrounded by lawyers who earned a fraction of what our law school classmates made in the private sector. We all worked long hours, suffered emotional fatigue, and watched terrible things happen to people we cared about. Nevertheless, we could achieve that standard of success and find each day a "good day." At the end of any case, we could say we did everything we could for each client. Regardless of the outcome, we did not contribute to a process that strips our clients of their humanity. Instead, we stood up to it and fought alongside the people we represented to resist it. Whatever the outcome, we always felt confident that through our representation, our clients' voices were heard. My career to date was filled with "good days"—as measured by this more nuanced understanding of my role. Based on this definition, poor people in the District of Columbia could not get better representation than they received through PDS.

During my tenure at PDS, I became convinced that the success of PDS was primarily about the lawyers who worked there. It takes a special person to care about people others find deplorable. It takes a special person to resist being beaten down by the terrible things they will experience in the criminal justice system.

As much as anything, I credited a recruitment program that identified and hired the most committed future public defenders from law schools across the country, a training program that gave them the skills they needed to act on this commitment, and a community that inspired them to maintain their passion. I soon became the training director for PDS and turned my attention to developing the amazing young lawyers we hired into defenders who could meet this benchmark and to nurturing the community to which they would turn for support. After a decade as a public defender in Washington, I was given the opportunity to help build a public defender system from the ground up, in a place where it was desperately needed. Armed with my understanding of what it meant to be a successful public defender and of the role that recruitment, training, and community play in developing these advocates, I was ready to embrace this challenge.

In 2004 I got a call from Stephen Bright, the executive director of the Southern Center for Human Rights, a nonprofit based in Atlanta, Georgia, committed to improving the administration of justice. Although Steve had left PDS more than a decade before I started, he was a former public defender there. I met Steve several times during my tenure at PDS, and I viewed him with great admiration, going back to my law school days.

Steve left Washington to do death penalty work in the South but quickly began challenging injustice more broadly. By the time I became a public defender, Steve was already one of the nation's best-known critics of America's dysfunctional approach to criminal justice. He worked tirelessly, taking on systems that failed to meet constitutional demands. He understood the central role that bad lawyering played in fueling unacceptable outcomes. To public defenders, Steve was inspiring. His was the loudest and most consistent voice calling attention to our nation's failure to ensure that poor people accused of crimes had adequate representation.

While I was at PDS, Steve would regularly return to Washington to rally support for his work in the South. He would often stop by the office, sharing stories of the abysmal lawyering that was tolerated outside of our Washington bubble.

It always felt as though he was challenging us to leave the relative comfort of PDS to do the work where the need was greatest. Steve had just finished leading an effort to develop a statewide public defender system in Georgia. The new regime was to kick in on January 1, 2005. He wondered if I would consider becoming the state's first training director.

Georgia has 159 counties, and at the time each had its own system for providing counsel for the poor. Only 20 had full-time public defender offices. The rest relied on judge-picked lawyers who agreed to handle criminal cases for a fixed fee. There were no standards that counties had to meet or statewide training requirements. Because cash-strapped counties were responsible for funding the lawyers, they crafted systems that would allow them to do it cheaply. The results were often frightening.

Steve's offer presented an amazing opportunity to replicate across Georgia what worked so well in Washington. I imagined a statewide model that could be exported to places most in need of reform. I began to think about how we could attract passionate lawyers to Georgia's public defender offices, train them to provide the highest quality representation, and infuse them into a community of advocates across the state committed to the promise of equal justice. My response clearly reflected what I saw as the success of PDS.

As excited as I was about this opportunity, I also had reservations. I had become quite comfortable in Washington. Illy was pregnant with our first child, Aaliyah. We had recently married and bought a house. I was certain I already had the greatest job in the world, and Illy had recently switched from teaching first grade to teaching high school English at a charter school, founded by two close friends, for court-involved kids. One of the friends was a former public defender, and our office had a very close relationship with the school.

Two brothers who attended the charter school had lived with me off and on for a few years. I met them when I was a law student volunteering with a tutoring program, and they became like foster children to me over the years. The other kids at the school were frequently at our home, and we regularly participated in outings and functions with the lawyers, teachers, and students. We had developed a second family made up of young professionals committed to social justice and of teenagers from the communities we served. These were the friends I imagined I would lean on forever, and they were the people I wanted my children to grow up around.

But I also felt an obligation to embrace this opportunity. I knew PDS was the ideal place to develop the kinds of public defenders who were always missing from Steve's stories. PDS was like a small public defender factory, investing its resources to produce the advocates America so desperately needed. Applicants from the top law schools in the nation, many of whom were being courted by the most prestigious law firms and federal clerkships, would compete for a handful of slots. Those selected would collectively participate in an eight-week training program before receiving their first cases. They would be closely supervised as their caseloads slowly increased, with opportunities to co-counsel cases with some of the most experienced trial attorneys along the way. Manageable caseloads ensured the opportunity to brainstorm every case with a collection of colleagues who treated every client as their own, guaranteeing that every person represented by the agency received the benefit of the institutional knowledge and creativity so unique to the public defender world.

But despite the amazing defenders the organization cultivated, farming those defenders to places where they were most needed was not part of its vision. Its mission was to provide superior representation to poor people in Washington, DC, not to save public defense in America. PDS did not contemplate that its lawyers would transition to continue their work beyond the DC borders. In fact, as wonderful as its recruitment model was, PDS often attracted law students who would spend a few years in public defense but who were not necessarily committed to a career in the field. Developing awesome lawyers to go really hard for a few years before moving on made sense, given PDS's objective.

Every year, incredibly talented public defenders would resign. Some would continue doing criminal defense work in private practice. Most stopped practicing criminal law. A handful would remain in indigent defense, but they were the exception, not the rule. I often bemoaned our organizational failure to transition alumni to places where they were needed. I was now challenged to do just that.

I also understood that PDS did not need me. While I was well respected as a trial lawyer and training director, the organization was filled with wonderful public defenders who could fill any void my departure might leave. Every year the agency would lose lawyers who were among the best criminal defense lawyers in the nation and would replenish them so seamlessly it never missed a beat. No poor person in Washington would suffer if I left.

The cost-benefit analysis led to one conclusion. I should seize the opportunity to take what I learned at PDS and transfer it to a place where change was desperately needed. Illy was supportive. We decided to move to Georgia.

I understood from a decade at PDS that a successful public defender program begins with hiring. PDS never hired experienced lawyers. It wanted public defenders with a specific mind-set, and it understood that the best way to ensure that is to develop them from scratch. I believed in this approach and saw recruitment as the key to reform. But I also knew that getting law students to consider coming to offices throughout Georgia would be challenging. As a law student, I had never considered moving to the Deep South, nor had any public defenders I knew. We all had our sights set on a handful of relatively well-resourced offices, in attractive cities like DC, New York, Philadelphia, San Francisco, and Seattle. When I decided to take the job in Georgia, colleagues wished me well but were skeptical. They were doubtful that we could open up a national pipeline of recent law graduates to join us.

But circumstances in Georgia offered an attractive opportunity that did not exist when I was a law student. Back then, the assumption was that places like Georgia were hopelessly broken and that there was no way for a new lawyer to succeed there. However, I believed there were law students who would relish the chance to be a part of what we were building.

Unlike some of the popular offices in the Northeast and on the West Coast, we in the Georgia system offered the opportunity to join a community that would be working to reform public defense in a place where it was most needed. Candidates could be in on the ground floor of meaningful change. I knew it would take a special breed of recent law graduate to be excited by this prospect, but I was certain we could recruit young lawyers who were every bit as talented and passionate as those who went to well-established offices. I knew there were law students who would welcome the chance to be part of a movement to tackle injustice where the need was greatest. They just needed the assurance that they would have training and support, and that they would not be alone.

I set out to create a blueprint to make this happen. It was called the Georgia Honors Program.

Through the Honors Program, we would recruit the most caring lawyers, provide them the training they needed to ignite their passion for the work, and build a community that would help them retain it. Each year, we would bring in a new class of public defenders who would commit to spending at least three years in offices throughout the state. They would begin this experience together, with a three-week training program that not only would provide them with the skills they needed to be excellent advocates but also with a set of strategies to resist the systemic pressure to simply process cases. They would be paired with mentors to give them support, and they would regroup for quarterly gatherings for the next three years. The meetings would provide additional training and foster the group's development into a supportive community committed to a shared vision.

The program's success depended on our ability to attract promising defenders to the offices we served. We conditioned admission into this community, and the promise of three years of training and support, on the applicants' agreeing to allow us to place them in any of the forty-three judicial circuits that were part of the state public defender system. Initiatives like Peace Corps and Teach for America demonstrated that there were dedicated young people willing to sacrifice quite a bit to do good work where it is most needed. I had faith that we could identify their legal counterparts.

I was quickly reassured. In its first year, the Honors Program attracted well over a hundred applicants from more than fifty law schools, representing roughly half the states in the country. Twenty-four lawyers made up its first class. They graduated from seventeen different law schools in twelve different states. More than thirty years separated the oldest from the youngest. They were male and female, African American, Caucasian, and Latino. Some were born and raised in Georgia, while others had no previous connection to the state. But they shared a commitment to join this exciting movement to reform indigent defense. This early recruitment success left me encouraged.

The inaugural class convened for the first time in August 2005. Its members met for three weeks. They were trained by supportive leaders from Georgia paired with a national faculty of seasoned public defender trainers. They did what so many young lawyers committed to public defense were unwilling to do, and what every skeptic I had talked to over the past year thought no student would do. They took a risk to become public defenders where the need was greatest.

Their presence validated what I believed we could accomplish when I agreed to move to Georgia. I knew that if we were going to reform public defense in the places where it was most broken, it would be because of new public defenders like these. I was sure we could identify these lawyers and encourage them to join us. But I did not appreciate the challenge they would be stepping into.

WITHIN A MONTH OF the launch of Georgia's new statewide public defender system, I organized a weekend of training sessions on the fundamental elements of criminal defense work, to be held on Jekyll Island, Georgia. The audience included hundreds of public defenders of varying experience levels, from a hefty collection of brand-new public defenders to nearly fifty chief public defenders tasked with running public defender offices across the state. The program was both an introduction to public defense for the newer attorneys and a refresher on the basic lessons for those who were more seasoned. One workshop focused on filing motions. We discussed litigating common constitutional violations—the type that defense lawyers routinely raise in every case—focusing on issues essential to preparing for trial and preserving a client's most fundamental rights. In a decade of practice, I never had a case in which I did not file similar motions, and I knew no competent lawyer who had not either. So I was taken aback when one of the chief defenders approached me afterwards.

"I really enjoyed that session," he said, "but we can't do that where I come from."

Perplexed, I said, "Sure you can . . . this is the United States Constitution." At the risk of stating the obvious, I continued, "It applies here in Georgia, I assure you."

He continued undeterred: "I understand that, but where I practice, if we file motions our judges get angry."

This was the first time I personally experienced the extent to which dysfunctional systems could warp the priorities of lawyers. I came to Georgia understanding client-centered representation as the foundation of public defense. Yet this practice was in marked contrast to what I was now hearing from one of the new leaders of Georgia's effort to usher in reform. In his worldview, the client's interests took a backseat to the desire of the judge. What he was advocating was a "judge-centered" mind-set. It was inconsistent with everything I understood about good public defense.

Later that weekend, we had a workshop on client-centered lawyering. After my discussion with this seasoned public defender, I realized the concept might be controversial. I soon learned I was right. During the panel, we got into a discussion about things public defenders may inadvertently do to reinforce the client's belief that we are not fully committed to them.

One public defender brought up how common it was to see public defenders socializing with prosecutors in the courtroom in view of their clients. To the client who sees the prosecutor as a person hell-bent on keeping him in a cage, this interaction could certainly suggest a lawyer who will be less than zealous in fighting for their liberty. Some lawyers shared that they actually are friendly with prosecutors, because it helps their clients. It certainly makes sense that a prosecutor who likes a lawyer is more likely to share information and give reasonable plea offers. But others chimed in that, in doing so, the lawyer must be conscious of how this may appear to the client. Some suggested the lawyer may want to explain to the client how the lawyers might act toward the prosecutor, and how it was designed to help achieve the client's objectives.

An older lawyer raised his hand. "I went to law school with the prosecutors and judges I work with. We are all brothers of the bar. The client is not. I will continue to be friends with the people I work with. Clients will come and go. Why would I care more about my relationship with the client than my colleagues?"

Over time I got to know many experienced public defenders who harbored similar attitudes. They did not get into the work because they cared deeply about the people they would represent. However, they did believe that poor people should have good lawyers and they were certain they were fulfilling that mission. They understood good lawyering as maintaining good relationships with the judges and prosecutors they would work with over time. If fighting too hard for a client in a case would damage those relationships, future clients would suffer. They believed good lawyers did not risk long-term damage to relationships that would help future clients. Those who fought too hard for individual clients were referred to as "true believers." The term was not meant as a compliment. The true believers were the lawyers who did not appreciate the need to get along with their "brothers of the bar."

We had set out to recruit true believers to the Honors Program. They included young lawyers like Janelle Williams, a member of the first Honors Program class. She was born and raised in an African American community in Brooklyn, New York. She graduated from Spelman College and Howard University Law School, two historically black colleges. She deliberately chose to attend schools committed to developing black professionals. She became a public defender because, as she said in her application to the Honors Program, she wanted to represent people who looked like her. For Janelle, public defense was about racial justice. She was accepted into the Honors Program and began her career in Bartow County, Georgia. Bartow County lies about fifty miles outside Atlanta, but it may as well be another world.

Janelle became one of two African American lawyers practicing in the courthouse. Her clients were predominantly white. It was the first time she realized the extent to which poor white people also suffered at the hands of the system. She loved her clients.

But she was routinely reminded that even in a world of white clients, race still mattered. Despite her business suits and briefcase, she was frequently mistaken for a defendant. It took some time before courthouse personnel stopped asking her where her lawyer was when she would enter the courtroom.

Undeterred by the challenges in front of her, Janelle threw herself into her new career and quickly won over the Bartow County legal community. Her spirit shifted their assumptions. The shift was gradual. Janelle got pushback for her client-centered mind-set from other defense lawyers in the community, who may have characterized her as a true believer.

One evening I received a phone call from Janelle. It was still very early in her career. She was representing a juvenile client and had prepared a seemingly obvious release argument that she had not heard made by any of the more experienced lawyers she watched in court. Her arguments were clearly supported by the law. However, when she consulted a veteran practitioner familiar with the court, she was advised that the argument would be a waste of everyone's time. The senior lawyer discouraged her. Janelle was determined to make the argument nonetheless, and wanted some assurance that this was not a mistake. Several of her Honors Program classmates encouraged her as she prepared for court the next day. Janelle made her pitch to the judge against a backdrop of snickers from some of the more experienced members of the bar. The judge agreed with Janelle and released her client. Soon, some of the skeptics adopted her argument in future proceedings.

Jason Carini was another member of that first class. I met Jason in the fall of 2004, when I was recruiting graduating law students at Boston College Law School. Jason grew up in Connecticut, and, aside from a family vacation to Florida, he had never been to the South. The first time he stepped foot in Georgia was when he traveled there to take the bar exam. The second time was to begin his public defender career.

Jason was placed in the Cordele judicial circuit, which had been the target of a 2003 lawsuit that led to legislation that formed Georgia's statewide public defender system. At the time the lawsuit was filed, almost half of the circuit's indigent defendants were pleading guilty without ever talking to a lawyer. The judges would allow them to negotiate pleas directly with the prosecutors. Presumably, lawyers would interfere with the efficient processing of cases.

In Cordele, public defenders almost never met their clients outside of the courtroom. Investigation, legal research, witness interviews, and motions practice were virtually nonexistent. As one could predict, the vast majority of people pled guilty, never receiving a meaningful day in court.[1]

Jason arrived in Cordele having just completed three weeks of training in Vidalia. He was ready to try to implement some practices that were foreign to the courthouses. He understood what kind of representation his clients deserved and saw no reason why he would not do his best to achieve this standard.

Soon after he received his first batch of cases, he filed several dozen suppression motions—the very types of motions we discussed that weekend on Jekyll Island. As Jason recalls, "The courthouse clerks were mystified. Evidently they hadn't seen many motions coming out of the public defender's office; they literally asked me what the motions were for and what was supposed to happen with them." Not long after he filed the motions, he was called into the circuit public defender's office.

The judge had called his boss to complain about all the motions Jason had filed. The circuit defender was far more reluctant than Jason to risk upsetting judges. As Jason recalls, his boss did not order him to reverse course but "suggested that it might be best to file far fewer motions in the future and to see if any of the ones that had already been filed could be dismissed." But Jason was unmoved. He refused to withdraw any of the motions and continued this practice when he believed there was a viable issue that needed to be explored. He certainly drew the ire of the judges. But over time, they began to become less hostile. Slowly, the idea of a meaningful motions practice became a little more accepted in the court-rooms where Jason practiced.

Lawyers like Janelle and Jason made me hopeful about change. But soon the legislature, which had become more conservative since the re-form legislation was enacted in 2003, began looking to cut funding for public defense. This was in the wake of a local case that had made national news. On March 11, 2005, Brian Nichols shot and killed a judge, a court reporter, and a deputy sheriff as he escaped from Fulton County Superior Court in Atlanta during his rape trial. Later that day, before he was cap-tured, Nichols killed a federal agent. The fact that Nichols committed the crimes was beyond dispute. The only real issue was the sentence he would receive. Early on, Nichols's lawyers proposed a resolution that would save taxpayers millions of dollars: Nichols would plead guilty and agree to a sentence of life without parole in order to spare himself a sentence of death. Paul Howard, the Fulton County district attorney, refused. He se-cured a fifty-four-count indictment and provided a witness list with three hundred names.[2] He was seeking the death penalty and was prepared to mount an expensive case to secure it. He insisted on going through a pro-cess that the new state public defender system was ill-prepared to afford. The cost of mounting a sufficiently responsive defense exceeded $3 mil-lion. Of that, $2.6 million came out of the budget for the new statewide public defender system.[3] The ensuing high-profile trial became arguably the single greatest factor in determining the course of indigent defense reform in Georgia.

Critics of the new public defender system decried the amount of money being spent by the defense. Georgia lawmakers blamed defense counsel for mounting such an expensive defense, and blamed the presid-ing judge for approving the defense requests for funding.[4] Yet no one crit-icized Paul Howard for seeking the death penalty in the face of an offer that would ensure Nichols would be imprisoned for life, or for mounting such a complex case, given a relatively straightforward set of facts. By the time the case concluded three years and eight months later, the jury had convicted Nichols on each of the fifty-four counts. Yet jurors refused to sentence him to death. The defense team's hard work revealed severe mental health issues that convinced the jury that executing Nichols would be unjust. Brian Nichols was given the sentence he agreed to accept several years and millions of dollars earlier.

The Nichols defense team gave him the representation that our Constitution guarantees. Yet, rather than seeing this case as evidence that the legislature needed to rein in prosecutorial spending or invest more in indigent defense, state lawmakers were miffed at the public defender system. Apparently believing it more appropriate to have a staff of public defenders simply agree to the execution of their client, they took their anger out on the tens of thousands of poor people across the state who relied on Georgia's public defenders. By 2007, the Georgia legislature cut the funding for the state public defender system 20 percent.[5]

The extent to which a culture of indifference toward the treatment of poor people accused of crimes had a grip on Georgia was reflected in the response to the budget cuts. Very few people outside the defense community expressed outrage. It became clear that the state's commitment to recruiting, training, and supporting public defenders would not be sustained. The Honors Program was seen as a luxury that Georgia lawmakers were no longer willing to fund. We had been meeting quarterly, using hotels and conference centers to accommodate training sessions, but the funding was cut. We continued the meetings at the private homes of local lawyers in Atlanta, with public defenders crashing at one another's homes in nearby counties. While I felt committed to continue to provide support to the first two classes, it was clear that the end of the experiment with the Honors Program had come.

Though a number of Honors Program members left once the program was terminated, many others continued to work in their offices. But those who remained became increasingly dispirited. Marie Pierre-Py was one who remained. She was a graduate of Cornell Law School who came to Georgia because she was interested in death penalty work. She agreed to spend two years with the state's newly formed Capital Defender Office. But her experience with Honors Program classmates caused her to reconsider her decision to focus on capital cases. She came to have a profound appreciation for public defenders who struggled every day in the trenches to represent the masses of poor people pouring into the criminal system. She felt pulled to do that work as well. So when she finished her two-year commitment at the Capital Defender Office, she moved to Walton County to become a public defender.

Thirteen months later she decided she had to leave. She had closed roughly nine hundred cases. She handled approximately 270 cases at a time, including felonies, misdemeanors, and probation revocations. Marie wrote a letter to the *Atlanta Journal-Constitution* in which she explained that "an attorney devoting 50 hours per week to case work, taking no vacation time or sick leave, would have only three hours to devote to an individual case, including court time and meeting with the client."[6] She described a culture in which attorneys in her offices routinely allowed clients to plead guilty without adequate consultation or investigation. They often ignored conflicts of interest among clients because of the cost of having to bring in another lawyer. She described an office with lawyers who worked hard and tried their best, but—because of inexperience and inadequate resources—watched as poor people were consistently funneled through the system without any real chance at justice. She shared how the elimination of the Honors Program impacted morale. She concluded that without that support she could not continue to be a public defender in Georgia. She left Walton County to move to Washington, DC, and work at PDS. It was a chance to go to an office that promised the support that brought her to Georgia two years earlier. To find that support, she had to go to an office where she was not nearly as necessary.

About the time Marie decided to leave, I received an email from Brett Willis, another of Marie's classmates. I first met Brett that weekend on Jekyll Island. He was full of self-confidence, clearly either not aware of the challenges that lay ahead or assured that he was ready for them. Brett was smart, passionate, and fearless. He went to the Hall County public defender office, one of the best in the state. It was one of the few that existed before 2004, and it was filled with excellent lawyers who dedicated their lives to public defense. However, that did not mean it was immune from the cultural pressures that begin to wear on even the best lawyers.

I read Brett's email. He sounded uncharacteristically discouraged. He lamented the end of the Honors Program. He continued, "[There is] still nothing I'd rather be doing, but it doesn't feel quite as pure as before." The last sentence stung. "I'm just becoming part of the machine."

I must have reread that sentence a dozen times, each time thinking of Brett, Janelle, Jason, Marie, and the dozens of other young public defenders who signed up to help bring reform to Georgia a few short years earlier. Brett's words so perfectly captured what I had come to understand as the challenge with public defense. As passionate and determined as any public defender may be, what is most critical to their development is a supportive community that will help them nurture that passion. They will be engaged in a constant struggle to resist being shaped by the system. Either they will maintain the fuel to rage against the machine or they will become part of it.

Meanwhile, the high cost of defending Brian Nichols, which by this point had been a regular discussion in the news, became a rallying cry for critics of a state-funded public defender system. Despite the fact that Nichols's prosecution needlessly spent millions to achieve the very result the defense agreed to accept in the first place, stories of the trial's expense fueled the rush to defund counsel for the poor. Predictably, there was no similar outcry to rein in the spending of prosecutors. The writing was on the wall: Georgia's experiment to ensure public defenders could put up a fair fight for poor Georgians accused of crimes was nearing its end.

We brought in only two classes through the Honors Program. I saw what this support did for these young lawyers, so committed to fighting injustice in the courts. I was devastated to realize the state would not provide the resources necessary to continue this program.

About the time I began to see that the hope to build a model system that brought me to Georgia was fading, I got a call from two former PDS colleagues. One was Ron Sullivan, known to friends as Sully. He and I had started at PDS on the same day and remained close friends. He went on to become the director of the agency while I was its training director and then became a professor at Harvard Law School, still involved in right-to-counsel issues nationally. The other, Steve Singer, was already a respected PDS attorney when Sully and I showed up as new lawyers in 1995. Steve went on to do death penalty work in New Orleans before becoming an instructor in the criminal defense clinic at Loyola Law School. Steve was uncompromisingly principled, ready to challenge any injustice. And, as Steve had come to know all too well, there was plenty in New Orleans.

After Hurricane Katrina exposed the deep flaws in public defense in New Orleans, Sully and Steve had agreed to help rebuild a public defender office there. Sully's experience and credentials made him an ideal choice to develop a theoretical blueprint for building an independent, professional office. Steve's knowledge of the politics that shaped criminal justice in New Orleans—coupled with the fearlessness necessary to stand up to judges, prosecutors, and politicians—perfectly complemented Sully's strengths. From their years at PDS, both understood the central role that recruitment and training played in building a client-centered public defender office. Both followed my work in Georgia and knew that I had given a lot of thought to applying these tools to foster public defense reform in challenging environments. They invited me to join their effort.

I asked Illy what she thought about moving to New Orleans. "It is a once-in-a-lifetime chance to build a public defender office from the ground up," I said, hoping she might overlook the fact that this was the same argument I made two years earlier.

"Hell no!" she said. "I agreed to move to Georgia for your last 'once-in-a-lifetime opportunity.' We sold our house. I left my job. Aaliyah was less than six months old. I am just settling in. I like my new job. You can go to New Orleans. But Aaliyah and I are staying here."

She was, of course, right. We had just bought a house and had started building a new network of friends. Illy had started a new teaching job and was committed to her students. While she was unwilling to move a second time in two years, she did appreciate the opportunity that was presented. She understood, as well as anyone, that developing caring, committed public defenders was critical if poor communities were to receive justice. She believed in the model I had begun to build in Georgia. She understood that Georgia's commitment to public defender reform was not what we imagined when we moved there and that the situation in New Orleans provided a chance to further advance the work I had started.

Over the previous two years, many public defenders supported our approach in Georgia. But when it came to those who controlled the purse strings, there simply was no dedication to the investment in public defenders necessary to ensure poor people had the lawyers they deserved. When fiscal pressures hit, training and mentoring public defenders—which I viewed as at the heart of sustaining these lawyers—would always be seen as a luxury. Ensuring warm bodies stood in courtrooms next to poor defendants was the convenient fallback position.

New Orleans presented an exciting new possibility. Rather than trying to tackle an entire state, we could focus on one office. With Sully and Steve at the helm, I knew there would be leadership that would not compromise on commitment to hiring and developing the best lawyers. And while Illy was not interested in moving once again, she agreed to support me if I chose to take this on. So I decided to join them.

With my family in Atlanta, relocating to New Orleans was not feasible. Illy and I agreed that I would spend a year helping to get the office off the ground. I would commute, so I could spend weekends with the family. I would make the six-and-a-half-hour drive to New Orleans every Sunday night and return after court on Friday evening. Steve had a friend who owned an apartment he used part time. I would be able to crash there during the week.

EVEN BEFORE MY FIRST TRIP TO NEW ORLEANS, I had studied the challenges public defenders faced there. Like so many of the public defenders I knew in Georgia, and their counterparts in most of the country, these lawyers were saddled with crippling caseloads and deprived of the resources necessary to do their jobs.

One young public defender, Rick Teissier, had tried to do something about it.[7] After being appointed to represent a man named Leonard Peart, who was accused of several serious felonies, Teissier told the trial judge that he could not provide the representation the Constitution demanded. He was already juggling cases involving seventy other active felonies and feeling overwhelmed. In the previous seven months he had represented 418 clients. Each had routinely been incarcerated thirty to seventy days before he met with them. Nearly a third entered guilty pleas the first time they met him, receiving virtually no assistance from counsel. Teissier described an office that handled more than seven thousand cases per year. Yet it had only three investigators on staff. He admitted that he learned to operate with virtually no investigative support. There were no funds for expert witnesses. The library was so inadequate it was impossible to do any meaningful research.

His concerns made it all the way to the Louisiana Supreme Court. As courts across the country have done when confronted with indisputable evidence of violations of the Sixth Amendment right to counsel, it agreed that Peart was not receiving constitutionally adequate representation before rendering a decision that would maintain the status quo.[8] While Teissier's concerns were representative of what every public defender in New

Orleans faced, the court limited its nominal relief to cases in the court-room to which he was assigned.[9] Eleven of the twelve criminal courtrooms in New Orleans were left ur.affected. Little changed for poor defendants in New Orleans. Teissier left the public defender's office. Another lawyer filled the vacancy. Business continued as usual.

When I arrived in New Orleans in the fall of 2006, I got a clearer sense of exactly what "business as usual" meant for public defenders in the city. My first morning, Sully and Steve took me to the "office" where the public defender program was housed. It brought the struggles Teissier described to life. Roughly a third of the space was taken up by a small kitchen, a con-ference room, a broom-closet-sized library, and two offices—one for the director and one for a staff member who handled finances. The remainder of the space, which measured approximately two thousand square feet, was used as work space for the rest of the staff.[10] Several cubicles were shared by the legal staff, with limited computer access. The office did not have access to any online research database, a standard resource for any law office, and the collection of law books was outdated. In addition to the space and resource limitations, the area was filthy. I quickly learned that none of the lawyers used the space for anything more than to drop off their bags before going to court. For all practical purposes, there was no public defender office in New Orleans.

The funding challenges facing these public defenders were acute. They mirrored what so many public defenders faced elsewhere. Yet there was reason for optimism when it came to funding. As Hurricane Katrina exposed so many of the city's problems, there was a new window of oppor-tunity to attract resources. Plans were under way to secure adequate office space, replete with phones and computers. There would be additional re-sources to hire more lawyers and investigators.

Inasmuch as the problems appeared to be primarily financial on the surface, I would quickly learn that there were other forces driving the sta-tus of public defense in New Orleans. The system was shaped by perverse structural characteristics that would not be so easily removed.

The system in New Orleans was designed to give judges control over the public defenders, a structural defect wholly inconsistent with pro-moting the fair administration of justice.[11] Public defenders should play the role of interrupting convenience when it interferes with justice. They raise legal issues and demand that they receive sufficient attention. Slowing down the swift conveyor belt from arrest to sentencing, to give everyone time to make more contemplative decisions about human lives, is an important benefit they provide. Naturally, they can become annoying to judges who see their role as ensuring the conveyor belt churns rapidly.

Judges invariably have priorities that are inconsistent with the interests of the accused. Judges face pressure to keep their dockets running quickly and economically. They often resent lawyers who push back too hard. They want to be able to tell the public that they help save tax dollars, process a high volume of cases diligently, and ensure bad people are off the streets. In New Orleans, political pressure can also be reinforced by personal interest. Court frequently concluded every day by noon. Afternoons at Tulane and Broad, the name given the criminal courthouse based on its location, felt like Sundays. Lawyers who fought too hard could disrupt what had conveniently become very short workdays.

A prominent hurdle in the way of our reform efforts was legislation that gave local judges control of the board charged with overseeing the public defender program.[12] The judges had enjoyed unfettered discretion in appointing board members of their choosing to serve limitless terms at the judges' pleasure.[13] The judges effectively controlled the public defender's office in Orleans Parish through the board they selected.

More important to the bench than zealous representation was a board that catered to the judges' demands. The judges used the board to ensure that the public defenders worked with the court to process poor defendants of New Orleans quickly. Public defenders who failed to cater to the wishes of the judge were advised to change their behavior, or they were reassigned, pressured to leave, or—in the rare case of true obstinance—terminated. Not surprisingly, termination was relatively rare, as most public defenders learned to quickly fall in line.[14]

To further pressure lawyers to cater to judges' desires, each public defender was assigned to a particular courtroom.[15] Tethered to that courtroom, the public defender in essence became part of the judge's courtroom team. The lawyer's relationship with the judge would impact their entire professional life. In this way, the board minimized the likelihood that a lawyer would practice in a manner inconsistent with the judge's wishes.

Because the lawyers' workloads were a function of judicial, rather than client, needs, an arrested poor person would not be assigned an attorney until after the state made a charging decision. It would take a minimum of six to eight weeks, a period in which the defendant who could not afford to hire a lawyer had no contact with any attorney.[16] This left poor defendants lawyerless during the critical period between arrest and arraignment, when the attorney-client relationship is most effectively nurtured and developed, when investigative leads are most fruitful, and when early lawyering can lead to bond reduction and dismissed charges.

To get around the constitutional right to counsel during critical stages in the prosecution, each arrestee would be brought to a first appearance hearing before a magistrate to determine bail. A "stand-in" attorney would be available to help the magistrate "process" arrestees whose cases would be heard that day. The stand-in lawyer would not talk to the lawyerless arrestee and would have no personal information about the accused; he or she had only a brief account provided by the arresting officer regarding the facts of the case. The public defender's role was pro forma—to routinely stand silent as the prosecutor's bond request was automatically granted.[17] To defenders of the status quo, the presence of a warm body with a law license in the courtroom was good enough.

A final disturbing feature of pre-reform indigent defense in New Orleans was the part-time status of public defenders. These lawyers were welcome to maintain a private practice to supplement their meager public defender salary, predictably creating a conflict between lawyers' responsibilities to their indigent clients versus their private ones.[18] Public defenders had an incentive to devote as little time as possible to their appointed clients, in order to maximize the time they had for private work.

AFTER VISITING THE PUBLIC DEFENDER office that first morning in New Orleans, I went to observe court. I walked into a courtroom in time to witness arraignments, the hearings in which the prosecutor's office would announce charging decisions. The scene was fairly chaotic. People, primarily men, in suits wandered about the well of the court chatting to one another. I assumed they were attorneys, although one could not discern the defenders from the prosecutors. The only players who could be readily identified were the judge, who sat on the bench in a black robe, and the prisoners, who were lined up in a row, wearing orange jumpsuits, off to the left side of the courtroom. The suited men had no contact with the men in jumpsuits. It was not clear that any of the lawyers had ever met any of the defendants before.

The judge began calling cases. As each case was called, a voice would rise from the mass of suits. None of the men in jumpsuits would be brought to his spokesman's side, and the lawyer often barely acknowledged his client. Almost as quickly as a case was called, it was disposed of. The judge would call another name.

The processing went on for several minutes, until the judge called a case with no suited spokesman. When it was clear that there was no lawyer claiming the client, the judge turned to the row of men in orange and asked the one whose case it was to stand. One of the prisoners rose.

"Where is your lawyer?" asked the judge.

"I haven't seen a lawyer since I got locked up," the man replied.

"How long has that been?" asked the judge.

"Seventy days," said the man, seemingly resigned to the treatment afforded him.

"Have a seat," was the judge's response. He moved on to the next case.

I sat stunned. I could not believe a man had been locked up seventy days without seeing a lawyer. As troubling as that was, I was even more shocked that not a single person in the courtroom was fazed. Not the judge. Not the prosecutors. Not even the defense lawyers charged with representing these men. This was business as usual in New Orleans.

Despite everything I had learned about the state of public defense in America over the past two years, it was jarring to watch as nameless human beings were efficiently processed and sent back to jail cells. Dozens of people accused of wrongdoing—some on the flimsiest of evidence—warehoused in cages for weeks without any ability to talk to a lawyer, contest the charges, or challenge their detentions. How many jobs and homes were lost? How many families were devastated?

I witnessed overwhelmed public defenders who did not have time to talk to the men they represented. I saw clients who sat in jail cells without lawyers. Many of the financial and structural problems plaguing the system in New Orleans were on display in that courtroom. But what I struggled with the most that morning was understanding the indifference displayed by this room full of lawyers—public defenders, prosecutors, and judges. These were men and women sworn to pursue justice, completely resigned to a level of injustice that would make any citizen shudder. How did these professionals become so lost? And what chance did we have at overcoming injustice as long as they remained so desensitized to it?

The financial and structural challenges facing public defenders in New Orleans were certainly as severe as any I had seen. But the more familiar I became with practice in New Orleans, the more I came to appreciate the cultural forces that shaped the system. While my eyes were opened to an accepted culture of injustice through my work in Georgia, my experience in New Orleans helped me understand this phenomenon more clearly. In Georgia, I worked with lawyers who were products of these systems. In New Orleans, I would work in the heart of the system. Everywhere I turned, there were indicia of an underlying corrupted culture.

One of the biggest problems involved investigations. Without a good investigator, the defense was stuck with the facts provided by the prosecution. They were never a complete set of facts, and they were always limited to those that promoted a theory of guilt. The prosecution's story was designed to cast the accused in the worst light; it was always a story of an antisocial other, someone unworthy of continued participation in society. There is always more to the story. A good investigator is essential to discovering the facts needed to show a more complete picture. Investigation is at the heart of good public defense.

Public defenders in New Orleans did not share this view of the importance of investigation. These lawyers did not visit crime scenes, interview witnesses, procure expert assistance, or conduct legal research. They were much more willing to leave the prosecution claims unchallenged.

Not only did public defenders in New Orleans eschew investigation, they often saw no value in spending time with the people they represented. One study reviewed eighty-seven interviews with public defender clients who had been detained pretrial immediately before Katrina. They were locked up on average for five months before the storm, yet "only three reported *ever* being visited by their attorney while they were locked up in the New Orleans jail."[19]

One interviewee described talking to his attorney for the first time while sitting at counsel table waiting for his trial to begin and discovering, to his dismay, that his attorney could not remember his name and apparently had not talked to his alibi witnesses.[20]

THIS VIEW OF PUBLIC DEFENSE completely devalued the public defender's role outside of the courtroom. It reduced lawyering to the ability to talk glibly and off the cuff. It placed no significance on the institutional knowledge that makes the best public defender offices successful. The absence of staff meetings,[21] formal training opportunities, or an office environment that encourages communication and brainstorming, made it difficult for lawyers to consult with each other about their cases or to learn new approaches to litigation. Attorneys learned their practice through a pervasive "'sink or swim' culture."[22] Out of necessity, these lawyers learned to practice without preparation. Those who survived in this environment were heralded as the best trial lawyers. A willingness to try cases with minimal preparation was seen as a qualification for a good public defender rather than as a sign of irresponsibility and dereliction of one's duty to their client.

We began to bring young, idealistic lawyers into the office to try to counter some of these attitudes. But resisting the prevailing norms would not be so easy. A young lawyer was assigned to a drug case one morning and was told to be ready to try it after lunch. We had been providing training to the new lawyers, and they understood the need to prepare for trial. The defender let the judge know that they could not provide constitutionally adequate representation in such short order. But the judge was unmoved, having seen countless lawyers try cases under similar circumstances. The judge assured the lawyer that it was only a simple drug case and demanded the lawyer be ready. Upon leaving the courtroom, the lawyer sought out a well-known defense attorney who had formerly been a public defender. The lawyer reinforced the judge's message. As I recall, the young lawyer said the conversation went something like, "It's a simple drug case. The police saw him throw the drugs to the ground. Any lawyer should be able to pick up that file and be ready for trial in four hours."

When I heard this, I was shocked. I had handled many drug cases. I, like every public defender I respected, never tried one without visiting the scene and testing the officer's version of events. Of course, there are honest police officers. But there are also those willing to make up facts to make cases stronger. Lazy lawyering gave police permission to make up facts without having them tested. Diligent lawyering forced police to be honest. Public defenders owed it to their clients to assume police might be wrong, and to seek confirmation.

I recalled any number of cases in which we would use a pretrial hearing to lock the officer into his story so he could not change it later, should a prosecutor's subsequent coaching pressure him to want to alter the facts. We would then go to the crime scene and learn that the officer could not possibly have seen what he claimed from where he said he was. This young lawyer in New Orleans was told to essentially trust whatever the officer said. The message was troubling: good lawyers do not challenge the version of events told by a prosecution fighting to strip their client of his liberty.

Later, I had a conversation with one of the lawyers who had been a public defender for approximately a year. I had just finished conducting a training session on the importance of developing client relations and discussed how the relationship can benefit case preparation. He approached me to say that he had never thought of the issues raised. He never saw client relations as central to the representation. He was brought up to believe you spend just enough time with the client to keep him from complaining, so you can be left alone to work on his case. He felt like he had been ineffective for not considering these lessons previously. He said it is easy for a new lawyer to simply adapt to the way things are being done and to consider the status quo as the standard of representation that they should strive to achieve.

The attitudes I witnessed from public defenders in New Orleans were not unlike those I had been exposed to previously. For the first time, however, I spent my days immersed in the very culture that produced this mind-set. My time in New Orleans helped me understand how structural and financial pressures could create a culture that would not be so easy to change. As the lawyers learned to practice without investigators and experts, a shoot-from-the-hip attitude became the norm. Without sufficient time to meet with clients and prepare outside court, triage could easily be mistaken for representation.

I BECAME INCREASINGLY CURIOUS ABOUT CULTURE. My experience in Georgia certainly helped me see how culture can shape public defenders.

I thought a lot about training, mentorship, and community building as tools that could be used to develop public defenders who could better withstand those systemic pressures. It was this model that encouraged Janelle, Jason, and other defenders like them in Georgia to resist the pressure to adapt. When I came to New Orleans, I already had thought a lot about how we could forge an army of defenders that could withstand these cultural pressures. But my experience in New Orleans helped me think about the relationship between culture and public defenders more expansively. As I came to better understand the forces that influence culture, I began to think about how public defenders could be organized into a force to actually transform it. My work to date, teaching lawyers to resist the status quo, was simply the first step—albeit a critical one—in a much more ambitious effort.

CHAPTER 4

A MIGHTY STREAM

CULTURE IS LIKE THE CURRENT OF A MIGHTY STREAM. The force of the current determines where the water will go. If a person wants to swim against the current, they may be able to for a while. But only for so long. Over time, the pull of the current will wear them down. The person will either get out of the water or be carried by its flow.

As I began to study culture, the metaphor of the mighty stream resonated with me. I studied how culture is created and how it could be changed. Like the current of the mighty stream, culture is invisible, yet powerful. We often don't even realize its impact on us, but eventually it leads and we follow. But unlike the current, it can be changed. Culture change is not easy. But it is possible.

I came to understand that culture is formed by the shared assumptions of the people who operate within a system. These assumptions, the deeply held beliefs about how the world is and ought to be, determine the perceptions and behavior of the system's members. They are a reflection of the values that the group collectively comes to embrace. Like the current of a mighty stream, these values lie beneath the surface, invisible to the human eye. The pull of these values is too powerful to resist.

Once culture is formed, it will shape those within the organization. Those who already are inclined to embrace the system's values will adapt to the culture quickly, while those who bring a counterweighing set of ideals will acclimate more slowly. But over time, if they remain in the system, culture molds everyone. We are often unaware it is shaping us.

Culture shapes our assumptions about the world and therefore how we believe things ought to be. It determines our biases and prejudices. It forges the stereotypes we embrace. Because our behavior is a function of our beliefs, and our beliefs a function of our internalized values, culture ultimately drives our actions.

Working in the Deep South and meeting so many public defenders, I realized most wanted to do a good job. They cared about justice. But they were molded by a system that did not respect justice. I met young public defenders who were entering systems that had come to accept an embarrassingly low standard of justice for poor people. It was only a matter of time before they had the passion beaten out of them. Most would either quit or slowly become resigned to the status quo. I was sure that so many of these lawyers would be very different public defenders if they began their careers in a client-centered environment.

Many of the most seasoned lawyers I met had come to understand justice as something very different from what they believed coming out of law school. They believed they were doing a good job. The system taught them how to practice, and they were rewarded for adapting. The most insightful lesson I took from the experts who study organizational psychology was that if we want to change the behavior of those who operate within a system, it is insufficient to mandate that they act differently. Changing rules and tweaking policies are no match for a strong cultural undertow.

For example, imagine a public defender office where demeaning client jokes are met with approval. Assume the office has a whiteboard where it posts the dumbest client story of the week. Lawyers compete to tell the tale of the stupidest client. This contest reflects deep-seated values about the lack of dignity and respect the lawyers have for the people they serve. The whiteboard is what is known as an artifact—a surface example of the office culture. Imagine a new leader takes over and is appalled at the lack of respect lawyers have for clients. That leader may make a rule that no lawyers talk badly about clients. The leader could ban the whiteboard. This rule might end the practice of badmouthing clients publicly, but it does not change the fact the lawyers do not respect the clients.

Culture change requires more than changes in rules or policies. As one management guru famously stated, "Culture eats strategy for breakfast."[1]

Any policy changes that are inconsistent with the underlying culture will be thwarted by that culture. Culture change is a long-term process.

I read with intense interest on how culture is created. The first step is to introduce a set of values to the people who make up a system and encourage them to act in accordance with it. As the group pursues these values and experiences success, its members begin to internalize them. As these values are internalized, they become assumptions. Finally, as the group begins to embrace a shared set of assumptions, culture starts to shift. It is this shared set of assumptions that is so defining. Transforming culture begins with introducing a new set of values into an organization.

With this new perspective on how culture drives our approach to criminal justice, I began to expand my thinking about how we could reform public defense. I knew that the values that were fundamental to client-centered public defense—and that were so much a part of the fabric at PDS—were largely missing from the public defender organizations I had studied since leaving Washington. The horror stories of inadequate representation I had come to know so well served as examples of what happens when lawyers had no use for these values. Foundational client-centered values—loyalty to the client, respect for the client's desires, thoroughness and preparation, and a commitment to communication—were absent from so much of the representation I witnessed. I started to understand that transforming a dysfunctional public defender culture would require infusing offices with values that I had always taken for granted. I saw recruitment and development of the next generation of public defenders as the ideal vehicle for this mission, and I had a renewed appreciation for the magnitude of the opportunity in front of me. This was not just about training lawyers to be better public defenders for their clients; it was a chance to build a movement to transform culture.

I WANTED TO BUILD on what I started with the Georgia Honors Program and use it to support public defenders across the South. I knew that the cultural challenges that faced public defenders in New Orleans and across the state of Georgia plagued defenders throughout the region. My study of organizational culture refined my understanding of how to address the problem. I believed the first step was to identify a cadre of public defender offices that shared a client-centered vision. From there we would recruit, train, and develop lawyers to embrace the relevant value set. Collectively, these lawyers would begin to inject those values into the fabric of the offices, leading to a culture shift.

Because I understood many public defenders had subtly been shaped into lawyers they never wanted to become, I was convinced that the success of this project would attract more offices to the movement; our success would remind these defenders of why they chose this work in the first place and give them an opportunity to return to that path. Partner offices would serve as examples to others of ways of providing more meaningful representation to communities. I called the project the Southern Public Defender Training Center (SPDTC).

My experiences in Georgia and New Orleans taught me that leaders trying to engage in culture change have to deal with three categories of staff members. The first category is made up of those who were around before the new regime and who are resistant to change. Members of this group will try to undermine progress. But in the early stages of culture change, some of the organization's staff will likely come from this group. Despite their resistance, some of these employees will be valuable to the organization because they have experience or institutional knowledge that is needed as the organization redefines itself. But their resistance will pose an internal challenge, so a reform-minded leader must try to minimize the size of this group and work to neutralize its negative impact on those who remain on the team.

The second category includes those who were around before the new regime who are receptive to change. These team members are invaluable, as they bring experience and institutional knowledge and are often eager to think about how to help the organization adapt to the new value set being introduced. They recognize that the office should aspire to a higher level of practice and are less defensive about self-critique. This group will be the key to shepherding the office toward its new vision.

The third group is made up of new members of the team. Assuming the leader makes appropriate hiring decisions, these employees will be brought on board because of their commitment to the institutional vision. They are poised to enthusiastically embrace the core values. If this group can resist the forces opposing change—both internally and externally—it will determine the future culture of the office. As waves of new staff members are brought on board and groomed to internalize the new organizational values, culture will start to shift.

When I decided to launch SPDTC, I understood that a comprehensive culture-change blueprint would require a strategy for working with all three groups of employees. I also appreciated that this plan had to include legal and nonlegal staff alike. But I was one person with a broad vision and no resources. The comprehensive culture-change model would have to be built over time.

I decided to start with what I believed to be the most critical piece of the model: grooming a generation of public defenders who had a revolutionary understanding of what justice looks like for poor people. Sadly, ensuring that marginalized communities receive the protections enshrined in our Constitution, and are afforded the dignity and respect in the process that we expect for the more privileged members of society, is revolutionary. Building a movement to fight for these ideals would require that we identify, mold, and support a new army of public defenders.

The model would have three components: values-based recruitment, values-based training, and values-based mentorship. The program would seek to identify public defenders open to embracing client-centered values. Training would focus on teaching the lawyers the values and providing them with strategies for resisting systemic pressure to abandon them. The mentorship piece would concentrate on helping lawyers in the field identify those pressures and working with them to practice consistently with these core values in the face of those challenges.

To launch the model, I was awarded a fellowship from the Open Society Institute (OSI, which would later become the Open Society Foundations) supporting the work for eighteen months. The Southern Center for Human Rights (SCHR) agreed to serve as the host organization, allowing me to use the office's printer and copier. But I needed help. The modest grant would not enable me to hire staff. So I solicited volunteers.

The first person I turned to was Illy. She was only in her second year as a teacher in South Fulton County, and she was advancing quickly as a member of the county's curriculum team and a first-grade team leader at her school. Illy loved teaching. Her students needed teachers like her. Only two years had passed since I asked her to leave her last teaching job to support my vision. So I knew I was asking a lot. But I also knew I could not do this without her.

From her personal experience, Illy understood what people who relied on public defenders needed from their lawyers. She served as a reliable reminder that training good public defenders was a means to a greater end—allowing impacted communities to be heard—not an end in itself. She was also incredibly well organized and charismatic. She would be essential to building an infrastructure to support our work and attract supporters. In addition, I knew that this effort would require working around the clock. There was no one else I could bounce ideas off as they came to me at three o'clock in the morning. I knew that with Illy on board we could get this project off the ground.

Illy and I spent a lot of time talking about her taking a year off from teaching to help me build this project. She went back and forth. But ultimately she agreed to help me—for just one year.

The second person I reached out to was Sean Maher. Sean began his career as a public defender in Atlanta. He had recently moved to New York to join the Neighborhood Defender Service of Harlem, a public defender office, launched with a PDS alumnus as its founding director, that had earned a national reputation for its client-centered approach to advocacy. We were introduced by a mutual friend when I first decided to move to Georgia. He was excited about the vision of the Honors Program and eager to help however he could. Sean told me that when he was a new public defender in Atlanta, he did not receive any training. He said young attorneys had been given a pile of cases and sent to court. He explained how new lawyers would try to teach each other, because there was minimal supervision. Sean also understood that Atlanta's was one of the better public defender offices in the state. He certainly knew how bad public defense was throughout much of Georgia. I remembered his reaction when I had shared my vision: "You want to try to change the way public defense is practiced all across Georgia? Good luck with that." Then he paused and slowly smiled. "Count me in."

For the next year and a half, Sean and I worked together to build the Honors Program. We designed a curriculum that not only taught lawyering skills but infused client-centered values into every lesson. We developed a series of exercises to teach every lesson in interactive sessions. And we very consciously planned the training sessions and the extracurricular activities to effectively forge a cohesive community. For three weeks, the group would do everything together. They would reconvene every three months to reinforce their commitment to client-centered lawyering. Like me, Sean was heartbroken when Georgia defunded the Honors Program.

He was excited to hear that Illy would take a year off to help me build the new vision. He would do whatever we needed.

We hoped to forge a strong community of client-centered public defender offices across the South. We planned to recruit a new class of lawyers each year. Lawyers would make a commitment to participate in ongoing training and development for three years as they learned to be client-centered in systems that were hostile to good public defense.

We would duplicate the Honors Program model but make some practical adjustments. Because lodging was such a significant expense, we would take the fourteen-day curriculum that had been spread over three weeks (we took weekends off) and teach for two weeks without a break. Because lawyers would be spread across the South, and travel was also costly, quarterly gatherings would be replaced by semiannual meetings. We received the OSI funding in the spring of 2007. Knowing it would run out in the fall of 2008, we felt pressure to start our first class right away. We would have to secure resources to replace the initial grant, and we knew we had to be well beyond the planning phase before we could successfully raise more funds. So we expected to welcome our first class in the summer of 2007.

However, there was a challenge. Illy had to finish the school year and would not be available full-time until June 2007. I had committed to my work in New Orleans through the summer of 2007. This left very little time to recruit our first partners. Fortunately, we had two offices that were eager to invest in the project—in New Orleans and Atlanta.

In New Orleans, a critical piece of our plan was to develop a pipeline for committed public defenders from across the country. Many who had been part of the system before Hurricane Katrina were defensive. We imagined a very different approach to public defense and wanted to bring in lawyers who would shake up the status quo. There were certainly some lawyers from Orleans Parish who were eager to be a part of the reform effort. However, many others were products of the strong judge-centered culture that shaped the way lawyers practiced. They were resistant to too much change and seemed threatened by our bold vision. We wanted to infuse the office with lawyers free of the toxic culture of Orleans Parish Criminal Court.

We hoped to bring in a new class of recent law graduates each year and develop them into future leaders. Katrina drew attention to the region, leading to grant opportunities that allowed us to recruit a first class of ten lawyers in the fall of 2007. The model we built in Georgia had already attracted a following of law students interested in joining an effort to improve public defense in systems on the cusp of reform. The promise to spread this work more broadly only made the project more intriguing. Advertising the office's partnership with SPDTC, and the promise of admission to the first SPDTC class, would be a valuable incentive for candidates.

We launched a national recruiting effort to identify graduating law students who wanted to become public defenders in New Orleans. The interviews were designed to identify lawyers who embraced client-centered values and understood the incredible challenges they would face in acting on them. That first year we would hire ten passionate recent law school graduates from across the country, all of whom would join the first SPDTC class.

I also tried to recruit from some of the offices I had worked with in Georgia for people to join this first class. But most offices relied on state funding for training, and funding cuts to indigent defense left them without resources. Only our biggest partner office in the state—in Atlanta—could secure county funding to support lawyers to join the first class. They would send five young public defenders. Along with one lawyer from a juvenile defender office in New Orleans, these were the sixteen lawyers who made up the SPDTC class of 2007. Their three-year experience would commence with our Summer Institute, the fourteen-day "boot camp" that would introduce them to SPDTC.

On July 28, 2007, all sixteen gathered on the campus of the Cumberland School of Law in Birmingham, Alabama, for an opening dinner to kick off the two weeks. They were met by a small group of volunteer faculty committed to helping guide the group during the most formative years of their development as public defenders. The program was designed for lawyers practicing for fewer than three years. Experience taught that within those formative years defenders develop habits—both good and bad—that are hard to break. We targeted newer defenders because we sought lawyers who would come to the program with completely open minds. Anyone who has trained public defenders has endured the seasoned attorney who is resistant to considering new ways of practicing. "That won't work where I come from" is a common refrain encountered by any lawyer trying to teach longtime public defenders new approaches to challenges.

The faculty was a special group. On top of handling full caseloads, all were frequently invited to teach and present at defender training programs nationally. But SPDTC asked even more of its faculty than other programs. Trainers would be expected to help work with our defenders twice a year, and they needed to learn the curriculum and how we expected it to be taught. They also had to agree to serve as mentors to the lawyers they trained. They understood that serving on the faculty was a commitment to helping build the organization. They believed deeply in the mission and the model. All spent many nights away from their families and devoted countless unpaid hours.

As we gathered for a kickoff dinner on the first evening, I explained the vision of how a generation of public defenders in the South would help raise the standard of representation across the region. I told the group that through this community, they would get the training they needed to have a strong sense of what their clients deserved. They would have mentorship and support to help reinforce the lessons when systemic pressures sent the opposite message. But, perhaps most importantly, we would give these lawyers a community of like-minded colleagues to continually support and encourage them in their effort—so often seen as Sisyphean—to roll that seemingly immovable boulder of justice forward.

"You are in the dawn of your careers," I said. "You have all chosen to become public defenders. This is the most important work a lawyer can do, but nowhere is it more important than in the places you have chosen to work. If you do this work right, it is the most difficult work a lawyer can do. But nowhere is it more difficult than in the systems where you will practice." Their success would depend on the success of this community to provide ongoing support and inspiration.

My appreciation for the value of a like-minded community stemmed from my years at PDS. When I was a young public defender there, a group of my peers and I would meet regularly to remind ourselves of the reasons we chose this line of work. These gatherings connected us to one another, helping to build a much-needed support network, and kept us inspired as we shared and nurtured each other's idealism. It was this community to which we would turn to reassure us of the rightness of our mission when outsiders exhibited so little respect for our work and our clients.

This community had helped expand my understanding of the role of the public defender. A few of us became public defenders because we believed the work was critical to protecting individual rights. We understood the danger of a tyrannical government and wanted to provide resistance to the institutional instinct to run roughshod over marginalized people. We wanted to fight against bullies who cared little for the liberty interests of the powerless.

Several others had very personal experiences that had given them a connection to those most impacted by the existing approach to criminal justice. They understood the human toll that mass incarceration had on people who have always been on society's margins. They wanted to work with the people whom those in power deemed expendable.

At one gathering, a close friend whose parents were active in the civil rights movement told us that he chose to be a public defender because he always wanted to be a civil rights lawyer. In his mind, public defense was our generation's civil rights struggle. At the time, I did not appreciate the importance and truth of this sentiment. I associated civil rights with efforts to desegregate the Woolworth's lunch counter in Greensboro, North Carolina, in 1960, or to register black people to vote in Mississippi during Freedom Summer in 1964. I knew the work we were doing was important, but I did not see it as civil rights law. Now, after my experience in the South, the connection was clear.

The next morning, we began the intense, fourteen-day program sitting in chairs arranged in a circle, a setup designed to promote collective learning. As an introduction, each person was asked to share a story about themselves that would help the group understand why they decided to become public defenders.

We started with the faculty. We wanted the group to know that there was nothing we would ask of them that we would not do as well. We wanted to reinforce the idea that we would all go through these two weeks together, as a community. The group would learn over the two weeks that we were more than faculty—we were family. We were bound by a common vision and a commitment to realize it together. Some of our differences were obvious—we were men and women of differing races and ethnicities. Other differences—such as our religions, sexual orientations, and professional histories—we would learn about over the course of the next two weeks.

After the faculty spoke, the sixteen lawyers took turns. There was no assigned order. Each person entered the circle to share as they were moved to do so. As each person entered, the group clapped. As they finished, the group clapped again. No one spoke except the storyteller. The stories ranged from humorous to tragic. Some evoked laughter, others respectful silence. Most were quite personal. We wrapped up feeling closer than we had ninety minutes earlier. In the coming two weeks, the lawyers would be on their feet, engaged in a variety of exercises in front of their peers.

The group pretty quickly recognized that the initial exercise was meant to be much more than a simple introduction of participants. It was designed to reveal several programmatic goals. The first was for the lawyers to understand their roles as storytellers. They would enter a system that had embraced a presumption that those accused of crimes were criminals. Without the presentation of an effective counternarrative, it would be easy for prosecutors, judges, and juries to disregard the humanity of their clients. In the absence of a more nuanced story, unjust outcomes were inevitable. As public defenders, they would be responsible for telling their clients' stories at bond hearings, plea negotiations, pretrial proceedings, trials, and sentencing hearings. They would literally be their client's storytellers at every point in the process when decisions were made about their lives. At every turn, when systemic forces encouraged lawyers to give in to case-processing, these lawyers would insist on reminding the system of the human life at stake. If we were going to effectively tell our client's stories, we had to learn the art of performance. The introductions foreshadowed an important component of the training: learning the art of storytelling and performance and how it applied to every aspect of their work.

But the exercise was also a first step to overcoming the obstacles that prevent lawyers from effectively learning and telling these stories. For many of the lawyers, simply being asked to perform in a circle, surrounded by peers, was scary. They were used to learning by sitting in a classroom or a conference while subject-matter experts lectured to them. They preferred that the spotlight not be on them. The process was made even more intimidating by the fact that they were asked to tell personal stories. The more personal the story, the more vulnerable they felt. The group would learn that forcing themselves to confront their aversion to vulnerability was part of the program design. It was a second goal of the morning's exercise.

Throughout the training, the lawyers would be asked to push themselves in other ways that were uncomfortable. As lawyers they had likely learned that vulnerability was weakness and that the best lawyers possessed no self-doubt. They had almost certainly learned to mask any uncertainty they might have. We now had to unteach that instinct. As a faculty, we understood that a willingness to try new approaches and to push oneself to learn new skill sets required a willingness to make mistakes. A fear of looking foolish would keep these lawyers from growing.

Becoming familiar with vulnerability was also essential to building relationships with the people they would represent. As public defenders, they would ask people who did not know them, and often did not trust them, to share very personal stories. They would meet the men, women, and children they were to represent at one of the most frightening times of their lives. The lawyers could not responsibly unpack their clients' powerful, and often painful, stories if they had no appreciation for what it feels like to make oneself vulnerable in front of a stranger.

A third goal of these introductions was to begin exploring what motivated public defenders to do this work and to find ways the lawyers could remain connected to those motivators when the challenges were greatest. The curriculum was peppered with opportunities to consider the many challenges public defenders would face in the field. They would come to understand how forces could drive the most committed public defenders to start to become numb to injustice. They would collectively brainstorm strategies to resist those pressures. They would learn that perhaps the greatest challenge they would face was maintaining a strong sense of why they did this work. If they were going to avoid being reshaped by the very systems we needed them to change, they would need to develop strategies to resist the pull to normalize injustice. And that starts with remembering what brought them to the work in the first place.

Finally, to remain conscious of their goals in the face of a system that depends on public defenders to keep the assembly line of justice well oiled, the lawyers would need a strong support system. For this reason, the introductions were designed to begin the process of community build-ing. Not only did every participant in the group learn something personal about each of their classmates, but everyone had to share something they may have told few, if any, others. It required a level of trust. We would continue to push them to trust one another as the two weeks progressed. To ensure we succeeded, the faculty was tasked with creating a safe and trusting environment.

Having the group collectively go through this exercise was the first step in forging bonds among the lawyers in the room. This network would be critical to their ability to do the transformative work that we envisioned. As they learned the personal experiences that brought each of them to this calling, they became closer. As they supported one another—empathizing with one another's apprehension about entering the circle—they became closer. Throughout the process they would have many opportunities to learn about one another and to prop each other up as they took turns tack-ling various exercises before the group. If we succeeded, this would be a group of peers they would lean on throughout their careers.

The first hour and a half set the foundation for the next two weeks. We would then turn our attention to exploring the unique "mind-set, heart-set, soul-set" at the heart of public defense.[2] This was the focus of the first few days.

The sixteen lawyers began by grappling with what it means to be a client-centered public defender. We unpacked the concept with guidance from faculty, using discussion prompts and hypothetical scenarios. The group examined how the role of defense counsel differs from that of the prosecutor; while the latter has a broad obligation to ensure justice is done for everyone, including the accused, the defense lawyer has singular allegiance to the client.

From there, we examined how the role of the public defender differs from that of retained defense counsel. Unlike a person who chooses to hire a lawyer and pay handsomely for their services, someone forced to rely on a public defender frequently does not want them. Often they neither trust the lawyer appointed to them nor the system itself. This dynamic brings a unique set of challenges for public defenders. When a person hires a lawyer, a level of trust usually comes along with the payment. The public defender has to spend considerable time overcoming preconceived ideas many poor people have about "free lawyers" and developing a trusting relationship. At the training, this morphed into a discussion of some core "client-centered" values: loyalty to the client, respect for what the client wants out of the case after being fully advised of options and potential consequences, thoroughness and preparation in all aspects of the case, and clear and ongoing communication with the client.

The group came to understand that the public defender must ensure the client has the assistance required to make important decisions about their life. The lawyer does not substitute their judgment for the client's. Rather, the lawyer makes sure the client has all the information and advice needed to make these decisions. Respecting the dignity of the client in this way is especially important for public defenders who routinely represent people whose voices and priorities are frequently disrespected. The public defender should not be seen as yet another authority figure telling the person they represent what is best for them.

A series of interactive workshops over the next several days used role-playing to present common challenges public defenders face as we explored various aspects of client-centered lawyering. In a workshop on obstacles to developing strong relationships with clients, the group brainstormed perceptions people often have about public defenders that make clients reluctant to trust their lawyers. For example, people often think public defenders are lazy, that they are incompetent, that they do not care about their clients, that they are part of the system, that they believe the client is guilty, and that they will work hard only if they are convinced of the client's innocence. Recognizing that such perceptions make it challenging to build trusting relationships, we work through hypothetical scenarios to consider how our words and actions often inadvertently reinforce these stereotypes.

We collectively brainstorm language and behavior to break down these hurdles. As an example, when a lawyer asks a new client, "Tell me what happened," the client may hear the lawyer saying they believe the client is guilty. Why else would the client know what happened? It may cause the client to get defensive and further distrust the lawyer. Instead, a lawyer might explain what the prosecution "claims" happened and ask if the client has any idea why the prosecution might believe this. "Do you have any idea what they are saying you did?" may cause much less defensiveness in a client wary of their lawyer's motives. This framing of the question gives the client an opportunity to share important information without feeling as though the lawyer had already assumed their guilt. Through a series of hypothetical scenarios that raise similar issues, the group brainstorms more conscientious responses.

A different workshop used role-playing to push the group to consider how the lawyers can live up to client-centered values in the face of routine ethical challenges. For example, the ethical rules prohibit a lawyer both from lying to a judge and from disclosing information they learned from the client. The rules can create a tension in practice. One role-play scenario: The lawyer knows the client has a prior conviction because the client told them, but the judge does not know this information. The judge asks the lawyer if the client has any prior convictions. A faculty member playing the judge would push the lawyer to disclose the information. Some participants shared the information learned from the client right away. This would be an ethical violation. Others lied and said the client had no prior record. That would also be an ethical violation.

We collectively worked through responses that protect clients in an ethical manner. "I do not have any information that I am able to share with the court," might be an option. It is certainly truthful, since the rule prohibits the lawyer from sharing the information. "I have no representations," might be another. The class began to understand how to advocate in ways that were both ethical and client-centered. Not only does the exercise teach the ethical rules, it introduces the lawyers to the kinds of pressures they will face to abandon client-centered ideals, and it provides space for them to work through appropriate responses.

We took time to help the group digest some foundational lessons on the unique obligations public defenders have to the people they serve, what it means to be client-centered, the care and thought that go into building a trusting relationship with people who have every reason to be distrustful, and strategies for navigating real-world pressures in ways that remain true to our duty to our clients.

About three days in, we turned to a session intended to help the lawyers appreciate the responsibility that comes with being entrusted to amplify another person's story. Lawyers were paired with a person they did not know and seemed to have little in common with to share stories about significant events in their lives. Each story had to be something personal that had nothing to do with law school or being a lawyer. The story was to be one they found impactful, and it was meant to evoke emotion. The pairs found quiet places to exchange the stories. When they returned, we sat the group in a courtroom setting. Each person had to advocate for their partner before a faculty member playing a judge. The only instructions were that they had to do their best to make the judge feel the power of the partner's story.

One by one we called names. The person approached and sat at the defense table in the seat of the accused. The partner, acting as the advocate, sat by their side. The judge asked them to rise and share the story. When the storyteller finished, the judge asked the "accused" how they felt as the story was recounted. Invariably, lawyers seated in the accused's chair expressed that they never appreciated how helpless it makes one feel to have another person tell their story. The judge then turned to the storyteller. A common theme was the overwhelming responsibility the teller felt to do the story justice.

The group collectively came to appreciate how vulnerable it felt to have someone else speak for you—and these were people they had spent three days with. Unlike actual clients, they chose the personal story they shared. We ask our clients to share potentially embarrassing information before they know anything about us. The lawyers at the training could withhold the most embarrassing events in their life. Our clients often cannot. The group discussed how the ability to build a relationship and help the client feel comfortable sharing information is interconnected with a lawyer's ability to craft a powerful narrative. They began to see their power as storytellers, and how their effectiveness was tied to the lessons of the past three days.

As a faculty, we watched the group come to understand that their ability to humanize their clients through storytelling was critical, whether talking to a judge at a bond hearing or to a prosecutor at a plea negotiation, or at any other opportunity to communicate with someone whose decisions can impact the person they represent. The public defenders in that room were beginning to understand something that is not taught in law school—effective lawyers are not simply legal technicians, they are powerful storytellers.

We pivoted to the next phase of the program, which focused on pre-trial practice. For the next few days the group's members were on their feet in simulated exercises as they learned the many tools available to lawyers as they prepare for litigation. Topics included preliminary hearings, investigation, discovery, motions practice, and negotiations, to name a few. The exercises were intended to teach discrete lawyering skills. They were also designed to continue to build bonds between the lawyers, who will struggle together and support one another during the exercises.

But there was another purpose. The sessions were not taught in isolation of one another; the lawyers learned that each topic adds a unique skill to the lawyer's toolkit as they begin to gather the information needed to craft effective stories. If the first phase of the program was about *why* it is so important that lawyers be powerful storytellers, the next phase was about *how* to construct the story. It taught the lawyers to view each skill as one more way to gather the facts needed to construct a story.

MANY LAWYERS HAVE VOLUNTARILY taken a trial advocacy class in law school. Others have had trial advocacy training as new lawyers. For the most part, those programs begin with a fact pattern that contains the universe of facts available to the lawyer in the case. The implicit lesson in this model is that lawyers have nothing to do with shaping the facts. The facts are given and the lawyering begins with a known universe of facts. However, nothing could be further from the truth. Good lawyers understand that lawyering skills designed to shape the universe of facts are critical to the representation.

Overwhelmed and under-resourced public defenders frequently make decisions based solely on the universe of facts as given to them by the prosecution. When there is limited time to investigate and litigate, evidence helpful to the client remains unknown, constitutional violations go uncovered, and the protections at the heart of our system of justice are unrealized. Roughly 95 percent of cases result in pleas because the lawyers are ill-prepared to challenge the allegations.

To address this problem, Summer Institute participants are required to use the skills taught during the pretrial phase of the program to build a case. They are given a hypothetical client. To mirror reality, all they get initially is a police report. The report is bare-boned and points to almost certain guilt. As the group is taught various pretrial topics, they participate in workshops where those skills are applied to the hypothetical case. In the workshops they can get information about the case depending on how well they execute the skills. For example, in the preliminary hearing workshop, a staff member, playing the testifying officer, is in possession of a set of information that they will share with the lawyer only if the lawyer asks the right questions. There are rules to what a lawyer may ask during a preliminary hearing cross-examination. A faculty member playing the prosecutor listens for objectionable questions and objects. Another faculty member plays the judge and rules on objections. This teaches the group that their ability to mine for the information in the possession of the officer hinges on their understanding of how to conduct a preliminary hearing.

Each workshop provides an opportunity for the lawyers to learn more about a case as they master a new skill-set. In this way, they can understand that all of the skills they are learning are to be used collectively to build a universe of facts that will be available to craft the story. At the end of this phase of the program, based on the information they have gathered, the group will draft a defense theory paragraph, which will lay out the story of the trial they will conduct in the final phase. The group understands that the more effective they have been at using the pretrial skills, the more flexibility they have to craft a powerful story at trial.

The final phase of the Summer Institute involved trial advocacy. The group used everything they learned up to that point to represent the client they were given on the first day. In workshops that addressed every aspect of the trial, the lawyers learned trial advocacy skills. They also continually revisited lessons from the first two phases of the program. As they built their case theory throughout the trial, they had to rely on previously gathered facts. If there were gaps, they were prodded to consider what they might have done differently during the pretrial phase to fill the void, reinforcing the connection between pretrial practice and trial advocacy. They also had to use the storytelling skills taught earlier in the program to make the story persuasive. The trainees were pushed to revisit challenges that can come up during trial and think about ways to resolve them consistent with client-centered values. Drawing from the first phase, the lawyers had to think about how they could most effectively humanize the client, respond to pressures from the judge to be less zealous, and bring to life the fundamental protections at the heart of our system of justice.

Unlike a traditional trial advocacy program, the training at this stage consciously wove earlier lessons into the trial advocacy phase, reinforcing the idea that public defenders are at all times client-centered advocates, storytellers, and legal technicians charged with resisting any forces that would seek to undermine a just outcome for the person they represent.

The program covered a vast amount of material, touching on issues the lawyers will work through their entire careers. The daily sessions often ran for ten to twelve hours each day, with evenings devoted to speakers, videos, and games that provide a chance to unpack the day's lessons.

Despite the incredibly long days, the lawyers attending the initial session were hungry to delve deeper. Each had many questions. Each night the lawyers and faculty gathered in a common area outside the hotel to explore some of the issues, or to simply unwind with a new community of friends. The running joke was that each day felt like a week, not only because of how much they covered but because of how close they became with one another. Throughout the process, faculty designed games and exercises to force the group to learn more about each other. It was like a summer camp for public defenders.

On the evening of August 10 the group gathered for a cookout. It was a Friday night. They had finished the trial advocacy portion of the program that afternoon. The evening would be a time to enjoy a last night together. Illy, Sean, and I sat at a picnic table. We were joined by Patrice Fulcher and Cathy Bennett.

I met Patrice shortly after I moved to Georgia. She began her career as a public defender in Atlanta with Sean, before she joined the newly formed Capital Defender Office to work on death penalty cases across the state. Patrice was acutely aware of the challenges facing public defenders in Georgia and excited about the vision of the Honors Program. She immediately volunteered to join Sean and me as early architects of the model. Patrice's race- and class-consciousness permeated her entire approach to lawyering. She always saw herself as an activist-lawyer.

Soon after meeting Patrice I met Cathy Bennett, the talented training director for the Commonwealth of Massachusetts. I had heard wonderful things about Cathy before meeting her. I knew they were all true the moment I met her. She exuded the compassion at the heart of our philosophy. I invited her to help as well.

Along with Sean, Patrice and Cathy had become two of my closest confidants in this endeavor.

Now we were gathered, watching sixteen lawyers who did not know each other two weeks earlier interact as though they were at a family reunion. "I can't believe we pulled this off," I said.

"If we could bring in sixteen lawyers each year, we could really make a difference," added Cathy.

"Maybe twenty?" Patrice chimed in.

"There is a big gap between Georgia and Louisiana," Sean noted. "Maybe we could add Alabama and Mississippi?"

Illy looked up wearily. "Stop encouraging Jon, everybody. I only took one year off. So unless one of you plans to quit your job and come help him, let's just enjoy the sixteen lawyers from two states for now."

Everyone laughed. We all toasted. We had pulled it off. We went back to sitting in silence, admiring what we had accomplished.

The next morning, we gathered at ten o'clock. The members of the class shared some skits they prepared to roast the faculty. We then gathered in a circle and gave everyone an opportunity to share parting words with the group. After the last person in the room spoke, we shared hugs, said some personal goodbyes, headed to our cars, and began the journey home. It was a bittersweet drive back to Atlanta. I was exhausted. I wanted to get in my bed and sleep for twelve hours. I thought about those fourteen days and how amazing they were. I wondered how we would keep it going. But mostly, I bemoaned the fact that the two weeks had to end. I thought about one part of a class skit in particular.

Barksdale Hortenstine, Danny Engelberg, and Zanele Ngubeni were three lawyers I recruited to New Orleans several months earlier. Zanele and Barksdale were summer interns at public defender offices in Georgia in 2006 when I met them. Barksdale was a graduate of Emory Law School and Zanele of the University of Tennessee. Danny was a graduate of Georgetown Law School. As a first-year law student, he spent a year as Illy's teacher's aide. He then spent a summer as my law clerk while I was still at PDS. None had any connection to New Orleans, but they all wanted to be part of the reforms we were implementing there.

Barksdale had played a district attorney version of me who had founded the Southern District Attorney Training Center. Barksdale even shaved his head and cut his beard into a goatee to mimic my appearance. Danny was a young prosecutor learning to promote the values of the program. Danny began his fictional opening statement: "Ladies and gentlemen, Mr. Jones is guilty—"

Before he could get another word out, Zanele, playing Patrice, interrupted. "No, no, no. You never call the defendant by his name. You might accidentally humanize him before the jury." Getting up to model what she was saying, Zanele continued by pointing directly at the lawyer playing Mr. Jones. "You point with a straight arm directly at the defendant, you give him a piercing scowl, and you say loudly, 'Ladies and gentlemen, *the defendant* is guilty.'"

The room broke into laughter. But the final remarks were more sobering. They reminded everyone that the message in the skit was a sadly accurate reflection of the system's adopted value set. They revealed a deep understanding of their duty to resist that message.

I recalled the words of one of the lawyers who would head to New Orleans. She had just finished the bar exam, the test that every lawyer must take to be allowed to practice law in a state:

> I spent three years being taught that lawyering is all about the ability to analyze a problem using a mechanical process. We were never taught to consider the people behind the cases we learned. There was never room to discuss feelings and emotion. We were taught that the law is rational. The people behind the cases became the vehicles through which we arrived at technical solutions. This experience helped me understand that over these three years, I lost the ability to empathize. How can we represent our clients if we don't have empathy? The most important lesson I learned from all of you is that being a public defender requires empathy.

And those of one of the Atlanta lawyers who had less than a year as a lawyer under his belt, as I recall:

> I could never have known how much I needed this. In law school I learned how to be a lawyer. But I forgot how to be a person. These two weeks reminded me that I cannot possibly be effective at the former without making sure I don't lose the latter.

———

ONCE THE CLASS WRAPPED UP their final thoughts, the faculty took turns saying their goodbyes. Toward the end, Sean got up. He invoked the story line from the popular science fiction movie *The Matrix*. He told the group of a simulated reality world inside the Matrix, and a meeting between two men, Morpheus and Neo. Most of us had seen the movie but were curious to see how Sean would connect it to our mission. He went on to explain that Morpheus offered Neo a choice between two pills: one blue and one red. It began to crystallize. Speaking from the perspective of Morpheus, Sean continued:

> If you choose to take the blue pill, you will return to the comfortable simulated reality of the Matrix. You will forget you ever met me. You will go on living a comfortable life. Everything will be easy. All will be blissful. You will never know pain or strife. On the other hand, you can take the red pill. You will experience sorrow and agony. You will know misery and injustice. But you will feel the world around you. You will experience reality.

Sean let the silence fill the room, then he continued:

> Over these last two weeks you have all come to the realization that you chose to take the red pill. You have all refused to sleepwalk through this work. You chose to get close to injustice. To feel the heartache. To shoulder the emotional toll it will take on you. But only by experiencing reality can you begin to change it.

CHAPTER 5

THE FIRST STEP IS RESISTANCE

FOR THE TEN LAWYERS we recruited to New Orleans, the red pill turned out to be pretty hard to swallow. Within the office, there were varying degrees of skepticism about our plan to bring in brand-new lawyers from outside city limits. Some felt that the most important quality for a public defender was to have a good relationship with the local judges. They were perplexed that we would not prioritize local lawyers. Others saw experience as the most important factor and could not understand why we would look for lawyers who were so green. Some just felt like they were drowning and longed for lawyers who could begin to take cases off their shoulders immediately, even if they were not the most qualified.

The bar exam is offered only twice a year. The ten recent law graduates took the exam in July 2007, their first opportunity upon graduation. Results would not be available until October. In the meantime, on their return from Birmingham, the lawyers could help with work outside of the courtroom, but they could not be assigned their own cases.

Criminal court judges in New Orleans were livid about this influx of outside lawyers. They knew it was part of a broader strategy to wrest from them control of the public defender office. The fact that these lawyers could not handle cases right away only added to their ire.

By the time we hired the lawyers we had opened a new office in a building down the street from the courthouse. For the first time, public defenders in New Orleans had their own desks in private offices with computers and phones. We hired a team of investigators and a handful of social workers. And we required that any lawyer who remained employed by the public defender office would no longer be allowed to maintain a private caseload. They could no longer trade on their indigent clients' interests for preferential treatment of their wealthier clients. This stripped judges of some of their leverage over public defenders. And it caused many of the lawyers who were most accepting of the former system to leave. The makeup of the office changed dramatically.

Recruiting lawyers from outside Louisiana had been seen as a direct attack on the fiefdom the judges had ruled. We were finding creative ways to provide representation to people who had previously been unrepresented. A year earlier, the Supreme Court of Louisiana issued a temporary rule to "permit [lawyers who are not members of the Louisiana Bar] to render temporary pro bono criminal legal services to indigent persons arrested or charged with a crime or crimes in Orleans Parish." The order further required that a "licensed lawyer . . . provide oversight and supervision," ensuring that Louisiana lawyers provided appropriate guidance to the outside lawyer, who might not know some of the jurisdictional idiosyncrasies. Through this rule, we attracted a number of experienced attorneys from other states to assist with reform efforts.

These lawyers were used to fill the void left when the Orleans Public Defenders (OPD) lawyers were assigned to represent clients at first appearance hearings. It was at those critical hearings that the amount of bail was decided. The hearings determined whether a person would spend the next several months in jail. Before Katrina, poor defendants went unrepresented in these proceedings, often losing their liberty with no advocate to fight for their release. Stories, such as the one of the man who had been locked up for seventy days without seeing a lawyer, were routine. We decided to address that by making sure lawyers were assigned immediately. With the help of the temporary rule, we were able to give lawyers to arrestees at arguably the most important point in the process. Despite the obvious benefit to the quality of justice, some of the judges still pushed back. They desperately wanted to stem the influx of lawyers from other jurisdictions who did not plan to remain in Orleans Parish for their careers, and thus were more immune to judicial pressure.

While these experienced lawyers were incredibly valuable to OPD's efforts, some judges were determined to interfere with progress. They argued that the rule required that lawyers practicing pursuant to it must have a barred Louisiana lawyer in court with them at all times. No matter how experienced and competent the lawyer, they could not handle even the most straightforward of matters without direct supervision. Such an interpretation would render the rule useless, as it was meant to allow the short-term use of out-of-state lawyers to provide coverage that was otherwise lacking.

I learned of the judges' attack on our progress when Steve stormed into the office we shared. "Can you believe these judges? They have no problem allowing civil lawyers from Louisiana to represent poor people facing lengthy jail time for serious felonies. They let bankruptcy lawyers and divorce lawyers do this all the time." As if I needed further convincing, he continued, "These civil attorneys from Louisiana are far less able to provide effective representation than experienced criminal defense attorneys from outside Louisiana. If you needed brain surgery, would you rather have a foot doctor from Louisiana perform it or a neurosurgeon from Illinois?"

SOME OF THE JUDGES did not try to hide their hostility toward lawyers from outside the parish. The new lawyers would describe a common ritual that would happen when they entered a courtroom for the first time. "What high school did you go to, counsel?" the judge would ask, intent on determining which lawyers did not have local roots. While there were local lawyers in the public defender office who supported reform, one's connection to New Orleans served as a proxy for which side one was on.

As we started to bring in lawyers who were less accepting of the system, and weeded out many of the part-time defenders who were more "judge-centered" than "client-centered," we also began to move away from having public defenders assigned to courtrooms. Under the old system, known as horizontal representation, as the client moved from judge to judge at various stages in the process, a new lawyer handled their case. Because public defenders under this system were assigned to courtrooms rather than to clients, as a client's case was passed to a new courtroom, the client had to rely on a new lawyer with whom they had no relationship. This system kept lawyers from getting to know their clients and having familiarity with the procedural history of the matter. It also gave judges more control of public defenders who must appear before them in every case. Lawyers understood that if they upset the judge in one case, every client thereafter might be punished.

Judges who prioritized the quick processing of cases preferred this horizontal system of representation. They never had to wait for a lawyer to be available. That the client would bounce from lawyer to lawyer, never assured that any of them really knew their case well, was of secondary concern. And the system was quite efficient. Dockets were wrapped up before lunch and judges left the bench. The luxury of such an abbreviated workday depended on horizontal representation.

But in this reform era, public defenders began to engage in vertical representation, the practice of meeting a client at their first court appearance and following the case until completion. This allows the lawyer to have a better understanding of the case and a stronger relationship with the client. It is what anyone who paid for a lawyer would expect. But to many of the judges, vertical representation was maddening. Like their private counterparts, public defenders would handle matters in several courtrooms. It frustrated judges who had come to believe the public defenders belonged to them. They had no patience for a lawyer who was not at their beck and call. When one of the public defenders had matters in two different courtrooms, you would frequently hear the judge yell, "Where is *my* public defender?" This was a further attack on their control. Many would never accept a regime in which the public defender belonged to the client, not the judge.

Many of the older public defenders, who had become accustomed to the way things were, were equally frustrated with this new system. They, too, had to spend more time in court as they worked between multiple courtrooms. It seemed completely inefficient. And through the lens of a legal professional most interested in efficiency, they had a point. But through the lens of a person who depended on a public defender, vertical representation was a big step toward ensuring they had an advocate who knew them, and their case, well enough to truly represent them.

As Steve railed at the judges' efforts to interfere with our ability to recruit lawyers to fill obvious holes in representation, he was concerned about the toll it would take on our new lawyers. He knew the lengths some judges would go to reverse the tide of reform. They resented the office for resisting the court's expectation that lawyers would stand lifelessly

as the court processed poor defendants through the system. They sought
to punish public defenders for the agency's insistence that the lawyers be
assigned to clients rather than courtrooms. At times, the judges even used
creative methods to declare poor people ineligible for a public defender,
forcing them to come up with money they did not have to hire a lawyer
who would offer less resistance, or go without a lawyer altogether. Steve
insisted the office push back at every turn, and he was repeatedly held in
contempt as a result.

In one case, a judge needed lawyers for three capital cases—complex
cases in which the accused faced the possibility of a death sentence. Steve
did not have enough lawyers to handle the cases, which were incredibly
time and resource consuming. The judge, knowing he could not move
forward with the case without a lawyer, simply wanted a warm body to
provide the veneer of meeting the right to counsel. Steve refused. The
judge scheduled a contempt hearing. Steve's crime, it appeared, was an
unwillingness to simply find a warm pair of hands in which to place these
three lives.

On another occasion, a judge ordered Steve locked up when the judge
grew impatient waiting for a public defender to arrive in court. The lawyer assigned to the courtroom was on her honeymoon and her replace-
ment was handling cases in several courtrooms. Feeling slighted that "his"
public defender was not available when he demanded, the judge drove to
the public defender's office with a deputy sheriff and brought Steve to the
courtroom before citing him for contempt. This power play was clearly
meant to send a message to Steve and the management team.

On yet another occasion, in an attempt to funnel defendants away
from OPD, a judge accused Steve of having a public defender represent
a man, arrested for copper theft, who the judge claimed was not technically indigent. The judge's assessment was based on his finding that "[the
man] owns a house, vehicles and dressed very nicely." However, OPD's
indigency determination revealed that "the house he owns was destroyed
by Hurricane Katrina, his car is a 1994 Buick, and he earns $9,600 a year.
That's half the annual income that presumptively entitles someone to an
indigent defender."[1]

Steve was used to such bullying. But he was concerned about what
these young lawyers would be forced to endure. The office was divided
over resistance to vertical representation, as well as the decision to recruit

idealistic lawyers from law schools across the nation. Judges built alliances with some of the older public defenders who had grown accustomed to the old system and were resentful of the changes. Spending a couple hours a day in one courtroom, effortlessly moving cases along, was easy. They now had to cover cases in multiple courtrooms, with an expectation that they investigated the case, raised legal issues, and met with clients.

No sooner did the new lawyers arrive than some members of the local bar began to refer to them as "carpetbaggers," interlopers from the North who came to challenge their way of life. Although only one of the ten new lawyers was a graduate of Harvard, the group became known as the Harvard Ten. The name even took hold among some of the more cynical public defenders in the office. With Harvard representing Northern elitism, the intention was clear: to let the new management team know that our efforts were a declaration of war. Outside lawyers were not welcome.

Judges who resented the changes decided to simply treat all public defenders as fungible. If a case was called and the assigned public defender was not in the courtroom, some of the judges would demand that any public defender present come forward and handle the case.

One afternoon I got a call from Danny, one of the ten new defenders. He had been sitting in the jury box of a courtroom, where lawyers sat as they waited for their cases to be called, when the judge called a case that was scheduled for an evidentiary hearing. The assigned public defender was not in the courtroom. That fact would not deter the judge. He had the defendant sit at the defense table and brought the testifying officer to the witness stand. He then ordered Danny to come to counsel table and handle the hearing.

Danny had been a lawyer for only a few weeks. But he knew that he could not handle a hearing in a case he knew nothing about for a client he had never met. Danny explained that the man's public defender was in another courtroom and would be there soon. The judge was unwilling to wait. He again asked Danny to come to counsel table. Danny refused, in as respectful a way as he could. So the judge started the hearing without a lawyer.

Danny called me the next day to talk about his experience. He shared that afterwards a more seasoned lawyer chided him for not doing the hearing. "That guy would have been better off with you there than with nobody," the lawyer opined. Danny struggled with that idea. As unprepared as he was, he was better than nothing. The judges and local lawyers who were opposed to our reform efforts would frequently claim that the changes were hurting poor defendants, that Danny refusing to handle the hearing was worse for the man accused, that Steve refusing to take more cases than the office could handle was leaving poor people without lawyers.

But Danny knew that what was really hurting poor people was a system that refused to reform. He understood that poor people were suffering as the public defenders resisted the unjust system, but he also understood that as long as public defenders acquiesced to unjust demands by judges, they enabled the existing system. They had to refuse to participate in unconstitutional practices. He referred to Sean's words back in Birmingham: "I know these lawyers who think we should be handling any case. I like many of them. But they took the blue pill. They are numb to the injustice the system causes. They don't even realize how unjust it is. I don't think they lose sleep at night. On the other hand, I couldn't sleep at all last night. I don't know what that red pill is, but it sure ain't a sleeping pill."

Every one of these lawyers had similar stories. Some of the judges were determined to make their lives as difficult as possible. But it was not only pushback from the judges that these lawyers had to deal with. The prosecutors were equally rankled by the public defender office's new vision of justice, a vision that cast their role as adversaries to state agents hell-bent on caging poor New Orleanians.

One of the changes that the district attorney hated was a renewed emphasis on investigation. When everyone accepted the facts set forth in the police report, there was no need to fight in court. Public defenders were much less likely to question their client's guilt or challenge the constitutionality of the actions of police. But that changed post-Katrina. We began to hire a professional staff of investigators. We did not look for retired police officers, as was common in many public defender offices across the country, because we wanted a team that would be sufficiently critical of police practices. We understood that, just like lawyers, police were shaped by the culture of their profession. They learned to embrace assumptions about police work that we wanted to vigilantly challenge. And so we hired a team of investigators who were smart, curious, creative, and committed. Many were recent college graduates who were passionate about criminal justice. We trained them to, among other things, canvass crime scenes and interview witnesses. Steve and I understood from our years as investigators—roles we each played at PDS prior to becoming lawyers—and public defenders that hearing a witness's story firsthand always uncovered details that were different, or missing, from the police account.

But the prosecutors were furious about this new practice. Despite the fact that New Orleans had the highest rate of wrongful convictions in the world, prosecutors took it personally—as if their integrity were being called into question—when the new public defenders examined the allegations behind their charging decisions. They did not seem to appreciate that the constitutional right to counsel requires lawyers to investigate cases. Defense counsel is obligated to talk to, locate, and interview witnesses.

They decided to try to put an end to this practice by intimidating the new crop of public defense professionals pushing for change in New Orleans. In one instance, the DA charged a twenty-two-year-old investigator with kidnapping after she talked to two young witnesses in a sexual assault case. The young investigator did what any of us would expect from our legal team should we be accused of a crime. She did what the defense team is constitutionally and ethically obligated to do. Her actions did not violate any laws or other authority. She never used trickery or deception to talk to the girls. All charges were dropped five months later.[2] But the move was never about prosecuting a young, idealistic investigator. It was about chilling a new brand of public defense in the city.

While there was plenty of resistance to reform in New Orleans, the office leadership fully embraced the vision of SPDTC. Leadership was committed to transforming culture internally as well as challenging injustice externally. In addition to Steve and Sully, the leadership team included Christine Lehmann, a smart and passionate lawyer who came to New Orleans to do death penalty work after receiving a law degree from Yale and a theology degree from Harvard. We would soon bring in Chris Flood, a former colleague from PDS who had been doing federal defender work in New York and was inspired to join the reform effort. Derwyn Bunton, who was originally on the board that ushered in reform, would soon become the executive director of the office, once a solid reform foundation was laid. Derwyn had come to New Orleans from New York University Law School to do juvenile justice work. Every person involved in leading the reform effort shared a common view of what justice demanded for poor people accused of crimes. The course was rocky, but the people in charge were clear about where they were heading.

Our difficulty in building alliances with many of the public defender offices throughout Georgia lay in the lack of a shared vision with many of its public defender leaders. While several leaders given the reins of reform in Georgia certainly welcomed real change, quite a few were lawyers who had for decades been part of the systems they were tasked with changing. There was little diversity. Of the first forty-nine chief public defenders in Georgia's statewide system, forty-five were white men. Three were women. Two were lawyers of color. In the "good ol' boy" world of Georgia criminal justice, a number of these leaders were comfortable with the way things were. They went to school with the judges and prosecutors. They were friends with the local sheriffs. Everyone socialized together. Their values were all shaped by the same system.

Many understood that there was a need to improve the systems where they worked but believed that being too critical was counterproductive. They certainly believed they were working toward justice, as they understood it. But they could not appreciate how broken their systems were and were unwilling to ruffle feathers as they ushered in a statewide public defender program. Shortly after I left Georgia, some of the young lawyers from the Honors Program told me that a few of the chief defenders would tell them, "The only thing Rapping was training you to do was to get fired." They saw any advocacy that upset the status quo as poor lawyering. This leadership perspective made reform impossible.

Of course, there were some leaders in Georgia who truly wanted transformative change. But any support they would need to push for it quickly disappeared. Soon after the legislation creating a statewide public defender system was passed, the Democratic legislature that ushered in reform was replaced with a much more conservative body of lawmakers that was far less sympathetic to reform. As the new statewide system struggled to get off the ground in 2005, the 148th Georgia General Assembly gathered. It was the first session since Reconstruction in which both houses were controlled by Republicans. Already hostile to public defender reform that would centralize any control, lawmakers were given, in the form of the Brian Nichols case, the fodder they needed to stall progress before it could begin.

Two years later, after the first director of Georgia Public Defender Standards Council (GPDSC)—the entity responsible for overseeing the statewide system—retired, the Republican governor of Georgia would appoint a Republican legislator who had served eight terms in the Georgia General Assembly. As the legislature threatened the public defender budget, a council committed to real reform pushed back. Relations between the GPDSC and those who oversaw state budgets grew tense. The new director did not have any meaningful indigent defense experience. He had no demonstrated commitment to the cause of public defense. The appointment was meant to improve the agency's relationship with the legislative and executive branches.[3] But improving relationships meant not fighting too hard for desperately needed funding.

However, while our progress in Georgia faced a setback, our new partnership in New Orleans left us encouraged. Eager to build on this momentum, we spent the next several months identifying new offices to work with. We continued a steady pace of growth, and as our reach spread, I quickly learned that the challenges I had seen in Georgia and New Orleans were far from the exception. They were the rule.

In the summer of 2008 we welcomed a new class of thirty public defenders. A second group from Atlanta represented Georgia. New Orleans sent thirteen more lawyers who, along with five lawyers from four additional parishes across the state, represented Louisiana. There were lawyers from three counties in Mississippi, a lawyer from Charleston, South Carolina, and two from Nashville, Tennessee.

Early in the summer program, as always, we started working through exercises designed to teach how to build effective client relationships. We discussed the many reasons clients often do not trust public defenders and some of the subtle ways we communicate that can easily reinforce this distrust. We talked about the importance of the first meeting, where we can begin to break down some of the negative perceptions clients often harbor about public defenders. We also pointed out many of the ways a less thoughtful initial interaction might inadvertently reinforce some of those negative stereotypes.

As we discussed a number of assumptions that can undermine effective attorney-client relationships, and some of the ways lawyers can blindly foster mistrust, a young public defender named Genesis Draper spoke up. Along with Sunny Eaton, she was one of the first two participants from Nashville.

"My problem is that I am not the first person to talk to my clients. We have investigators that initially meet them. By the time I meet them, much of this damage may already be done."

It was as if a collective light bulb went off in the room, as the lawyers shared stories of how their offices were structured in ways that ensured that the first point of contact would be made by a person who was solely focused on gathering information without any thought about building relationships. They all knew of first meetings with clients who did not trust the interviewer and had provided inaccurate and unhelpful information. Often the damage to the relationship was done before they ever met the client. The conversation reflected a subtle culture that saw the role of the public defender more as a gatherer of information to facilitate a process than someone who developed the trusting relationship necessary to truly work with the client to solve a panoply of problems that led them to this point in their life.

Later that evening Genesis came to talk to me. She had been thinking a lot about the earlier workshop. She understood that our discussion reflected a broader cultural challenge. Public defenders faced such great pressure to handle overwhelming caseloads that it became easy to lose sight of the need to learn about the person behind the case and what their priorities might be in the process. She realized she was not always sufficiently attentive to what her clients would tell her, and wrestled with the harm that she may have caused.

But the day's lessons helped her understand that the emotional toll of her shortcomings were a sign of strength, not weakness. She understood that a lack of concern about her participation in this injustice would be a much greater threat to her ability to serve her clients. She was grateful to have the opportunity to work through similar challenges in a supportive community. She was committed to learning how to listen to the people she would represent and how to establish relationships that would enable her to feel more like an ally than part of the problem.

FIFTY MORE LAWYERS JOINED US over the next two years. Greenwood became the second office in South Carolina to join. Knoxville became our second Tennessee partner. We added lawyers from two more parishes in Louisiana. Dallas became the first Texas office to send a lawyer, and we added one defender from Virginia. Three more Georgia offices joined Atlanta.

We were growing, both in our reach as well as in the depth of our partnerships with a number of offices. In addition to adding new partners, we continued to add lawyers from Atlanta, New Orleans, and Nashville—our largest urban partners. But we were attracting lawyers from much smaller offices, such as Greenville, Mississippi; Shreveport, Louisiana; and, as mentioned, Greenwood. Wherever these lawyers came from, the types of challenges they faced were similar.

For young public defenders, sustaining oneself in a hostile environment was no easy task. It meant being constantly reminded that your value is measured by your ability to facilitate a system that mistreats your clients. Judges and prosecutors let you know that they would prefer that you just sit down and shut up.

In the summer of 2009, we were training our third annual class of public defenders. We had just finished a class trip to the Birmingham Civil Rights Institute. In a debriefing with the lawyers following that experience, we reflected on how their work was an extension of the important civil rights struggles documented in the museum. We spent the day thinking about America's history of state-sponsored oppression and its connection to the battles the public defenders were fighting in courtrooms in the present day. As we discussed how those in power still had very little regard for justice for our society's most vulnerable members, my mind went back three years to my time working in New Orleans.

I was waiting to observe evening first appearance hearings when the magistrate took the bench at 6:35. There were approximately forty arrestees whose cases needed to be heard. A private attorney represented one of the defendants. The rest were left to a team of two public defenders. As a professional courtesy, the judge called the private attorney's case first.

After about ten minutes of discussion, the judge granted the requested bond, then turned to the public defender in the courtroom and said, "You better talk fast because we are going to finish the rest of these by seven o'clock."

IF YOU SPEND ANY time watching how justice is dispensed in most courthouses in America, it is easy to see how public defenders can start to accept their role as cogs in the system's machinery. These are systems that have low expectations of public defenders. They are designed to forge public defenders who do not interfere with the routine injustice. If a person stayed in these systems long enough, he or she could begin to morph into the caricatures so often portrayed in popular culture.

When I was a young public defender, the head of the trial division had a button on her office desk that read, "Don't tell my mother I am a public defender, she thinks I play piano in a whorehouse." The not-so-subtle message—that there is no less respectable job a lawyer could have—is one that every public defender has confronted. The lack of respect for these advocates is directly related to the image we have adopted of those accused of crimes. In a world that continually tells public defenders that the more faithful they are to the people they serve the more despicable they will be deemed, it can be easy to lose sight of the nobility of this calling.

We do not assume that recent law graduates understand the role of the public defender. Law schools do not teach it, popular culture aggressively distorts it, and the legal profession disrespects it.

I recently had an exchange with a graduating law student who struggled to understand why anyone who cared about justice would become a defense lawyer. The student asked me whether lawyers who defend criminals are supposed to "seek justice or get their clients off?" The student did not understand one of the most basic aspects of our justice system: that when a person is presumed innocent, having a lawyer who forces the prosecution to establish guilt beyond a reasonable doubt by pointing out holes in the state's case is *fundamental* to justice. This student got through three years of law school and still believed that a defense lawyer who does not participate in proving the case against their own client is somehow acting inconsistently with justice. Implicit in the student's question seemed to be that justice demands that the defense lawyer should presume the allegations true and work to help establish their client's guilt. The question also suggests that law schools do not do a very good job preparing lawyers to promote justice.

That's why the Summer Institute is so crucial: it provides a chance to examine many assumptions that are incompatible with serving justice. It is why the lawyers are pushed to consider whether public defenders have roles that differ from those of prosecutors or of their private counterparts. It is why we ask them to grapple with whether public defenders have an added responsibility, and a challenge, that comes with representing a person who never asked for their help.

As the group unpacks the various layers of duty they owe to the people they represent, they are asked to consider situations that may challenge their ability to live up to these duties. Are there certain types of cases that they would struggle with—perhaps rape or child abuse? Are there particular types of clients they would struggle to represent—maybe a white supremacist or a crooked police officer?

As they ponder these questions, many will draw from some of the quotes written on large poster boards adorning the walls of the central meeting room. Each is a quote relevant to public defense. They serve as examples of the higher ideals public defenders are tasked with upholding in every case.

We then introduce a model designed to help them answer these tough questions. We introduce it using some of the quotes. The group is asked to consider three in particular and to vote on which most resonated with them.

The first is the quote attributed to Sister Helen Prejean that hung on my office wall a dozen years earlier:

> The dignity of the human person means that every human being is worth more than the worst thing they've ever done.

The second is from Margaret Mead:

> Never doubt that a small group of thoughtful, committed citizens can change the world; indeed, it is the only thing that ever has.

The third, from Friedrich Nietzsche:

> Distrust all in whom the impulse to punish is powerful.

The votes are always fairly evenly divided. We then work through a model, developed by faculty member Jeff Sherr, called the public defender motivation triangle. Jeff was the training director for the State of

Kentucky, a system well respected for its creative approach to public defense training. I was introduced to Jeff when I first moved to Georgia,
and he generously shared ideas as I worked to create a statewide version
of the PDS-style training model. He was one of the early members of the
Honors Program faculty and had been a person I consulted with often as
I continued to reimagine the outer limits of what we could accomplish
through training and mentorship.

While we had been discussing the various motivators for being a public defender since I was a young lawyer at PDS, Jeff put these ideas into a
model. We adopted this paradigm in our curriculum.

Jeff taught that every client-centered public defender is driven to this
work primarily by one of three overarching motivators.[4] Some of us are
"social workers."[5] We do this work because we want to help people who
have never had a fair chance in life. We want to address the issues that
brought them into the criminal justice system and help them to move on
with fulfilling lives. We do the work because of the people. We are the
counselors.

Some of us are "warriors." We are offended by the idea of an all-
powerful government using its might to target an individual in an unfair
fight. When we see such an uneven fight, we want to be on the side of the
underdog. It doesn't matter who is in the state's crosshairs; we want to be
on their side. We hate bullies. We are the warriors.

And some of us are "movement builders." We understand the criminal justice system as racist and classist. We believe it has fallen far short of
our most cherished democratic ideals. We want to be part of a community
of activists committed to creating a better world for our children. We are
movement builders.

The model is represented by a triangle with one of the three motivators illustrated on each side. While every client-centered public defender
likely has some of all three of these motivators in them, each is likely
motivated by one primarily. It is their default motivator.

Jeff teaches the lawyers that the public defender who is able to move
around the triangle and successfully tap into all three motivators will sustain themselves the longest in this work. No one motivator will work in
every instance.

For example, a lawyer may primarily embrace the social worker motivator but still have that one client they just cannot seem to connect with

at all. They may struggle to develop the relationship necessary to nurture their social worker instinct. But if they can pivot to their warrior motivator, for instance, they can feel like even if they cannot connect with the client on a personal level, they are offended by the prosecution's attempts to run roughshod over him.

Because the ability to tap into each motivator provides a powerful way for a public defender to overcome a wide range of challenges, we work with the group to nurture the instincts that are not predominant. For any given challenge, we push them to view it through different lenses. The exercise with the quotes gives some insight into what their primary motivator may be. We work with them to hone the other two.

Pushing public defenders to remain conscious of the reasons they chose this career path, working with them to tap into other powerful motivators for continuing to do this work, fostering in them a client-centered outlook that respects the dignity of the people they represent, and reinforcing the critical role they play in our system of justice are all foundational goals we begin to tease out during the first few days of the Summer Institute. We understand that no matter how technically sound they may be at lawyering, if they lose sight of their purpose they will always reinforce a corrupted status quo. And so this piece becomes foundational to everything we teach about preparing and trying a case.

I was regularly reminded of the cost of our failure to ensure public defenders understood this purpose. A 2012 meeting with Steve Bright over a cup of coffee back in Atlanta was one such time. We were talking about the state of public defense in Cordele, the original target of the Georgia lawsuit that led to the statewide system, and the circuit where Jason Carini began his public defender career. Jason completed his three-year commitment even though Georgia defunded the Honors Program that brought him there in the first place. But he soon left, feeling he did not have the promised support he needed to continue to push back against the culture there.

Steve saw the promise that came out of the lawsuit against Cordele slipping away. He shared a letter with me that SCHR received from a man represented by a public defender in Cordele. The man was being held on a bond he was unable to afford. He asked his lawyer to try to get his bond reduced and to request a preliminary hearing to force the state to demonstrate that it had the evidence required to continue to detain him.

As we taught our public defenders, these hearings are incredibly valuable. At this early stage in the representation, the defense likely only has a police report from which to understand the allegations. The opportunity to get more information from the prosecution, through a process known as "discovery"—so critical to uncovering legal issues that can be litigated and to providing investigative leads—would not likely arise until after there were formal charges. This could take weeks. The preliminary hearing provided a chance to learn about information necessary to begin preparing a defense. It could also potentially reveal problems with the prosecution's case that were left out of the police reports and that could lead to the client's release or dismissal of all charges. We teach our lawyers that there needs to be an incredibly good reason to waive that hearing.

The letter Steve shared was from the man's public defender, responding to his request. In it, she explained to the man that she would not file a motion to reduce his bond for ninety days. She added, "Explain to me why you are requesting a preliminary hearing. I would like to know why you feel a preliminary hearing is needed in your case."[6] The letter appeared to reflect a practice in the office of routinely waiving preliminary hearings and requiring a client to convince the lawyer of a good reason to do otherwise. Taking advantage of these hearings was the exception instead of the rule.

The letter revealed the mind-set of a public defender who was accepting of a system that cared little for the human lives it impacted. She was unwilling to challenge the detention of a man presumed innocent, seemingly comfortable with him rotting in a cell for three months. She too easily accepted the allegations against her client as true, apparently unable to comprehend the value of testing those charges through a preliminary hearing. Finally, she completely abdicated her role as a lawyer, demanding that her client—unschooled in the complexities of criminal procedure—explain to her why he felt this critical hearing was important.

These lessons reinforced in me the importance of our approach to grooming public defenders. We could teach lawyers how to effectively cross-examine or explain the procedure governing preliminary hearings. But none of those lessons would matter if they failed to appreciate the importance of these hearings and gave such little weight to their client's priorities. What chance did a poor person have when the public defender they were assigned had little desire to be a zealous lawyer?

But as Steve told me about this public defender in Cordele, I thought of a story I had recently read about a young public defender in Savannah, Georgia, that had reinforced my belief that populating public defender offices with the best lawyers the profession had to offer was not easy. The article described a dedicated public defender who by all accounts was developing into an excellent lawyer. He appeared to possess a wealth of skills and passion—the kind of lawyer we would hope to have as part of this fight for many years to come. Then came the line that felt like a punch in the gut. It was a quote from a senior public defender who worked with the younger advocate: "'I'll be very surprised if he's not a top notch, high echelon politician or DA or a very, very—'"

I was hoping the next potential profession on the list was "visionary head of a public defender office," but I was not optimistic. I read on:

"'—successful private-practice attorney,' [the seasoned lawyer] said. 'It's his choice.'"[7]

The importance of our work could not have been clearer. In too many public defender systems, the mind-set of the Cordele public defender was the accepted norm. The expectation was that an advocate would be anything but zealous. Those who did set themselves apart as good lawyers were expected to leave public defense once they got some trial experience. In fact, they were encouraged to leave. Almost anything was seen as a step up. The idea that the best lawyers would ever aspire to be career public defenders was laughable. For the most part, public defense was either for lawyers who hoped to gain trial experience on the backs of poor people or those with few other options and little sense of pride in representing the most vulnerable among us. The best lawyers left the profession, while those willing to adapt to the prevailing norm would end up running offices.

IN JANUARY 2010, nearly a hundred public defenders gathered in Montgomery, Alabama, as SPDTC held its first graduation. Thirty courageous public defenders would be honored. Members of the first three SPDTC classes were joined by more than a dozen members of the Georgia Honors Program. Georgia never fulfilled its promise to these young lawyers. They never got to graduate from the Honors Program. Without the continued support, some left. Others hung in there, trying to develop into the public defenders they desperately wanted to become. I felt personally responsible to these defenders as the person who recruited them to join that effort. Within a year of launching SPDTC, we scraped together enough money to support any of them who wanted to become part of what we were building. They, along with the class of 2007, would become our first graduating class.

These lawyers had been meeting every six months for the last three years. Each year, as they were joined by a new class, the community grew stronger. Many could not fathom doing the work without this support.

As graduation weekend closed, we sat in a circle listening as recent graduates shared parting words. By now, they all had at least three years under their belts. They maintained a strong sense of what kind of lawyers their clients deserved, tempered by an understanding of how far short they routinely fell from this standard. It was an understanding one could gain only through experience. But this experience could also easily drive a lawyer to overlook the gap between aspiration and reality. These lawyers refused to be blind to it. This community helped them remain aware. They were grateful for this group but also struggling with what they perceived as failure.

Barksdale stood up and talked to his peers. "I closed over five hundred felonies last year, and I have a hundred and sixty-five pending cases right now. They're all felonies," his voice cracked. "And I cannot be an effective attorney at those numbers." He sat down. Claps filled the room—a custom developed in part to show a struggling colleague support and understanding but also an expression of appreciation that another lawyer shared a struggle. Every lawyer in the room had similar challenges. The applause was a badly needed reminder to the rest of the room that they were not alone.

Diana Davis, an original member of the Georgia Honors Program, stood up next. "Without this group I would have quit a long time ago," she shared. "It's a hard job and nobody's helping you," she continued. "Other lawyers are telling me, 'You work too much.'" She could not slow down when so many people who counted on her needed so much. Her work ethic had been met with derision.

Jason Clark, another member of the 2005 Honors Program class got up. "When people keep telling you that you are crazy, you can begin to wonder if it is true," he started. He shared how he was often told not to push so hard. He was told that his ideals were too ambitious. He was constantly reminded of the local standard of practice. "I am so thankful to have a group that also believes in the standards that I try to live up to. You help me know that I am not crazy at all. I am in good company. The larger this group gets, the more strength I feel to resist the way things have always been done."

And so it went on. One after the other, public defenders shared victories and struggles, every testimonial punctuated with a round of applause.

Zanele was the last to speak.

"I do this work six months at a time," she told the group. Heads unanimously nodded.

"This work is so hard. I leave these get-togethers feeling like I can take on the world, and within three or four months I am starting to get beaten down again. Just when I think I can't do it anymore, it is time to get together with my SPDTC family. And then I am recharged. I know I have six more months in me."

That afternoon, after the hugs and the farewells and the tears, as the last of the young defenders drove away, the faculty met with Illy and me for the ritual debrief. We all had graduates asking us if they were welcome to come back in six months. Young lawyers like Janelle, Brett, and Danny, who could not imagine losing the support of this group. They promised they would find a way to cover their expenses. We all agreed that we would find a way to accommodate any of the graduates who wanted to come back, even if we had to come up with the funding ourselves. We also decided we needed to schedule a faculty retreat to discuss the direction of the movement that was blossoming.

Several weeks later, Illy and I sat with Sean, Cathy, Patrice, and Jeff. We were joined by other faculty members who would become instrumental to the development of Gideon's Promise—each of them among the best public defenders I knew from across the country—including Violeta Chapin, William Montross, Mary Moriarty, David Patton, and Dehlia Umunna. We knew the lawyers who were graduating from the Core Program, the name we gave the three-year training and mentorship experience for new public defenders, were exactly the kind of public defenders we would need to transform this system. We had thought a lot about how to support them as they worked toward a collective vision throughout the South. In addition to reconvening every six months and providing each lawyer with a mentor, we developed a virtual community through which the group shared success stories and reached out when they were feeling defeated.

But we were now realizing we needed to plan beyond the first three years. The lawyers obviously needed the continued support. The closing session a couple months earlier reminded all of us that they would struggle without this community. Resisting the cultural pressures of the systems where they worked would only get harder. And they could certainly still benefit from the training.

As the group continued to grow we would need more faculty. We would also have to supplement a curriculum that was designed for newer public defenders. We recognized the opportunity that was presented by the graduates' desire to remain connected to the community.

These were the lawyers who would become supervisors in our partner offices. They were also a readily available corps of trainers and mentors for the influx of new lawyers joining SPDTC. We decided we needed a program for alumni to help graduates develop as more experienced lawyers, supervisors, trainers, and mentors. It would allow us to continue to grow graduates into the public defenders the system desperately needed and develop the human resources needed to accommodate organizational growth.

But we also understood that we needed to work more closely with the leaders of the offices we partnered with to think about how to promote the values we were teaching in their organizations, and to pull in respected lawyers and supervisors from those offices to reinforce these lessons with the newer lawyers.

Our vision of continued growth required that we develop more trainers and mentors to help us spread this vision more broadly, and that we develop a pipeline to get the most committed future public defenders to our partner offices—many of which would never be on the radars of these budding advocates training in law schools throughout the country.

After three years of tireless work, the Core Program exceeded all of our expectations. Yet we were realizing that if our goal was a movement of public defenders that would truly transform culture, we were far from being able to claim success. Transforming culture would take more than a coordinated effort to develop young public defenders in their formative years. It would take a comprehensive model that strategically worked with partner offices at every level.

We spent dozens of hours over a long weekend, fueled by passion and caffeine, mapping out what this model would look like.

As the hours passed and the vision gained clarity, we all began to get excited about what we were outlining. But we also knew that one of the keys to moving to the next level was Illy. She had proven indispensable to our accomplishments thus far. We had already convinced her to stretch her one year leave of absence from teaching into three.

As the weekend went on, we had realized our vision called for four additional programs to accompany the one we had launched for newer public defenders. An Alumni Program would allow us to continue to support our lawyers as we shaped them into tomorrow's public defense leaders. A Leadership Program would bring the defenders who ran our partner offices together to consider how to strategically shift office culture. A Trainer Development Program would provide an opportunity to build a larger stable of faculty to support our growth. And a law school partnership would create a pipeline for future public defenders to gravitate to offices that they otherwise would not consider.

As we all got increasingly excited, we noticed Illy in the corner of the room shaking her head.

"Illy, what's wrong?" Dehlia asked. "Don't you like it?"

"I think it is great, but I would like it better if I didn't have to figure out how to build it."

Illy realized she might never return to the classroom.

CHAPTER 6

DAVID'S SLINGSHOT

GUY WILKINSON WAS THE head public defender for the Twenty-Fourth Judicial District of Tennessee, and one of thirty-one district public defenders in the state, when he testified before the Tennessee House Committee on Finance, Ways and Means. As the elected president of the Tennessee Public Defender Conference, he served as the group's spokesperson. When asked if he had enough resources, he was given the rare opportunity to help the committee understand the plight of public defenders across the state. Focusing on his own district, he responded:

> I probably am blessed. . . . You all probably could get up here and you're always asking for more and more; but in my district . . . I think I have enough assistance to cover the caseload that I have. I have a five-county district. I have an attorney for each county. What I have done is converted one of my investigators into an attorney position so I could cover all the courts. And uh, then I have one investigator for my five-county district. And our caseload, we do about four thousand cases a year. I have been blessed with retention of my staff which means I have experienced attorneys, which really helps a lot in being able to process cases, it's a time saver in a lot of cases, I think more efficient. . . . They get good quality representation. Of course, I'm bragging. I guess I'm biased. For one district in the state . . . I think you have supplied what I need.[1]

Although Wilkinson's lawyers each handled an average of eight hundred cases per year, he seemed to think he was "blessed." With that volume, and one investigator for all five counties, it is clear that his lawyers put little, if any, effort into challenging the allegations against the people they represent. Yet he did not feel he needed any additional help.

I am sure Wilkinson did not come out of law school thirty-five years earlier thinking, "You know what I want to do with my life? I want to help process eight hundred people a year into cages . . . I think I will become a public defender."[2] No, he was slowly and subtly shaped into a lawyer he never would have recognized when he was a law student by a system that had come to accept an embarrassingly low standard of justice for the poor. I don't believe he was an especially weak individual. Rather, the power of culture is so strong that most of us, as well-intentioned as we may be, will be shaped by it if we do not have the awareness and support to resist its undercurrent.

Wilkinson's testimony highlights the cultural challenge of reforming public defense. He ran an office with five lawyers who presumably, like him, grew to believe the level of service they provided eight hundred clients per year was all that justice demanded. They obviously had dire financial challenges, and almost certainly operated in a system in need of some structural reform. But even if they were given all the money and independence required, these lawyers had lost sight of what it means to be a public defender. They would continue to ignore critical aspects of the work, invariably not recognizing its importance. With fewer cases, they might just go home at lunchtime feeling like they had nothing else to do after processing the reduced caseload. Increased resources and freedom to be the lawyers their clients deserve are certainly necessary conditions for them to be the public defenders *Gideon* envisioned. But they are not sufficient. Real reform demands a change of one's heart and mind.

Some problems can be addressed by changing an existing rule or making a new policy. Scholars in organizational psychology call these technical problems. But others require organizational actors to reshape the core values that drive them. These are adaptive challenges. Experts understand that the ability to distinguish between the two is critical to effective leadership.[3] The reformer who tries to alter behavior by modifying governing rules or policies will fail at achieving true change.

For example, with eight hundred cases per year, one can assume the public defenders in the Twenty-Fourth Judicial Circuit spend little time, if any, with their clients outside of court. Any group of lawyers who believe they are doing a good job with that caseload have certainly lost all appreciation for the importance of an attorney-client relationship. Reformers could implement standards that require lawyers to spend fifteen hours per week visiting clients at the jail. This solution might force lawyers to spend more time in the physical presence of the people they represent, but it will not ensure meaningful communication. Instead, lawyers who have no idea how to effectively use the time will resent having to go through an exercise they deem futile. It will be a wasted fifteen hours for both the lawyer and the client.

Experts understand that we work to achieve outcomes consistent with our guiding values. Establishing new rules can impact our ability to achieve desired outcomes. But they do not change our worldview. For lawyers who embrace a value set consistent with justice, tweaking policies that interfere with their ability to act on those values will encourage improvement. But if lawyers are driven by a misguided set of values, creating policies that make it more challenging for them to live up to their warped value set will only make it harder for them to achieve their desired outcome. It will not prompt them to pursue a new vision.

For members of an organization with the right set of core values, technical solutions—changing policies that may hinder the ability to live up to those values—are a useful vehicle to facilitate desired behavior. But when professionals are guided by forces inconsistent with the organization's core values, technical fixes will fail. An adaptive solution that reshapes team members' guiding values is required.

Guy Wilkinson is not an isolated example. There are many public defenders who have accepted situations similar to his. After all, he was elected by his peers as a leader in their community. There are also many public defenders who would bristle at Wilkinson's testimony. They practice in systems where the challenges are not this great. They recognize that complacency with eight hundred cases is problematic. But they almost certainly still work in systems that have normalized practices that are inconsistent with justice. There is a lot of room along a spectrum from eight hundred cases per year to being able to provide every accused person what they deserve.

Challenges facing public defenders in America fall all along this spectrum. Offices across the country are populated with well-intentioned lawyers who have been shaped by these corrupted systems. Nearly every public defender in America has more clients than they can possibly represent competently, is forced to work with inadequate resources, and faces pressure to move cases quickly. Learning to triage becomes an indispensable survival skill for public defenders. Those who do this well are held up as the most capable. Sure, Guy Wilkinson is an extreme example. But it is virtually impossible to have worked very long in these systems without being shaped by the culture.

As I spent more time working with public defenders in the South, my understanding of the forces that shaped so many became clearer. When I first left Washington, DC, I was quick to assume that the lawyers I met who fell short of the public defender standard I learned were never truly committed to the cause. There were certainly plenty of lawyers who agreed to represent poor people who had no business doing so. But there were many others who cared very much—who tried very hard—but who were forced to adapt to practices in a broken criminal justice system.

The longer one remains in a system the greater the chance one adapts. With few exceptions, even the best of us have been shaped by less than ideal systems. For this reason, an adaptive approach to reform is required. Fixing public defense in America requires a cultural transformation. And this requires reimagining a set of core values that must drive public defense and working to get every defender to internalize these values.

Obviously, populating a defender agency with advocates who assume a common set of core values can be done a couple of ways. Leaders can work to get those already in the organization to recalibrate their existing values, or they can recruit new members and groom them to accept the desired value set. In reality, most offices will employ some mixture of both.

But organizational psychology teaches that learned behavior can be hard to abandon. Most of us, when told that the way we have been doing things is flawed, can become defensive. We can become vested in endorsing accepted practices. It can be more difficult to view the challenge with a truly open mind. Leaders can expect some degree of resistance to change from existing staff. While certainly not always the case, the level of resistance is often correlated with the seniority of the person being challenged and the perceived success they have enjoyed under the old regime. Of course, seasoned staff can bring a wealth of benefits that outweigh the effort required to overcome resistance. But the easiest way to populate an organization with folks who embrace a desired value set is to hire and develop them.

To successful business leaders, the importance of recruiting and hiring consistent with the organizational vision is obvious. This idea is surprisingly ignored in public defense. When I began helping to reform the public defender's office in New Orleans in 2006, one of our first tasks was to hire attorneys. Frustrated that the positions were not filled more quickly, one judge volunteered his opinion; he told the office chief about an unemployed lawyer who was working as a server at a local restaurant and expressed concern that, even with out-of-work lawyers in the city, the office still had vacancies.

Without knowing anything more than the fact that the server had a law degree, the judge concluded this person was qualified to represent poor people charged with crimes. Rather than seeing public defense as a highly specialized field of law, this judge viewed it as an occupation of last resort for lawyers who cannot get hired elsewhere. With the tremendous pressure to help move the conveyor belt along, public defender leaders can be excused for sometimes overlooking the importance of being selective in the process of hiring and developing staff. When there are overwhelming caseloads, there is a strong sense of urgency to fill the position quickly when a lawyer leaves the office. The lawyers who remain in the office are already drowning and can ill afford to take on more cases themselves. The immediate priority is finding a lawyer—any lawyer—willing to take over the excess caseload.

Many chief public defenders, when faced with a staff vacancy, begin and end their list of requirements with "admitted to practice law in [the state]," limiting their applicant pool to local, unemployed lawyers. Others demand slightly more: they seek a licensed lawyer who has experience trying cases. However, because only a small fraction of a public defender's cases end up in trial, the latter strategy is hardly better than the former.

Values-based recruitment, with an eye toward hiring advocates both to raise the quality of representation immediately and to develop leaders in the organization in the future, is at the heart of our change model. But when leaders are focused on constantly putting out fires, this approach is oft-ignored. This problem is compounded by the fact that many law students with the most potential to become excellent public defenders have traditionally competed only for placements in a handful of the best-resourced offices. Those offices—which were primarily in the Northeast and on the West Coast—built relationships with law schools. They were able to control caseloads to some extent so that when they had an opening, they could hire a stellar graduating law student who might not be licensed for several months. They promised training, support, and a community.

For the nation's best public defender prospects, working in Georgia, Alabama, Mississippi, or Tennessee was not attractive unless they had some previous connection to the region. Although I certainly met some great public defenders in these places, those states lacked the national reputation, and a national pipeline to law schools, to attract graduating law students from across the country. We aimed to change that. Through our Core Program, we offered ongoing training, support, and an amazing community of like-minded defenders. We launched a summer law clerk program to introduce students to opportunities with our partner offices early in their law school careers, in an effort to inspire them to join our movement. Once they were inspired, we were able, through a postgraduate fellowship program we developed with a number of the nation's top law schools, to overcome obstacles to getting many of these future lawyers into public defender offices in some of the most resourced-strapped counties.

The promise of doing the most meaningful work in places with the greatest need attracted many students who would otherwise never consider working in such challenging environments. And as the leaders of our partner offices saw the promise in the young lawyers we attracted, their entire vision of hiring shifted.

Fielding Pringle, the chief public defender in Columbia, South Carolina, was one of those leaders. She was highly regarded as a trial lawyer and a respected leader in the criminal defense community. She had been a committed public defender since 1998. But until she began working with Gideon's Promise to bring new public defenders to her office, she did not prioritize recruitment.

In the first three years of our partnership, she would hire eight new lawyers to join the Gideon's Promise Core Program. Several learned about her office through our summer law clerk program. Most were lawyers she would not have been able to bring on without our law school partnership efforts. They included law graduates from the University of California at Los Angeles and Berkeley, Washington and Lee University in Virginia, and American University in Washington, DC. The young defenders would make up nearly a third of the office's legal staff, and they would be at the heart of Fielding's effort to transform the culture of the office.

The defenders opened Fielding's eyes to the importance of values-based recruitment. Fielding thanked Illy and me in an email. "When we became involved with [Gideon's Promise] we began looking at potential applicants in a different light," she wrote. "Rather than hiring the next 'warm body' we could get our hands on to fill a slot to manage a caseload, we began looking for applicants who possessed the same kind of commitment and dedication to indigent defense that we were seeing in our [Gideon's Promise] hires."[4]

For the first time she realized how her past hiring practices damaged her office. "While this seems like an obvious goal for any public defender office, it was not one to which we had devoted a tremendous amount of time and effort," she admitted. "As a result, we had constant turnover and attorneys with questionable judgment who did not come from a client-centered place."

These new lawyers were foundational in her effort to transform culture. "Since the change in office practices and our involvement in [Gideon's Promise], our retention of attorneys has ceased to be a problem. For the first time in years, we have not had the rapid turnover issue," she said before sharing retention rate comparisons to emphasize her point.

Regarding the impact on the office, Pringle said, "The impact of retention on the quality of representation, continuity of representation, morale, organizational structure, and overall smooth running of my office has improved dramatically as a result.

"I attribute this change to better hiring practices but also, and largely, to the culture shift that the Gideon's Promise attorneys have brought to our office community."

She concluded the letter saying, "They are a different kind of public defender and they infuse the attorneys around them with their spirit, their confidence, their commitment, their excitement, and their drive. They are a changing force."[5]

Illy and I were frequently peppered with similar stories of how these young, idealistic public defenders, through the support of their Gideon's Promise community, were driving change in broken systems across the

South: Gabe in El Paso, Texas; Adofo in Jackson, Mississippi; Jessica in Knoxville, Tennessee; Alexia in Augusta, Georgia; Dee in Lumberton, North Carolina; Arienna in Birmingham, Alabama. The stream of stories about idealistic public defenders forging more humane justice systems in a growing collection of counties always proved uplifting. But we also knew that each of these young warriors were—in Zanele's words—doing this work six months at a time. The Core Program was sustaining them. But Guy Wilkinson's testimony highlighted the challenges that await them should they remain in public defense.

Without ongoing support and guidance, our graduates would almost certainly become subtly reshaped into lawyers who were part of the problem. Wilkinson's story served as a strong reminder that, while the three years of training and mentorship we provided our lawyers might be a critical first step in molding a client-centered outlook, it would not be enough to enable our lawyers to withstand cultural pressures for an entire career. His adopted vision of public defense illustrated why we could not end our relationship with our lawyers once they completed the Core Program. We had to keep working with them to reinforce the very mind-set we were trying to foster.

At the faculty retreat soon after our first class graduated, we began to put form to our vision for an Alumni Program. We decided that these rising leaders would serve as apprentice faculty during the Summer Institute and would be assigned mentees from the new class. They would also continue to meet every six months as our larger community gathered, to participate in a curriculum designed to further their development as lawyers as well as to give them skills to become better trainers and mentors. They would enjoy the support that they had grown to expect from SPDTC, but they would also begin to provide much of that support to the less experienced lawyers in the community.

This corps of lawyers would be an invaluable resource to future classes. They were new enough to the work that they were still very familiar with the struggles a young defender faced. However, after three years of trying to practice client-centered values in heavily resistant systems, they were well prepared to help these lawyers apply what we taught to the realities they would face.

The Core Program and the Alumni Program provided a path to developing young public defenders into seasoned lawyers who embraced a desired set of values. But we also needed to work with public defender leaders to marry this approach with a strategy to gain buy-in from other members of the office. These young lawyers would be idealistic. They would challenge everyone in the office to rethink some common practices. But there would surely be pushback from more seasoned lawyers if the message that they might do things differently came from the young defenders.

For this reason a critical component of the blueprint we created that weekend was a Leadership Program for the heads of our partner offices. These leaders would gather every six months to consider how to best support their newer public defenders as they struggled to become the lawyers their clients needed and to develop adaptive strategies to infuse their offices with a more client-centered vision. They would learn management and leadership tools and think about how to apply them in the public defender context. It required that leaders shed all defensiveness about acknowledging past mistakes. It demanded that these defenders look in the mirror and own their shortcomings. It would be up to these leaders to make sure every member of the team remembered the status quo is not OK.

The final piece of the model was the Trainer Development Program, to introduce seasoned public defenders to the way we teach and support values-based lawyering. This multiday program would introduce attendees to the curriculum and show how we teach the values in workshops and reinforce them in the field. We were growing rapidly. Demand from our existing partner offices was increasing and new offices were asking to participate. The program would help us develop faculty and mentors to support growth.

In addition to developing defenders to help serve as our faculty, we hosted seasoned lawyers from our partner offices who could offer guidance and supervision to these lawyers back home. They would see what we were teaching and think about how to weave it into the support they provided. This allowed many lawyers to feel greater ownership of the culture-change process and helped to minimize internal resistance.

After a couple years of running the Trainer Development Program, we invited law school criminal defense clinicians to attend. We wanted to inspire good future public defenders to join our growing movement. We would work with the clinicians in an effort to move beyond preparing future defenders to work in relatively resource-rich offices. The clinicians could help their students think about how to apply what they were learning in challenging environments and inspire them to consider joining the public defender reform movement where change was most needed.

Through our law school pipeline, we were matching eager future public defenders from across the country with offices that desperately needed them. Through the Core and Alumni Programs, we ensured they would receive continuous training and mentorship as they developed throughout their careers. The Leadership Program guided chief defenders in their efforts to support these lawyers specifically, and then transform office culture more generally. And the Trainer Development Program helped us develop more trainers and mentors, promote values-driven lawyering among partner-office staff, and collaborate with law school teachers to continue to funnel future defenders to our community.

And as the public defender community learned more about our culture-change work, the demand to join increased. Not only did public defense organizations want to send young lawyers to Gideon's Promise, they wanted to learn the model and bring it back to their organizations. As a result, we began to open the Leadership Program and the Trainer Development Program to public defenders beyond our partner-office community. Many programs would take aspects of our model and weave them into their own structures. We were working toward strengthening the depth of our involvement with our current partners, expanding the breadth of our partnership network, and exporting our culture-change model beyond our network of partners.

As we planned to expand from a single program for new public defenders into a comprehensive model for reform, Illy and I decided to create a formal nonprofit. Without any experience in building organizations, we knew we needed help. We turned to my sister, Alison. She had spent two decades leading nonprofits and was well established as an expert in building start-ups. She had not worked in the criminal legal arena, but she shared my passion for social justice. She was deeply committed to Illy and me. We were struggling financially and did not have much to offer. Alison would not ask for much. With her help we built a board, obtained office space, developed a strategic plan, and charted a fundraising strategy.

Alison worked around the clock for two years guiding our organizational development and teaching Illy the ins and outs of nonprofit leadership, while I focused on program and curriculum development. Thanks to Alison's tireless efforts, in 2010 the Southern Public Defender Training Center was legally established as a nonprofit.

Alison gave two years of her life to start the organization. It was time for her to return to her life before SPDTC. Before she did, she left us with one piece of final advice: "You need a better name. No one can say SPDTC."

The year 2013 marked the fiftieth anniversary of *Gideon v. Wainwright*, the watershed decision reminding us that lawyers for the poor are the only vehicle through which justice can be realized. That same year, an award-winning HBO documentary about our work, called *Gideon's Army*, premiered. To coincide with these events, we changed the name of the organization to Gideon's Promise, in recognition of the fact that we were building a growing movement of public defenders who, through their advocacy, would make the promise of equal justice a reality.

Our decision to "rebrand" in 2013 was, in part, a response to the perception that we were an organization that merely "trained" public defenders. What started as a single program for new lawyers blossomed into a full-blown movement of advocates working in public defender offices across many states, bound by a common vision of client-centered representation. Every six months these defenders would gather, with cohorts attending various programming tracks designed for new lawyers, graduates, supervisors, trainers, and leaders. They would spend some of the weekend in workshops targeting their specific needs, while other sessions would bring them all together for communal presentations and interaction. It was awe-inspiring to look over a room filled with hundreds of public defenders working together to promote a common vision of what their clients deserved.

The organization was six years old. It had evolved from a single program focused on the early development of passionate new public defenders to a comprehensive model aimed at transforming the culture of public defense. What started as a nascent effort involving two offices and sixteen young lawyers had grown into a movement of roughly thirty public defender offices across thirteen states.

While the heart of our work was concentrated in the Deep South, we began to add partnerships beyond the region that shared similar challenges. A hub that included Georgia, Alabama, Tennessee, Louisiana, Mississippi, and South Carolina now had spokes touching Texas, Kentucky, North Carolina, Virginia, West Virginia, Pennsylvania, and New York.

In those first six years we brought 228 new public defenders into the community through our Core Program. By now, we had more than a dozen chief defenders committed to meeting semiannually. A couple dozen supervising attorneys from our partner offices had attended our Trainer Development Program to learn to better support these young lawyers. Alumni of the Core Program were serving as mentors. The support system we were building for our new defenders was blossoming.

The next year we added partnerships in Sioux Falls, South Dakota, and Lincoln, Nebraska, as well as our first tribal defender office at the Gila River Indian Community outside Phoenix, Arizona. In late 2014 we added over five hundred public defenders to our community when we announced our first statewide partnership in Maryland.

Paul DeWolfe had been the chief public defender for the State of Maryland for only a few years when he attended our inaugural Leadership Program session. He had recently completed a strategic plan for his system of nearly one thousand employees and understood the need to center his leadership efforts on a set of core values. Every office in Maryland had a poster with the core values Paul developed for the state public defender system on display. But for many of the public defenders throughout the state, there was a glaring gap between Paul's vision and the accepted standard of practice.

Paul had already been fairly successful at building a leadership team that shared these values. But he understood that leaders cannot simply mandate a change in the tenets that guide staff practice. Paul knew he had a challenge: getting hundreds of public defenders across the state to embrace the values. He recognized our approach as the way to do just that.

Paul immediately understood the connection between core values and culture change. He saw how we used recruitment, training, mentorship, and community building to promote client-centered organizations. He asked Illy and me if we would be interested in a statewide partnership.

In 2014 I took a leave of absence from teaching and went to Baltimore to launch the partnership. We began training staff across the state, from the newest lawyers to the leadership team. We also brought in the Gideon's Promise faculty to develop a cadre within Maryland to train and mentor under this model. Once this foundation was laid, Patrice Fulcher agreed to join Paul's leadership team to oversee the process and usher in our first statewide partnership. She was one of the architects of Gideon's Promise and the ideal person to spearhead the effort. She was joined by Lori James-Townes, who was the head of the public defender social work division in Maryland. Lori had since joined the Gideon's Promise faculty as well and was the person who introduced Paul to our organization. Together, Paul, Patrice, and Lori brought culture change to the Maryland public defender system.

The next year, Paul issued a challenge to the twelve district public defender offices across Maryland. Each would receive one hundred and fifty dollars to create client-centered reception areas. Paul understood that the physical appearance of an office provided some insight into its guiding values; the reception area is the public's first contact with the office and shapes community perception about the professionalism and commitment of the organization.

Whether in the waiting room of a healthcare clinic, a social service agency, or a public defender office, low-income people frequently expect to sit on folding chairs, talk to clerks through bullet-proof glass, and stare at drab-colored walls with peeling paint. Everything about these environments contributes to a sense of dehumanization. It was this way in public defender offices across America, and it was certainly the case in Maryland.

One hundred and fifty dollars is not a lot of money. Many of the Maryland offices were in buildings that were old and unappealing, but the idea was not to create the ideal environment; it was to force public defenders to consider what it meant to be client-centered and to think about ways the office subtly undermined this value. The exercise was a way to awaken staff to objectionable practices that had become accepted.

The districts had an opportunity to share pictures of the revamped reception areas at an annual conference in Ocean City, Maryland. The ballroom was filled with hundreds of public defender staff members as the presentations began. Inspirational quotes, children's artwork, fresh paint, goldfish tanks, throw pillows, kiddie tables, and library books filled the screen. I choked up as I considered the care that went into creating spaces that assured impacted communities that they mattered.

I thought back twenty years, to when I was a graduating law student in Washington, DC. Maryland was right next door, yet I never considered applying to a public defender office there. I had been taught the importance of client-centered representation and offices in Maryland did not enjoy such a good reputation in that regard. Had I sat through these presentations as a law student, I surely would have made a different decision. In fact, in the ensuing years, hundreds of soon-to-be lawyers from law schools across the country would apply to join the Gideon's Promise movement in Maryland. Applicants frequently explained during interviews that they were anxious to join Gideon's Promise. Clearly, many would have never considered Maryland but for the partnership. They relished the opportunity to be part of what we were building.

IN 2008, SOON AFTER GENESIS AND SUNNY returned to Nashville following their summer in Birmingham, Dawn Deaner became the new chief public defender at the office following the untimely death of her predecessor. She had spent more than a decade as a respected trial lawyer in the office and was one of the lawyers most admired for her trial prowess. She was cultivated into a trial lawyer in that office, which was known for having great trial attorneys. Still, in retrospect, she acknowledges that she never considered what it meant to be a client-centered lawyer.[6] That was never seen as part of what made a great lawyer.

Like every lawyer in the office, Dawn had started in general sessions court, where the vast majority of cases that came into the system were resolved the day they were assigned to a public defender. She learned to meet clients, very quickly assess the merits of a case based on the limited information provided, and determine which approach to attempt. The presumption was that most cases would be resolved by plea to avoid jail time. Noncriminal consequences—such as the ways in which a criminal conviction might affect a person's housing, employment, eligibility for public benefits, or immigration consequences—were not investigated or considered.

In retrospect, Dawn acknowledges that as she went through the experience, she never considered that there was anything wrong with the practice. "Cases were resolved quickly. We did not consider collateral consequences. We did not look beyond the facts of the case and were never taught that we needed to," she recalls. "That is just the way it was. I never thought about trying to address the caseload problem; I just assumed part of the job was getting the majority of the cases resolved quickly so we could focus on the few that we would really fight. . . . It was what we knew." Dawn had fallen into the trap that awaits public defenders everywhere. Routine injustice was normalized.

She certainly did not come into the new position thinking of herself as a reformer. But as she started to focus on some of the accepted practices with a critical eye, it was evident that there was much that needed to change. She did not bring that critical eye with her into the job—she had a lot of help nurturing it. But to her great credit, she was open to considering how things could be improved.

As soon as Dawn took the reins, Genesis and Sunny began to talk to her about SPDTC and the client-centered community we were building. They began holding training sessions internally to try to teach the lawyers in the office some of what they learned, and they urged Dawn to send more new lawyers to the organization's training.

Dawn's interest was piqued. Like most of her colleagues, she had become a public defender because she wanted to help people. But the people behind the files quickly got lost in the deluge of cases. She saw SPDTC as an opportunity to keep her new lawyers from becoming desensitized in this way.

In 2009 Dawn found funding to send Martesha Johnson, a lawyer from Nashville who was incredibly committed to public defense in her city, to SPDTC. As a law student, Martesha had been an intern for Genesis, so she had heard all about SPDTC. She was excited to come to Birmingham. The next year, 2010, Dawn sent four more lawyers to SPDTC, including Aisha McWeay. Along with Genesis and Sunny, Aisha and Martesha would become strong advocates supporting Dawn in building a pipeline from Nashville to SPDTC.

Dawn would talk to Illy and me frequently about what she could do internally to reinforce some of the lessons we taught her younger lawyers. When we decided to launch our Leadership Program, Dawn was among the first to join. She already had a core of young lawyers who were questioning whether things could be different in Nashville. She wanted to understand how to nurture and spread this vision.

Over the next several years, Dawn completely embraced the need to engage in culture change, and Nashville quickly became one of our strongest partner offices. During Dawn's tenure, twenty-eight more lawyers went through the Core Program, and most of her management team participated in the Trainer Development Program. She developed the young lawyers she hired into leaders of the office. Many Gideon's Promise graduates became supervisors. In 2016, when her first assistant retired, Dawn made Aisha second in charge at the office. When Dawn left the office after a decade as its leader, Martesha became chief public defender.

Genesis left Nashville for personal reasons soon after Dawn took over, but she saw that change was on the horizon. She continued her work as a public defender in Houston and remained a part of the Gideon's Promise community. She followed the evolution in Nashville closely.

"Nashville is a completely different office thanks to Dawn," she would later tell me. "Lawyers coming to that office now can't appreciate the change. We were great trial lawyers, but 'client-centered' was never a concept we considered. Now it is the defining theme of the office."

Through adaptive leadership practices, Dawn worked on shifting the office's mind-set. Staff came to understand that practicing the organization's core values required spending more time with each client. Processing was no longer accepted; it was resisted at every turn.

Nashville became a perfect example of how to effect culture change. But it was only one of the many public defender offices in our network where the norms were shifting.

IT WAS A CLEAR FALL DAY in October 2016 when the Orleans Public Defenders Office led its first Second Line for Equal Justice. Over two hundred people, representing dozens of community organizations, would parade over two miles. They would march from Treme—America's oldest African American neighborhood[7]—to the courthouse steps. Revelers would carry signs that read "Equal Justice for All" and "Fund Public Defenders Now."[8] Derwyn, who had been the chief public defender for the last eight years, spoke as the crowd assembled at Tulane and Broad. "Th[e] constitutional guarantee [of a right to counsel] is violated every day inside this building," Derwyn told the crowd. He had plenty of examples to back it up. In Louisiana, 85 percent of people thrown into the criminal justice system are too poor to afford a lawyer.[9]

In New Orleans, "second line" parades are a cherished musical tradition among African American communities that have "helped generations of African Americans preserve their cultural identity and sense of community in the face of racial injustices dating back to the days of slavery."[10] The Second Line for Equal Justice was Derwyn's brainchild. The second line was at the heart of the cultural identity of black New Orleanians. Sadly, mass incarceration had also become a fixture in that community.

It was not the first time he would mobilize public defenders to join the communities they served to protest injustice. Two years earlier, Derwyn had gathered his staff on these same courthouse steps, where they stood in solidarity with 250 clients and community members to shine a light on the routine injustice happening daily at Tulane and Broad.[11] He told a reporter about Bernard Noble, who had been sentenced to thirteen years in prison for possessing two joints worth of marijuana.[12] Noble's case served as a symbol of draconian sentences that discarded poor people for relatively minor mishaps. In a system under which the routine disregard for some lives had become normalized, the community stood with Derwyn as he expressed his view that his office was the "only entity in the courtroom defending [impacted communities]."[13]

Derwyn and his lawyers used every opportunity they could to raise awareness of the plight facing the people they served. They told the stories of their clients in op-eds published in national news outlets including the *New York Times* and the *Washington Post*.[14] They shared the stories on *60 Minutes* and *Last Week Tonight with John Oliver*. They took advantage of the attention focused on New Orleans in the wake of Hurricane Katrina to raise awareness nationally about the challenges plaguing public defenders.

When caseloads became overwhelming, and his budget was significantly cut, Derwyn refused to take any more cases. As people accused of serious crimes sat without lawyers, the magnitude of the constitutional crisis was brought to the public. Derwyn's actions led to an American Civil Liberties Union lawsuit forcing the system to confront its blatant disregard for the constitutional right to counsel.[15]

This was a new brand of public defender. Rather than sitting by passively, going along with a broken system and helping to normalize the injustice, Derwyn saw his obligation differently. He refused to be complicit, and in resisting shined a bright light on the problems in New Orleans.

This was indeed a new vision of public defense. It was a vision that understood the role of public defenders more broadly. These lawyers not only battled judges in courtrooms but also mobilized community members to push back against systemic injustice. They used their skills to raise awareness of injustice and to galvanize support. Their obligation was not to facilitate an unjust system, it was to resist at every turn. Less than a decade after Katrina hit, an office that was once seen by the community as symbolic of the injustice in New Orleans was leading the charge for reform.

Client-centered public defense was not always welcomed by those in power. In Jackson, Mississippi, a judge, frustrated by the public defender's zealous advocacy, decided to reassign public defender cases to more compliant private lawyers. When a Gideon's Promise graduate named Greg Spore refused to abandon his client, the judge held him in contempt. When Michele Purvis-Harris, the head of the office, stood up for her lawyer, she was held in contempt as well. All of this was legal.

In Houston, Alex Bunin found himself threatened with termination by an angry county commissioner after he was accused by the county attorney of helping a group of criminal justice reformers in a lawsuit challenging unconstitutional bail practices in the county.[16]

And in New Orleans, angry prosecutors threatened to bring charges against a public defender investigator for a trumped-up offense after she sought evidence from a security guard to help her client. The prosecution suggested she had impersonated a police officer and told the witness that she worked for the prosecutor, despite the fact that she left her business card with the security guard when they initially talked. The charges were ultimately dropped.[17]

While the advocacy rankled those who administered the existing system, it was refreshing to those who had always seen public defenders as part of the problem. Before I understood the power of culture, it would have seemed illogical that highly regarded public defenders could be viewed by members of impacted communities as part of the problem. But in time, I viewed it as a pattern repeating over and over and over again. Public defenders often measured their value in their ability to assess the facts of a case and, taking into account the legal consequences of various courses of action, make a decision about the best course of action for the client. That this decision should be the outcome was then assumed. The goal was then to convince the client to make the "right" decision. Communicating with the client, to understand their concerns and priorities, was often devalued. This was especially true in a high-volume practice, in which taking too much time with a client might be chided as "hand-holding" that kept the lawyer from efficiently working through other cases. The effort it would take to help the client understand all the considerations that went into the lawyer's conclusion might be seen as a poor use of time.

I came to understand exactly how a lawyer could believe they were doing a great job for a client while the client felt the lawyer did not care about them or their case. When the client complained that the lawyer was neglecting them, the lawyer might chalk it up to the client being "needy" or "difficult." The lawyer might even get offended: "Doesn't this client appreciate everything I am doing for them?" The lawyer might wonder, "Does the client think I do not know what I am doing?"

For a client, perhaps the most important thing a lawyer can do is to be the one person in the system who cares. The client's life is on the line, and they may need the comfort of believing there is someone who is truly looking out for them. That cannot be done by a lawyer simply saying "Trust me." That trust must be gained through relationship building. Trust from a client has to be earned, as does trust from the communities that public defenders serve.

Like Derwyn, Dawn had thought a lot about how her office could more effectively be a voice for the community it served in the drive for equal justice. She knew this required "an earnest reckoning with the way her own office is perceived by the poor criminal defendants they represent."[18] She decided to create a Client/Community Advisory Board.

Dawn began her announcement of the new board with the following words:

> How can I accept a status quo in which our clients—the individuals and families we are here to serve—have so little faith and trust in us? Shouldn't we at least try to understand how the relationship between public defenders and our clients got to this place of distrust, and identify how we contributed to that problem? And once we do that, isn't it our obligation to work on doing better and repairing that harm?[19]

The client advisory board would be a forum that would allow client feedback and input about the agency's work.

The board grew out of an initiative Dawn started called Defend Nashville.[20] This initiative included a series of "listening tours" in which clients and families were invited to share their experiences and concerns. Public defenders also shared their experiences witnessing injustice. Dawn's vision was bold. She wanted to "unite our office, our client community, and other Nashvillians into a grassroots movement powerful enough to bring meaningful reform to our courthouse."[21]

Rahim Buford was one of the first people Dawn asked to join the client advisory board. At the age of eighteen, Rahim had been sentenced to serve life plus twenty years for his role in a robbery that led to a man's death. He spent twenty-six years in prison. He had to rely on a public defender who he felt helped "microwave [him] through the system."[22]

Once released, Rahim threw himself into criminal justice reform work as an organizer and author. He was impressed with Dawn's listening tour and admired how she "was always at events where marginalized people spoke."[23] He attended a community meeting Dawn organized. They began to talk about their shared vision for a community/public defender partnership.

As Rahim observed the public defenders in Dawn's office interacting with impacted people, he saw a different approach. Rather than lawyers "talking at" people, as if they had the only perspective that mattered, these public defenders asked, "What do you want to happen?"

Reflecting on the experiences of those who went through the system with him, Rahim said, "We never saw our lawyers. It was traumatic."

He saw a change under Dawn's leadership. "These public defenders actually visited their clients," he told me.

Rahim understood as well as anyone what the new brand of public defense meant for the people who depended on it. He credits Dawn with the change.

Dawn decided early in her tenure as chief defender that she would not simply go along with the status quo, and she has described her approach as one "meant to bring about a healthy amount of disruption."[24]

"To not stand up and do something about it is to enable the system to provide as little as it wants to provide," she said.[25]

These are the kinds of partnerships that are important to build between public defenders and the communities they serve. It is a critical component of our work to transform justice in America. We often partner with people who can help reinforce this vision. Raj Jayadev is one of those people.

Raj is a community organizer and activist from San Jose, California. He has dedicated his life to working with communities impacted by the criminal justice system and ensuring that their voices are heard. I was drawn to Raj's message that the community voice is the engine necessary to challenge our assumptions about justice. But I was especially drawn to Raj's work because he saw the connection between these communities and the public defenders charged with speaking for them in the system as indispensable to real change.

Raj developed a model called participatory defense to forge alliances between communities crippled by criminal justice policies and the public defenders who represent them. The model seeks to tear down the walls of distrust that have been built up between the two and foster productive and cooperative relationships.

Under this model, public defenders are pushed to embrace their role as spokespeople for the communities. While their primary obligation is to the individual they represent, they must understand the power of the family and community in helping them provide that representation. Organizationally, public defenders enjoy community support and can marshal community power to advocate for policies that strengthen the office.

Meanwhile, community members come to appreciate the power of public defenders to voice their concerns and fight for their loved ones. They are encouraged to see public defenders as allies, rather than adversaries who are just part of the system designed to rip them apart.

Raj first experienced Gideon's Promise when he joined us for a weekend in Birmingham. He would later write an article about the public defenders he met at Gideon's Promise, saying they reminded him of the X-Men. He wrote:

> In the X-Men movie series, the superheroes are misunderstood, even vilified at times by the public, but nonetheless are charged with saving humanity. The budding heroes, who already have the innate abilities within them, develop their skills at a special school to be prepared for the high stakes battles they are charged to engage in.[26]

Raj understands that our criminal justice system suffers from a lack of humanity, and that transforming it requires an army of superheroes to restore that humanity. He appreciates that a movement of public defenders has the ability to infuse the system with that humanity. And he recognizes that without the necessary support and preparation, these champions will not be able to survive "the high stakes battle" of resisting routine injustice.

But he also recognizes that to effectively play this role, public defenders have to work closely with the communities they represent. And he understands that this requires tearing down walls that divide advocates from the people they serve.

It would take a shift in perspective to see public defenders and the communities they serve as critical allies in the fight for justice.

Public defenders often view themselves as lone underdogs in a battle against an oppressive system. We frequently describe ourselves as David in the battle against Goliath. Anyone who has been a public defender can appreciate the analogy. But if we take a step back and unpack the analogy, it renders the communities public defenders serve invisible. The battle is between lawyers in the criminal justice system. It is a very lawyer-centric view of the work.

Raj pointed this out to our community several years after he was introduced to our work. We were hosting a public panel discussion called "Public Defenders: Islands, Bridges, or Arteries" at one of our gatherings in Atlanta. The ballroom was packed. The panelists discussed how some public defenders are like islands, with very little connection to the communities they serve; they focus narrowly on the individuals they represent and look internally for the resources to do the job, with the courthouse as the narrow arena in which they operate, and the resources provided them by the criminal justice system as the universe of tools available for the representation.

The panel also discussed how other public defenders recognize that there are community resources that can be marshaled to help represent individual clients. They develop relationships with community-based organizations and serve as a "bridge," connecting individual clients to services and opportunities beyond what the system provides. They help clients secure housing, employment, and social services. It is a more holistic approach to representing an individual client.

But under each of these models, the public defender's role is limited to representing the individual client. The difference is in the extent to which the legal team connects to the broader community to help provide support in this effort.

The panel suggested a third role, in which the public defender is committed to the representation of each client and understands the power of the community in helping with this goal. The organization also understands itself as a resource for the larger community. It is the vehicle through which that community voice is infused into the system. While the priority of any client-centered public defender must be to the individual accused, public defenders advocating for the third role understand that their clients cannot be treated justly if their collective voices are not heard. This voice is the necessary lifeblood of a system that treats them humanely. Public defenders are the channel, or artery, through which that voice is amplified.

During the panel discussion, Raj used the David and Goliath analogy, but he put a twist on it. He said that the community was David and the public defender is the slingshot David uses to slay Goliath. In this view, the people who are being attacked are those targeted by our justice policies. The public defender is the instrument, or weapon, the attacked community can rely upon to fight the battle. The community needs the public defender to fight for it in this arena. And the public defender exists as an instrument to help the community in this battle.

As we began to understand the power that a movement of public defenders could have when they saw their role this way, Raj's work became invaluable to our efforts. He became a regular presence at our semiannual gatherings, teaching our leaders how to build effective community partnerships and giving our lawyers ideas for injecting client stories into the system's consciousness.

This model of public defense is exhibited when public defenders in New Orleans organize a second line march for justice or a demonstration on the courthouse steps to ensure community concerns are being amplified around routine practices inside. It is on display when the public defenders of Nashville engage in listening tours.

But it is also present in the day-to-day work of individual public defenders. Take Kelly Pretzer in Memphis.

Kelly was growing frustrated by the lack of appreciation for the challenges people who appeared in Mental Health Specialty Court faced trying to fulfill court obligations. She knew that they were frequently not believed when they claimed to have missed an appointment because of a bus schedule.[27]

The vast majority do not have cars and must rely on public transportation. In an effort to help her colleagues better advocate for these clients, Kelly organized a trip through Memphis to sites where clients are mandated to receive treatment.

She rounded up her Gideon's Promise colleagues and led a dozen public defenders armed with bus passes as they simulated what a client might experience on a typical day of treatment.[28] They were given assignments, including a handout prepared by Kelly that read "Today you will be taking on the role of a treatment court client. You will have to use the MATA bus system to get to different facilities where our clients often receive services."

The lawyers found that even with all the planning, navigating the bus system was challenging. They frequently had long waits at bus shelters and long walks from bus stops to treatment sites. They were often late for appointments. To get to the three locations, the lawyers found that, on average they rode seven buses, walked a mile and a half, and endured an hour of waiting between rides.

When the lawyers told me of their idea to replicate the struggles so many of their clients encountered to fulfill court obligations, I was amazed. They understood that the people they represent were assumed to be lazy or unconcerned about court orders when they tried to explain why they were late for appointments. They knew that it was up to them to effectively tell these stories. It can be easy to accept the assumption that the client who was late for an appointment did not care. These lawyers refused to do that. They understood that client-centered lawyering required understanding the people they were charged with speaking for.

Kelly was part of a new way of thinking about public defense in Memphis. Like the offices in New Orleans and Nashville, the Memphis office has become one of our larger partnerships. These lawyers are part of a new wave of advocates helping to spread the message that public defender offices could become the nucleus of the ongoing struggle for civil rights.

THE MESSAGE RESONATED with Dr. Charles Steele Jr., the president and CEO of the Southern Christian Leadership Conference (SCLC). In 2017, he asked Illy and me to attend as his guests when the organization hosted its fifty-ninth annual convention in Memphis, and he invited the local public defenders. The SCLC was Martin Luther King Jr.'s organization, and Memphis is where King was assassinated. We were honored to have our defenders recognized at this event.

Earlier in the year, Steele had attended a fundraiser for Gideon's Promise where we honored his wife, Cathelean Steele, for her work in the community with young girls. After the event, he explained to me that for the first time he understood how public defenders are indispensable in the broader struggle for civil and human rights.

Now, in Memphis, with civil rights leaders from across the country filling the room, Steele asked the two dozen public defenders who were his guests to stand. He explained why the advocates were so important.

"Our struggle for civil and human rights is far from finished. Nowhere is this truer than in our criminal justice system. It is a system that is almost exclusively reserved for the poor and disproportionately for black and brown people," said Steele. "Public defenders serve as the advocates for these men, women, and children. If they do not have support, they cannot help our most vulnerable communities fight back against this unjust system."[29]

Illy and I listened. We smiled at each other. We were making progress.

PART III

TRANSFORMATION

CHAPTER 7

CLOSING THE GAP

IMAGINE YOU ARE A PUBLIC DEFENDER in a system with crushing case-loads and too few resources—in short, you are a public defender in America. It is your turn to handle "first appearance court," which means you will take on the representation of all recent arrestees who qualify for a public defender. You receive the list of your new clients. For each client you are given a one-page police report, containing the barest of facts—just enough to make out the allegation. You know from experience that these reports almost never include facts that might help establish a defense, even when known to the officer preparing the report. Today you have twenty new clients. It is 10 a.m. and initial hearings begin at 1 p.m. You know that once initial hearings begin things move pretty quickly, as the judge is anxious to get through the docket. Therefore, you have only a few minutes to meet with each client and will not have an opportunity to talk further once court starts.

In one of your cases you are appointed to represent Mr. Jones, who is charged with robbery. As you read the police report, it seems to raise more questions than it answers. The allegation is that Mr. Jones robbed the complainant on the street at 3 a.m., after the complainant decided to go for a walk because he could not sleep. The report indicates that Mr. Jones allegedly took ten dollars from the complainant at knifepoint. The complainant immediately reported the robbery to an officer, and Mr. Jones was arrested ten minutes later. There is no indication that either money or a knife was found on your client at the time of his arrest. The complainant positively identified Mr. Jones as the man who robbed him.

You recognize the area where the robbery occurred as a block notorious for drug activity. You also note that the complainant's address is about a mile from the scene of the alleged robbery. You know that robbery carries a potential sentence of twenty years in your jurisdiction. Before you go to talk to your new clients, the prosecutor tells you she will offer Mr. Jones a plea to attempted robbery if Mr. Jones will take the plea at the initial hearing this afternoon. The prosecutor will not oppose a term of probation. The plea will be off the table once the hearing ends. You know that Mr. Jones will go home today if he takes the plea, but that he will be given a bond he almost certainly cannot afford and sit in jail if he chooses to take the case to trial.

You have an investigator call Mr. Jones's wife, and you learn that they have two young children and they live in government-subsidized housing, and that Mr. Jones works for the county as a trash collector. You know that with a felony conviction, Mr. Jones will likely be evicted from his apartment and will possibly lose his government job. This is all you have time to learn about Mr. Jones and the case before you sit down to talk to him.

When you meet Mr. Jones and tell him what he's charged with he looks surprised. He insists he never robbed anyone. He tells you that the complainant is a known crack addict. Mr. Jones says he was on his way home after playing pool with some friends when the complainant approached him and two other men. The complainant gave one of the men ten dollars to find him a "rock." The man took the money. Mr. Jones says at that point he just kept walking. Ten minutes later he was arrested.

You explain the plea offer and tell him he has to decide in the next three hours. Mr. Jones has a lot of questions. What about the fact that he didn't have any money or a knife when he was arrested? Can you talk to other people who were out there who can confirm his story? Is it not unbelievable that the complainant would go for a walk a mile from his home in a drug area at three in the morning? Did the police search the complainant to see if he had drug paraphernalia on him to show what he was really doing out there? What are his chances of being convicted? If he takes the plea, how will that impact his housing situation? His job?

You cannot answer these questions . . . but you know Mr. Jones deserves these answers before having to make such an important life decision. You wish you could find out some of these answers before 1 p.m., but you have nineteen other clients to see. If you do not eat lunch you can give each client nine minutes, and you are already approaching fifteen minutes with Mr. Jones. Mr. Jones will have to make this decision without the answers to these questions.

Mr. Jones is clearly being pressured to give up his right to a trial, a jury, a judge. He is being asked to give up his right to look into whether any other constitutional rights were violated in the course of the investigation. He is giving up his right to the assistance of a competent lawyer. Everyone knows he is being pressured to abandon these rights. No one is concerned.

DAYS LIKE THIS OFTEN precipitated a phone call. In the early years of SPDTC, within weeks of concluding the Summer Institute, my phone would frequently ring. It would be one of our lawyers. The call would always start the same way, with a defeated voice saying to me: "Rap, I think I'm going to quit." The defender would continue: "I now know exactly what my clients deserve and there is no way I can give it to them. I have three hundred cases."

I always shared with them a story from a book called *Freedom Summer*, by Bruce Watson. It's about college students from across the country who went to Mississippi in the summer of 1964, thinking they could change the world. They joined heroic civil rights activists from the South to register people to vote and to build Freedom Schools to help Mississippians pass literacy tests required to do so. Watson tells the stories of these young people through interviews conducted forty years later. You learn that the students began knocking on doors only to have them closed in their faces. The people in the homes were afraid; they could be targeted by the Ku Klux Klan if they were seen cooperating with the civil rights activists.

As the summer went on, the once-hopeful students despaired. "Maybe my family was right," they would say. "Maybe I can't make a difference." Watson then fast-forwards forty years to a conversation with Congressman John Lewis, one of the architects of Freedom Summer. Lewis said that if it weren't for Freedom Summer, Barack Obama wouldn't be in the White House. Lewis makes the point that sometimes change can be so incremental, those in the middle of engineering it may not even recognize it is happening.

I share that story with every lawyer who calls me ready to quit.

As all faculty members started getting more calls like this, we realized that while we were teaching our defenders what every client deserves, they were feeling that to be successful as public defenders they had to live up to this standard in every case. They were setting a benchmark for themselves that no lawyer could possibly meet.

We teachers implicitly understood that even the best lawyers could not give every client the representation our Constitution demands in systems that were so broken. Too many factors beyond their control kept them from realizing this goal, from crushing caseloads to inadequate resources to judges who would not allow them the time necessary to ensure their clients' rights were protected to prosecutors who worked to circumvent the process necessary to ensure fair outcomes. We taught a gold standard because to teach anything less would be to train public defenders to help reinforce a substandard status quo. But we also recognized that our lawyers could not achieve this all the time—or even most of the time.

Nevertheless, always working toward what our clients deserve and not accepting the norm was important. We believed that every time a public defender stood up to a judge who just wanted them to sit down and shut up, it mattered. We believed that, even when that lawyer could not get the result the client deserved, as more and more resisted the status quo, collectively they could begin to raise expectations of what justice means for poor people.

Being a public defender in most of America—and certainly in the places our lawyers were working—necessarily meant having to triage. But when one has to triage every day, those shortcuts can become normalized. Exposure to so much injustice will cause moral injury—"a deep soul wound" or trauma to one's spirit from constant exposure to circumstances that are antithetical to one's deeply held moral beliefs.[1] Defenders can subtly become desensitized to it. It is much easier to sleepwalk through the process, to become numb to the injustice. But once we do that, we have become part of the problem.

While triage may be necessary as we work to forge a truly just system, being a good public defender means resisting the pressure to see the triaging as justice. It requires that we remain vigilantly aware of what justice truly demands while maintaining the ability to forgive ourselves for our failure to reach that ideal for reasons beyond our control.

We wanted to do a better job of helping our lawyers continue to believe they could collectively improve the system without becoming paralyzed by the slow pace of progress. We came up with a model we called Close the Gap.

We taught that our lawyers had to be very conscious of the gap that exists between aspiration and reality—or between what every client deserves and the level of representation they are actually able to provide. They then learn to view success as doing whatever is in their power each day to close that gap, if only incrementally. They understand that as hundreds of public defenders did what they could to close that gap, collectively they would make progress.

To sustain themselves as they pushed forward, they had to learn to forgive themselves for all of the injustice they were unable to address. The size of the gap each of them faced varied depending on the challenges in their individual jurisdictions. We worked with the lawyers to help them understand these hurdles and to prioritize the ones that they could realistically take on. We helped them come up with strategies to tackle those obstacles, and to keep those they could not address from wearing them down.

Our faculty/mentors learned to work through this model as our lawyers came to them with challenges. We would methodically walk together through the steps. First the lawyer would articulate the problematic situation that fell short of the ideal. Next, they would imagine how they would ideally like to practice. At this point they had identified the "gap." We would then catalogue all of the obstacles that kept them from achieving the ideal. Finally, we would brainstorm strategies to address the obstacles and identify what the lawyer could realistically take on.

Sometimes a lawyer could engineer a significant success, for example by convincing a judge to grant a motion that altered the course of a trial, developing an investigative strategy that led to information that prompted a dismissal, or winning a not-guilty verdict. Often the success seemed less seismic. Often it involved simply remaining client-centered against the constant pressure to move cases. It meant helping the lawyer understand that even when they could not overcome corrupted forces beyond their control, they could work with the client to make important decisions under the circumstances. For a person who would otherwise be processed without any regard for their dignity, simply knowing someone values their input can be quite meaningful.

We wove exercises into the curriculum intended to help defenders understand how they could practice client-centered lawyering even in the most difficult circumstances. The "exploding plea offer" hypothetical was one such exercise. Frequently prosecutors use "exploding" plea offers—offers that expire if not accepted in a very short time— to pressure defendants to resolve cases quickly and cheaply. Judges, joining the charade of pretending the client's decision is informed and voluntary—a constitutional requirement for a guilty plea—put their stamp of approval on these pleas.

The lawyers understand that each client is entitled to a lawyer who can adequately investigate allegations, conduct legal research to identify issues that might impact the outcome, take the time to develop a trusting relationship and glean information that is critical to preparing a defense, and advise the client sufficiently to make important decisions. They are responsibilities that require a significant amount of time, expertise, and resources. But to get that level of representation, the client has to give up the offer on the table. Taking the offer means forgoing their right to a constitutionally effective lawyer. It is a terrible predicament for a client. But a decision has to be made. Even when the advocate couldn't be the lawyer the client deserved, they could still help the client make the best decision under the circumstances.

Young lawyers are often taught that good attorneys rely on their experience to quickly assess what they believe is the best course of action. The limited time with the client is then spent trying to convince the client to go along with that predetermined course of action. They may neglect to mention important considerations for fear that it might eat up the precious time they have to get the client on board. Often, a lawyer will fail to even explore whether there are any factors important to the client they may not have considered.

In the exercise, we teach our lawyers that the best course of action can never be determined without the client's input. Rather than decide the right course based on the lawyer's values, the lawyer must help the client understand the decision in front of them. Both courses of action have adverse consequences. If the client takes the plea, he will go home.

But he will have to accept responsibility for committing the crime in open court, an experience that can be very difficult for some people, especially if they are in fact innocent. He will have a criminal conviction that may cost him his home and his job, and possibly his standing in the community. The conviction can also make any future contact with the criminal justice system more costly, as sentences are often enhanced based on prior convictions.

On the other hand, if he declines the plea, he will have a chance to have the lawyer investigate and research legal issues that might help him walk away from the experience without a conviction, or negotiate a better plea that could minimize some of the collateral consequences. If he is innocent, he will have a chance to demonstrate this at trial, an opportunity that is important to many people accused of wrongdoing. But he will have to wait in jail in the meantime.

How a person prioritizes getting out of jail, avoiding a conviction that may render them forever unable to live in government-subsidized housing or get certain jobs, fighting to prove their innocence, and maintaining their reputation is a very personal decision. The lawyer cannot presume to know how a person balances these factors without first developing a cohesive relationship.

The exercise is meant to demonstrate that even with limited time, the lawyer must try to help the client understand the costs and benefits of each option, and make an informed decision based on the client's priorities. A commitment to giving the client some agency over this critical decision in a system that so often disregards the client's concerns beyond the criminal case is itself incremental progress.

It is unconscionable that public defender trainers have to design programs to help lawyers navigate a system that makes it impossible to provide the representation each client deserves, but it is the reality for poor people accused of crimes in many American courthouses. Lawmakers create rules that undermine the value our Constitution places on individual liberty.

In this example, the defender is placed in an impossible position—and her client in an even worse one. They know their client is entitled to have them investigate, seek discovery, and conduct research to understand how a variety of legal issues might impact the case. They know they need time to research how a conviction might impact other factors so important to their client, like his housing, employment, and parental status. But they also know that if they take the time needed to do these things, the client will lose the option of the plea offer. All they can do is advise Mr. Jones of the services to which he is entitled from his lawyer and the fact that he will give that up if he takes the plea. They can explain the potential punishments that each course of action brings, while explaining that they have little information at this point to help the client assess how likely success at trial will be. Should Mr. Jones accept the plea, the defender can try to make a record highlighting their ineffectiveness by laying out all of the things they did not have time to do and the advice they did not have time to provide given the exploding plea offer. What they cannot do is give the client the representation he deserves.

In the world envisioned by those who drafted, and later defined, clauses of our Constitution and Bill of Rights, Mr. Jones would have the robust assistance of a lawyer with the time and resources required to provide the necessary representation. The facts necessary to determine guilt would be weighed and decided by a jury. The appropriate punishment, should there be a need for one, would be decided by a neutral judge after evaluating aggravating and mitigating circumstances. This is not that world.

One cannot look at the details of the case without wondering how the public defender should appropriately respond to this seemingly impossible challenge. But it is not only the role of the public defender that needs to be addressed here. This hypothetical case study should also be part of a training curriculum for judges, who know people pleading guilty the day they meet their lawyers do not have the assistance of counsel the Constitution demands. They have an obligation to not look the other way when important constitutional rights are being blatantly ignored. It should be part of a training curriculum for prosecutors who are responsible for thinking about much more than the outcome of any given case. For it is their job to ensure that justice is served in each case they consider prosecuting. And it should be part of a training curriculum for lawmakers who willingly give prosecutors the tools they need to force poor people to give up their constitutional rights out of fear of draconian outcomes.

Each of these actors behaves consistently with a culture that values the efficient processing of poor people through the system over respect for our foundational democratic ideals.

POLITICIANS

Ansche Hedgepaeth was a twelve-year-old seventh grader when she was arrested for eating french fries in a Washington, DC, Metro station, in violation of a rule that prohibits eating in a transit station. Ansche's crime led to her being searched, handcuffed, booked, and fingerprinted. When questioned about whether his officers went too far, the chief of the Metro Transit Police unapologetically responded, "We really do believe in zero tolerance."[2]

The men who constructed our criminal justice system would have urged far more tolerance. They were wary of government overreach. They envisioned a system that curbed the enthusiasm of its agents, not one that promoted the search and seizure of children eating fried potatoes.

They would have also been appalled at the jailing of Kelly Williams-Bolar, a caring mother living in a dysfunctional school district, for sending her children to a nearby higher-performing school in her father's neighborhood.[3] They would have shuddered to hear of the arrest of Gail Atwater in Lago Vista, Texas, a mother driving her two young children home from soccer practice when she was handcuffed and taken to jail for failure to wear a seatbelt.[4] Or the arrest of nineteen-year-old Jordan Lloyd, who was arrested after police stopped him for riding his bicycle on the sidewalk,[5] and of eighteen-year-old Bryce Snell, for attempting to record Lloyd's arrest on his cell phone.[6]

In the modern tough-on-crime era, criminals—largely defined by class and race—became public enemy number one. There was no political benefit to embracing the ideals at the heart of our democracy that eschewed criminalizing citizens. Our foundational aversion to the use of criminal punishment morphed into an addiction.[7] Lawmakers went on a criminalization frenzy, making it increasingly easy for law enforcement to justify the surveillance and detention of the people.

At the time the framers first cobbled together the protections so central to our criminal justice system, relatively little conduct was criminalized. By the beginning of the twenty-first century, more than four thousand criminal offenses would be defined under federal law with a similar explosion across states.[8] As a result, stories like those of Ansche Hedgepaeth, Kelly Williams-Bolar, Gail Atwater, and Jordan Lloyd became commonplace.

Not only did lawmakers go on a crime-creation binge, they enacted increasingly severe sentencing structures. Prior to this new tough-on-crime approach, the focus was on rehabilitation. Sentencing ranges and parole schemes allowed for the flexibility to release people who no longer needed to be locked up. This world gave way to a more draconian system of punishment. Penalties became harsher. Mandatory minimum sentences deprived judges of the discretion to be lenient. And a slew of sentencing enhancements for a variety of factors drove already harsh sentences even higher.

At the age of twenty-four, a pregnant Kemba Smith pled guilty to conspiracy to distribute crack cocaine. She was in an abusive relationship with a man who was a notorious drug dealer. While she never sold drugs herself, she benefited from his illegal income.[9] Smith, who had no prior criminal record, admitted her minor role. Because of mandatory minimum sentencing, she received twenty-four and a half years in prison with no possibility of parole.[10]

William James Rummel was charged with obtaining $120.75 by false pretenses.[11] He allegedly cashed a check for repair work he had not completed.[12] Although the charge carried a sentence of two to ten years, Rummel had two prior convictions at the time of his arrest: fraudulent use of a credit card to obtain $80 nine years earlier and passing a forged check in the amount of $28.36 four years earlier. Based on these two prior convictions, Rummel was convicted and given a life sentence for the theft. Similar sentencing enhancement statutes led to life sentences for people convicted of stealing a bicycle,[13] a slice of pizza,[14] three golf clubs,[15] and two videotapes.[16] In Louisiana, after receiving probation for three prior marijuana convictions, thirty-five-year-old Cornell Hood II was sentenced to life without the possibility of parole after being convicted of attempting to possess and distribute marijuana.[17]

Not only have legislators implemented laws that punish a sweeping range of behavior for untenable amounts of time, they have also sanctioned statutory schemes that allow the government to hold people in jail on unaffordable money bonds based on a mere accusation. Because there is such a strong correlation between communities we view as "others" and their economic depression, using money bonds is an easy way to ensure targeted populations can be detained pretrial.

Shadu Green was charged with a series of misdemeanors stemming from a traffic stop.[18] The court set bail at a thousand dollars. A bondsman agreed to post the bail if Green paid a nonrefundable four hundred dollar fee. Green did not have it. He sat in jail for six weeks before his family could raise the money. Meanwhile, he lost his apartment and his job, and six weeks with his daughter.[19]

Green was the victim of lawmakers who have so lost sight of the priority our Constitution places on liberty that they are willing to authorize people deemed undesirable to be locked away before being proven guilty. Green's story is not unique. Nearly a half million people who have yet to be convicted are sitting in jail on any given day.[20] This number is more than the entire United States incarcerated population in 1970.[21]

These are just a handful of countless stories that reflect a national mind-set about criminal justice that has become completely unmoored from our fundamental ideals. They are about lawmakers who have co-opted a system that was designed to restrain government oppression and reconfigured it to maintain a caste system to control otherized people. This misuse of crime policy has become so accepted that even lawmakers who believe themselves to be champions of marginalized populations have no appreciation for how disconnected they have become from our most cherished ideals.

One of the protections at the heart of our democracy is an independent judiciary, free from the influence of the executive and legislative branches. Judge Harold Baer learned a difficult lesson about how little leaders of the latter two branches had come to value the hallowed separation of powers doctrine. Judge Baer suppressed drug evidence and a confession after finding that the police violated the Fourth Amendment when they stopped and searched Carol Bayless's car.[22] The decision created a public firestorm. Robert Dole, at the time the Senate majority leader and a Republican presidential candidate, criticized President Clinton for appointing liberal judges who coddled criminals. Dole called for Baer to be impeached. Clinton responded by criticizing Baer's ruling and announcing his regret for appointing Baer to the bench. Less than three months after his initial ruling, Judge Baer succumbed to pressure and reversed his ruling.[23]

That the nation's most powerful politicians were unwilling to stand up for the importance of an independent judiciary so critical to checking the power of the other branches of government speaks volumes. Proving one's bona fides as tough on crime had become far more important to political campaigns than demonstrating respect for our constitutional protections.

Long gone were the days of politicians like John Adams, who famously agreed to defend the British soldiers accused of the Boston massacre. There was no less popular case at the time. He risked his political future to take on the representation. He would remember it as "one of the best pieces of service I ever rendered my country."[24]

We have strayed far from this thinking. The latter part of the twentieth century saw a rise in politicians with prosecutorial backgrounds. Touting a career as a prosecutor lent credibility to a tough-on-crime platform.[25] Even politicians who branded themselves as progressive have felt the need to tout their crime-fighting credentials. In 2004, while Senator John Kerry was running as the Democratic nominee for president, Tom Brokaw asked him whether he was proud to be a liberal. Kerry did not answer the question directly. Instead he emphasized that he was tough on crime. "I'm an ex-prosecutor. I've sent people to jail for the rest of their life," he boasted. "I led the fight to put a hundred thousand cops on the streets of America. What does that make me?"[26]

Meanwhile, service as a defense attorney has become a political liability. In 2014, Barack Obama nominated Debo Adegbile to head the Department of Justice's Civil Rights Division. At one point in his career, while working for the NAACP Legal Defense Fund, Adegbile participated in an appeal on behalf of Mumia Abu Jamal, convicted of killing a police officer in Pennsylvania.[27] The team successfully argued that Abu Jamal's death sentence should be converted to a sentence of life without the possibility of parole due to constitutional error during the sentencing phase. He faithfully did what defense lawyers are sworn to do; he pointed out flaws in the procedure designed to protect life and liberty. Forcing us to ensure the civil rights of every citizen are protected is exactly what we would want from the head of this department. His nomination was blocked by a bipartisan collection of senators.

Two years later, when Hillary Clinton selected Tim Kaine as her presidential running mate, the Republican National Committee attacked him for his previous work as a defense lawyer, in particular his volunteer work three decades earlier on behalf of men on death row. In an attack ad at the time, a narrator said, "Long before Tim Kaine was in office, he consistently protected the worst kinds of people."[28] When asked about the ad afterwards, Sean Spicer, then Republican National Committee spokesman, said, "There are rapists and murderers that he defended [to] keep out of prison that had done horrible things."[29]

That same year, critics attacked Hillary Clinton for her representation of a man accused of rape in 1975.[30] John Adams would have proudly reminded his attackers of the noble and indispensable role that defense lawyers play in our democracy. Hillary Clinton felt it important to assure voters that she did not take on this representation enthusiastically but rather only did so after she unsuccessfully tried to get off the case.[31]

Our tough-on-crime mind-set, and accompanying disdain for the lawyers who represent the accused, influences even local politicians across the country. In state after state, public defenders are expected to handle ever-increasing caseloads while legislators refuse to adequately fund them.[32] Without an army of lawyers who have the support necessary to check them, prosecutors have taken advantage of the expansive arsenal lawmakers have given them—more criminalized conduct and harsher potential penalties, and the ability to easily detain people before trial—to get around the protections the founders put in place to ensure just outcomes.

PROSECUTORS

I recently read a post on social media from a former student who had become a prosecutor in Atlanta. I had not talked to her since law school several years ago. But at the time, she was thoughtful about her reasons for wanting to prosecute and seemed to have a strong sense of justice. I frequently urged future prosecutors I taught to never forget the dignity of the people they have power over. She had seemed to take this to heart. So I was troubled when I read the post she titled "stupid defendant stories." It catalogued condescending accounts of people she prosecuted. I couldn't help myself. I sent her a private message:

> As a former student at John Marshall it will not surprise you to know my thoughts about this post. Those of you who choose to prosecute have a high responsibility to justice and I believe treating people with justice requires first treating them with respect. I would never allow my child to be taught by a teacher who shared "stupid student stories" online, nor would I choose a doctor who shared "stupid patient

stories" online. I can't imagine a citizen who must depend on you for justice could feel confident they can get it after reading your accounts of stupid defendants. I certainly get that as an overwhelmed and under-resourced prosecutor, you can get jaded. This makes it easier to let off steam by mocking those you prosecute. But it is a slippery slope before you no longer have respect for the citizens you are responsible to. I would not trust prosecutors, judges, or defense lawyers who mock the accused. I certainly hope we are producing prosecutors, judges, and defense lawyers at John Marshall who respect the citizens whose lives they have such power over. I hope this post just reflects a really bad day at work.

While she never responded, an hour later the post had been taken down. I understood that as her recognition that she was subtly becoming a prosecutor she did not want to become.

In his book *Let's Get Free: A Hip-Hop Theory of Justice*, legal scholar Paul Butler talks about the cultural pressures facing prosecutors.[33] He knows from experience. Butler came out of law school with a strong respect for civil liberties. As a black man from the south side of Chicago, he was aware of the disproportionate impact mass incarceration had on African Americans and believed in redemption. He started his career as a prosecutor in Washington, DC. He was critical of the criminal justice system and believed he could use his power as a prosecutor to make it more just. But soon Butler's concerns about civil rights and second chances gave way to a belief that his job was "to send as many people to jail as [he] could."[34] He went from seeing the young men he prosecuted as inherently redeemable to being something less than human. He honed his skill at convincing juries that "[the defendant] on trial was a piece of garbage."[35] He began to sit around with his colleagues and call young black defendants "cretins" and "douche bags."[36] Butler thought he could change the system. He came to realize it had changed him.

Butler could have benefited from a program designed to prevent the moral erosion that impacted him as a young US Attorney, a Gideon's Promise for prosecutors, to help them remain conscious of the values that should guide them. But no such program exists.

Unlike the defense attorney, who has a duty of loyalty to the accused, the prosecutor serves as a minister of justice, duty-bound to look out for everyone impacted by his actions—including the accused.[37] The prosecutor's obligation to ensure justice is done trumps his interest in winning a case.[38] The prosecutor is required to pursue a just outcome, even where doing so might jeopardize his chance of winning. He must never intentionally engage in conduct that undermines those tenets at the heart of our democracy. Yet culture drives prosecutors all across the country to do this. Every day prosecutors help perpetuate a system that over-prosecutes and over-incarcerates. They do so in a way that disproportionately targets the most vulnerable. Yet most truly believe they are acting consistent with justice.

Justice requires our confidence in the fact that all constitutional rights are respected before a person is deprived of their liberty. The prosecutor must take the time to examine police conduct to be satisfied they followed proper procedures, and the accused must have an opportunity to explore and raise any improprieties with the court. Justice envisions that guilt is determined by a jury, at a trial with a judge to ensure the proceedings meet constitutional muster. And justice depends on the accused having counsel with the time, expertise, and resources to adequately protect their rights throughout the process. Any attempt to bypass these constitutional protections or to exploit a violation of them is surely inconsistent with the minister of justice role.

But in a society that has come to see so many of its members as criminals, prosecutors have flooded the system without regard for the fact that there are not sufficient resources to handle them all. One recent study looked at prosecutor caseloads in major urban areas. The results were sobering.[39] In Houston, prosecutors with less than two years' experience handled about 500 open cases at any given time, and about 1,500 throughout a single year. In Chicago, the average felony prosecutor handled about 300 cases at a time, and between 800 and 1,000 in a year. In Philadelphia, prosecutors handling the most complex cases in the Major Trials Unit or the Family Violence and Sexual Assault Unit carried 250 cases at a time. In Las Vegas, in 2009, ninety prosecutors handled nearly 800 cases each. With caseloads this high, the prosecutor who works fifty hours a week for fifty weeks per year will be able to devote between 1.66 and 3.125 hours to each case per year. This includes time to meet with witnesses, review police files, engage in the charging process, consider legal issues critical to the just resolution of the case, meet with defense counsel, handle in-court hearings, and many other obligations necessary to ensure the prosecutor is engineering just outcomes.

With caseloads like these, prosecutors cannot handle every case in a manner that is consistent with what justice requires. Prosecutors have unfettered discretion when it comes to charging decisions. They literally control the spigot that determines how many cases enter the system. They know that an overburdened system inevitably leads to unjust outcomes.

Faced with the choice of refusing to prosecute more cases than the system can handle or flooding the system with far too many cases, knowing justice will not be done, prosecutors have opted for the latter. Their desire to lock away folks they believe are dangerous has trumped their fidelity to the Constitution they are sworn to uphold. They have used the tools lawmakers have given them to circumvent the process the founders put in place.

With so much criminalized behavior to choose from and the ability to ensure the consequences of conviction are severe, prosecutors have learned to pile on charges and threaten stiff punishment. By making the cost of going to trial high enough, they have been able to coerce most people into giving up their constitutional rights and saying they did something wrong in order to avoid the risk of far greater punishment after trial.

Consider what happened to Paul Lewis Hayes.[40] Hayes was charged with forgery to the tune of $88.30, a crime that carried a penalty of two to ten years. The prosecutor wanted him to agree to serve a five-year sentence. Based on two prior felony convictions, the prosecutor threatened to re-indict Hayes as a habitual offender if he did not plead guilty, which would subject him to a mandatory life sentence under Kentucky's recidivism law. Hayes rejected the plea offer and the prosecutor made good on his threat. Hayes was convicted and sentenced to life imprisonment.

This was forty years ago, as the government was just starting its experiment using criminal laws as a much more potent weapon against its citizens. But it set a precedent that has largely defined criminal justice since then. Roughly 95 percent of all cases end up being resolved through plea bargaining. Many of those convicted never have a lawyer with the time to fully examine the allegations before they are forced to make this life-altering decision. In courthouses across America, people can be seen accepting plea offers the first time they appear in court. It is obvious to everyone involved that the lawyer who met the client that day did not have time to do any of the work the Constitution requires. The charade is even more blatant when the pleas are entered en masse, as they were in Johnnie L. Caldwell Jr.'s Spalding County, Georgia, courtroom, and countless courtrooms across the country.

When I was a public defender in Washington, DC, it was a common practice for prosecutors to condition a plea offer on the defendant's agreement to give up important procedural rights. Prosecutors would routinely take back plea offers if the accused refused to waive a preliminary hearing, insisted on litigating a pretrial motion, or demanded the production of discovery. These practices clearly valued securing convictions over giving the accused their fair day in court.

The pressure to give up one's constitutional rights are only increased when people are detained pretrial because they are poor. Shadu Green spent six weeks in jail insisting he was innocent.[41] But the prosecutor refused to agree to his release unless he pled guilty. Green was desperate to get out of jail. He was on the verge of pleading guilty to something he did not do when his family came up with the money to bail him out. Green was able to resist the pressure to plead guilty and could demand his constitutional rights.

Unfortunately, many are not so lucky. With hundreds of thousands of people sitting in jail on any given day simply because they cannot afford to pay bond, prosecutors have been able to coerce guilty pleas. Many are innocent but unwilling to risk wrongful conviction with much more grave consequences.[42] For the rare few who refuse to plead guilty, the consequences can be devastating. Marissa Alexander, a victim of domestic abuse, was prosecuted in Jacksonville, Florida, for firing a warning shot into a wall during an altercation with her husband. Believing she did only what she had to do to protect herself, she rejected a plea bargain to serve three years in prison. She went to trial and was found guilty of aggravated assault. She received a mandatory minimum twenty-year sentence.

Sixteen-year-old Kalief Browder was accused of stealing a backpack in the Bronx. Although he consistently maintained his innocence, he was held at Rikers Island for three years waiting to have a trial. He suffered beatings at the hands of prison guards and other detainees. He spent two and a half years locked in solitary confinement. Finally, after three years, the state acknowledged it did not have enough evidence to try Kalief and dismissed all charges. But the psychological damage could not be undone.

Kalief never recovered. He ended up hanging himself in his mother's home two years after his release.

As anyone who spends any time in the criminal justice system learns, this is how criminal justice is dispensed in America.

THE PRACTICES OF OVERCHARGING, threatening incomprehensible prison terms, and taking advantage of oppressive pretrial detention to compel nineteen of twenty accused people to plead guilty could not be more inconsistent with the founders' ideals. Thomas Jefferson said: "I consider [trial by jury] as the only anchor ever yet imagined by man, by which a government can be held to the principles of its constitution."[43] The jury trial is now virtually nonexistent. It has been replaced by the plea bargain, a resolution never imaginable to our founders. Plea bargaining did not even exist in colonial America.[44] It became a practice after the Civil War, and its prevalence has skyrocketed over the past fifty years.[45]

Prosecutors have come to view the use of plea bargaining to clear dockets as effective prosecution. They have become so concerned with racking up convictions efficiently that they almost certainly have never considered their lack of fidelity to these protections. In fact, we are all so used to an assembly-line criminal justice system that none of us blinks.

New Orleans provides one example of prosecutors rushing to rack up convictions without regard for the ability of the accused to adequately defend themselves. The city found itself in a constitutional crisis in February 2012, after the district attorney's office elected to charge 85 percent of all cases brought to its attention.[46] As the number of cases in the system ballooned, the public defenders were not given the resources needed to keep up. During the previous two years, as the DA's office was busy charging more cases, Derwyn Bunton warned city officials of the emergency, threatening to have to refuse to take on more cases.[47] The plea for more funding fell on deaf ears.

Public defenders in New Orleans were already handling roughly twice the number of cases recommended by national standards.[48] But the district attorney refused to change course. The Orleans Public Defenders found itself faced with a budget shortfall of about a million dollars.[49] It had to lay off nearly a third of the public defenders on staff.[50] The office, which represented approximately 80 percent of criminal defendants in

New Orleans and where staff were already working overtime to try to provide clients the representation they deserved, could no longer continue to absorb the crushing caseload.[51] As a result, 543 people accused of crimes, ranging from misdemeanors to murder, found themselves without lawyers.[52] Many of these citizens were jailed.[53] Anyone could see the crisis toward which the system was heading. There was no money available, yet prosecutors continued to pump cases into an overloaded system. The district attorney's office had been on a charging binge without regard for the scarcity of resources available.

The story of public defenders sounding an alarm about overwhelming caseloads and inadequate resources happens across the country. It is bad enough that prosecutors continue to charge cases without regard for resource limitations. In many places, it is common for district attorneys actually to oppose the public defenders' efforts to get relief.

In 2008, Miami Public Defender Bennett Brummer asked the court for permission to refuse some cases.[54] His lawyers were handling roughly five hundred cases each, two and a half times the maximum recommended by Florida's public defender association.[55] The state's attorney for the county opposed Brummer's motion.[56]

When Judge Stanford Blake agreed with Brummer and gave his office permission to turn down future, less-serious felonies, the state attorney's office appealed Blake's decision, fighting it all the way to the state Supreme Court.[57] The Florida Prosecuting Attorneys Association also weighed in, filing an amicus brief, to oppose Judge Blake's decision.[58] When the American Bar Association decided to weigh in on behalf of Brummer's office, the state attorney wrote a letter urging it to reconsider.[59]

In 2012, Missouri public defenders won a victory when the state Supreme Court agreed that they were entitled to refuse cases when existing caseloads threatened their ability to perform ethically.[60] In response, the Missouri Association of Prosecuting Attorneys issued a press statement disagreeing with the decision and challenging the idea that public defenders need caseload relief.[61]

An oft-cited National Advisory Commission (NAC) on Criminal Justice Standards and Goals standard recommends public defenders handle no more than 150 felony cases per year and 400 misdemeanors.[62] In 2016, public defenders in eleven of the thirteen counties in New Mexico carried between 165 percent to 364 percent of this recommended caseload.

Lawyers can sometimes spend only minutes with clients before they must make life-altering decisions. The district attorney responsible for Lincoln County, where public defenders have nearly three times the NAC standard, accused public defenders of fabricating the crisis.[63] The president of the New Mexico District Attorneys Association suggested public defenders turn to charitable donations and fundraising to supplement their budget.[64]

Sadly, this is precisely what public defenders in New Orleans had to do. The office started a crowdfunding campaign to make up the million-dollar budget deficit.[65] Whenever these resource crises threatened the citizenry's ability to seek justice, no prosecutor ever demanded their brother and sister ministers of justice refrain from enthusiastically continuing to charge more cases.

The disregard prosecutors have for the protections at the heart of our democracy are directly the result of systems that shape them to see those they accuse as more worthy of ridicule and derision than of dignified treatment. The same culture that shapes young prosecutors forges seasoned district attorneys who prioritize efficiency over justice. It also shapes judges.

JUDGES

Tim Young, the director of Ohio's state public defender system, was at a meeting of judges from across the state when he was introduced to a judge he had never met. Upon learning who Tim was, the judge responded, "Oh, the dark side." Tim immediately realized the judge was not joking, and that he was "offended by my presence."

Unfazed, Tim responded, "Judge, I am not sure I understand. If you mean defending the Fourth Amendment, the right to remain silent, the right to due process, and most of the other fundamental rights in the Bill of Rights that have been assaulted by the government, then I guess I am not sure what is so wrong with what I do." This comment was met with a "diatribe," as the judge complained that "his" money was being wasted on lawyers for the poor.[66] This rant shines a light on how little respect this judge had for constitutional rights when forced to apply them to people he has demonized.

And the comment about the money being "his," as opposed to the public's, is evidence of a judge-centered, rather than a justice-centered, mind-set. It is an attitude that prioritizes judges' own convenience over ensuring just outcomes. Ensuring things run smoothly in "their" courtroom becomes the goal.

Most judges are neither as conscious of nor as outspoken about their disdain for lawyers who challenge them as the Ohio judge who complained to Tim Young. But as with lawmakers and prosecutors, many have also been subtly primed to see poor defendants as criminals, so the most hallowed ideals meant to protect "us" are of secondary importance when applied to "them."

As I began studying criminal justice more broadly, I learned that it is common for judges to tolerate, or even encourage, substandard lawyering in an effort to keep their dockets moving without the healthy friction zealous counsel introduces into the process.

When Georgia refused to adequately fund public defense in the wake of the Brian Nichols case, a couple of judges offered solutions to the funding crisis. One judge suggested that we go back to offering the "many eager and [some starving]" local lawyers $50 per case, regardless of the time they invest.[67] A second judge suggested that the state require that all civil lawyers, regardless of their lack of experience handling criminal cases, handle a certain number of criminal cases free of charge.[68] These judges could offer these views without a trace of shame only if they understood the exercise as being about how to process people, like widgets, as cheaply and hassle-free as possible. These judicial attitudes reflected a culture that would not be so easy to shift.

At times, judges seek to punish public defenders for daring to demand reasonable workloads. For example, in New Orleans, when the resource-challenged public defender's office began to decline cases, some judges threatened to hold the lawyers in contempt.[69] In response to questions about the constitutional implications of overwhelmed public defenders, one judge responded, "*Gideon* says you're entitled to a lawyer. It doesn't say you're entitled to a great lawyer."[70]

Similarly, in New Mexico, when chief public defender Ben Bauer refused to appoint overburdened public defenders to additional cases, a local judge held him in contempt. Bauer cited his ethical duty to provide constitutional representation.[71] That was clearly not the judge's primary concern.

One need not visit too many courtrooms before seeing judges pressure lawyers to proceed with cases they are clearly not prepared for. In

Ohio, Portage County Municipal Court judge John Plough ordered public defender Brian Jones to try a case to which Jones was appointed the day before.[72] When Plough ordered the trial to proceed, Jones requested more time, explaining that he had had only twenty minutes to meet with the client to date. The judge denied the lawyer's request for a continuance and held him in contempt of court when he refused to proceed.[73]

In New Jersey, Terrence Miller met his public defender for the first time the morning of trial.[74] The two spoke for only a few minutes in the courthouse stairwell. The lawyer, who had been appointed four days earlier, had not tried a criminal case in seven years and needed time to get up to speed. When the lawyer met Miller, he had not yet talked to Miller's previous lawyer or interviewed any witnesses. Twice, the lawyer asked the judge for more time. Each time the judge denied the request. With the defense completely unprepared, proceedings began that day. Miller was, predictably, convicted and sentenced to a five-year term of incarceration.[75]

In some courtrooms, rather than deal with a resistant lawyer, judges engineer the wholesale deprivation of counsel. More than a dozen of the best defense lawyers in Houston, Texas, protested against a judge who was pressuring defendants to plead guilty without having their lawyer present.[76] One Houston lawyer described being in court when a judge brought out eight unrepresented accused men at once and got them all to plead guilty without providing them counsel.[77] Sadly, this is a practice that happens across the country, as judges understand that keeping defendants lawyerless and ignorant of their rights helps move cases quickly.[78]

As I saw in New Orleans, there are judges who bend over backward to find that a person owns anything of value, or has the most meager of income, to justify denying them counsel. A news story out of Orlando, Florida, lauded a judge for her willingness to scrutinize people accused of crimes to determine if they were truly worthy of a court-appointed lawyer. The piece was entitled "Lawyer: Taxpayer Money Wasted on Undeserving Defendants."[79] As I watched, I realized the "undeserving" included a man whose only source of income was mowing lawns "off the books" on occasion. After he asked for an appointed lawyer, the judge angrily accused him in open court of trying to bilk the taxpaying audience of their money. Following the public comeuppance, the judge denied him counsel.

Despite all of the taxpayer dollars used to mindlessly police, prosecute, and incarcerate poor people, this judge seemed most concerned with the possibility that people who were barely making ends meet might obtain court-appointed lawyers. The story reminded me of countless anecdotes I have heard from public defenders across the country about judges who deny court-appointed counsel because a defendant has a decent watch, jewelry, or nice clothes.

One spring morning in 2016, Chris Routh accompanied his client to court in Jackson, Mississippi. The state was asking the judge to revoke her bond. The young client had her three-month-old baby with her. The two began to sob as the judge prepared to jail the young woman. As the woman and the baby cried, Routh requested that the judge explain his reasons for revoking bond. Apparently finding the public defender's persistence unacceptable, the judge had him jailed.

This was the same judge, Judge Weill, who held Greg Spore and Michele Purvis-Harris in contempt.[80]

According to a press release issued by Purvis-Harris following Routh's detention, since Purvis-Harris's appointment in 2012, nine public defenders had been assigned to Judge Weill's courtroom. All had been either held in contempt or threatened with contempt "for simply doing their job." None had faced any disciplinary action nor held in contempt prior to being assigned to Judge Weill's courtroom.[81]

Greg and Chris were both products of Gideon's Promise. As they shared their stories with other members of the community, they were met with a level of understanding that could only come from a group accustomed to resisting bullying judges.

Shortly after his release from jail, Chris sent the community an email message through the Gideon's Promise listserv:

> I want y'all all to know how amazing my office has been through this entire shenanigan. The entire office was there to greet me at the jail last night, replete with mardi gras beads and cake. I have not doubted for a second that that office has been behind me full force and remain steadfast in our advocacy not only for our clients, but for each other. WE WILL NOT STAND DOWN.[82]

Chris's Gideon's Promise community sent messages of support. A group of judges would not likely have been as encouraging. In a system in which judges expect everyone to comply with their efforts to reduce friction and move cases, zealous public defenders are often not welcome. Passionate advocacy that slows things down is often seen as a personal slight. Justice is secondary to respect for the rules they have put in place for their own convenience.

Every lawyer has experienced judges who tell litigants and lawyers to be in court by 9 a.m. but who often arrive much later themselves. Because the judges' convenience is paramount, they often will not hesitate to punish the latecomer. Because a judge likely does not consider the inconvenience to the working men and women who have been waiting for them to arrive, it is the rare judge who issues a sincere apology when they are late.

It is easy for a judge to become desensitized to the humanity of the people who shuffle through criminal courts. The human processing can easily have a numbing effect.

Shelley Chapman, a bankruptcy judge, learned this on a recent visit to a criminal courtroom. Her daughter, a public defender, invited her to come to court. Judge Chapman was a jurist, but her exposure to criminal courts nevertheless shocked her: she was shocked by the lack of concern the judge had for the people whose lives her decisions would impact that day. The judge neither smiled nor acknowledged the audience as she took the bench. She chatted only with the court officers and the prosecutor, "as if they're all on the same side."[83]

Judge Chapman described the case of a very shaken young woman who was accused of assault by her husband. The prosecution was asking that she stay away from her husband and ten-month-old baby. The public defender tried to calm the woman as she explained that her husband had a drinking problem, that the woman feared for her child's safety, and that her husband made up the allegation after she threatened to leave him.

"Application denied, counselor," replied the judge coldly. The woman cried as the judge ordered the court officers: "Get her out of here."

In another case, the judge issued a stay-away order to a Hispanic defendant, explaining, "If the complainant calls and invites you over for rice and beans, you cannot go." She was equally offensive to others, telling them that "most young men with names like yours have lengthy criminal records by the time they reach a certain age." The blatant racial bias from the judge was something Judge Chapman had not experienced in bankruptcy court.

She was shocked by the rapid pace of the proceedings and the way the judge even "giggled" as courtroom personnel mocked the defendants. Judge Chapman concluded, "While we all may not be able to agree on what justice looks like, surely we can agree on what injustice looks like."[84]

Yes, we can. It looks like what happens in criminal courtrooms every day across America. The only people who do not recognize it are those who administer it.

It is a system that produces judges like Louisville, Kentucky's Sandra McLaughlin.[85] While arraigning a man accused of stabbing his wife, McLaughlin sneered, "She should have cut you." The man turned out to be innocent and the victim's wounds self-inflicted.

In another case, in which a man accused of a drug offense explained that he had a job and attended school, McLaughlin asked, "How do you do all that? Go to school, work, and traffic cocaine? You're very busy."

One defendant was accused of shoplifting. He asked to contact his family for money to post bond. Judge McLaughlin had a retort, "You should have contacted them for money instead of stealing."

Another was charged with theft. "So that's your job? Stealing from people when you clean their house?"

When asked about her clearly inappropriate remarks, the judge chalked them up to "'frustration' with defendants' refusal to comply with the law. . . . Sometimes I just want to shake them and say, 'What were you thinking?'"[86]

All of these are men and women who our Constitution requires we presume to be innocent. Judge McLaughlin was unable to do that.

Every time I hear another story of a judge who so reflexively disregards constitutional protections for those without means, I think back to my early days in Georgia. I remember the judge who complained about Jason filing motions. I think about the accused men lined up in dark green jail uniforms to take mass pleas in Judge Caldwell's courtroom. My mind gravitates to those judges who proposed to address Georgia's public defender funding crisis by appointing "starving" lawyers for $50 per case, or conscripting lawyers with no experience in criminal law.

In those days, I understood each of these as anecdotes about bad judges. My knee-jerk solution would have been to elect different judges. I now appreciate how this oversimplification of the problem misses the mark. These are less stories about individual judges than they are about a criminal justice culture. These judges are the products of systems shaped by corrupted values. They are systems that corrupt some more than others. But everyone who participates in the criminal justice system is capable of being molded by it.

This is true for judges. It is true for lawmakers. It is true for prosecutors. And it is true for public defenders. When we see that one of these professionals is acting in a way that undermines justice our reflexive response is to replace them with someone else or to craft rules to limit their ability to misbehave. But this reaction fails to appreciate the power of culture. It overlooks the reality that these men and women are driven by a value system forged by a toxic system. Changing the culture is the key to reform. And that begins with transforming the values of the people who drive it.

My work started with a focus on public defenders. I've come to understand that the lessons I learned apply to criminal justice reform more broadly. We must understand criminal justice reform as an adaptive challenge. We must identify the fundamental values that should guide these professionals. We must use recruitment, training, and mentorship to transform mind-sets that fuel injustice. We cannot simply make new rules and expect people to change who they are. A focus exclusively on technical solutions will never bring about the change that is needed.

CHAPTER 8

UNTIL THE LION LEARNS TO WRITE

AN AFRICAN PROVERB WARNS, "Until the lion learns to write, the story will always glorify the hunter." As lawyers, we too are shaped by a narrative that ignores the voices of the most marginalized. It is our responsibility to make sure those voices are heard so that the story can be complete.

In my criminal procedure class, the students learn that one of the factors police consider when determining whether a person's actions are suspicious is whether the neighborhood is a high crime area.[1] I ask my students to name high crime areas in Atlanta. They predictably sound off a list of low-income neighborhoods populated largely with black and brown people. When I suggest we include the campus of Georgia Tech, eyebrows go up. I remind them they have all been to college. I ask them to consider how many students engage in underage drinking or recreational drug use. They nod as if it is starting to make sense. I ask them why there is a significantly greater police presence in poor, urban communities than on college campuses. Why, I ask, are we more likely to see a young, African American man who is carrying a bag of marijuana outside a low-income housing complex as a criminal than a white college student who has the same amount of weed on his way to class?

Roughly half of my class each semester is made up of students of color. But the reaction of the students to these questions doesn't seem to depend on the race of the student. If they are being honest, they admit that class and race play a role in how they have come to understand criminality.

This is the implicit racial bias that shapes the criminal justice story in America. It accounts for how so many well-intentioned professionals, who believe they are contributing to justice every day, are actually perpetuating systems wholly divorced from our foundational ideals.

This narrative not only explains why police are more likely to monitor and arrest people of color.[2] It explains why federal lawmakers enacted sentences for crack cocaine, a drug more often associated with black communities, that were significantly more severe than those for similar amounts of powder cocaine.[3] It explains how once-idealistic prosecutors can come to call defendants "cretins," or joke publicly about "stupid defendant stories." It explains how a judge can giggle as her staff mocks a helpless defendant, or allow racist remarks to roll off her tongue as she addresses the accused. And it explains how a public defender can honestly believe lawyers handling eight hundred cases per year are doing an adequate job for their clients.

The most powerful strategy for challenging biases and assumptions is to use storytelling. Our assumptions about people in the criminal justice system have been formed by a narrative that never includes their stories. This one-dimensional story casts them as less human, as dangerous "others." Infusing the system with their humanity requires that their whole stories be told. Public defenders, who speak for these marginalized populations when they are accused of crimes, are the necessary vehicle to do this.

Public defenders can force us to see beyond the one-dimensional story of the accused as a criminal. They can open our eyes to the obstacles the accused has overcome in life, or the challenges with which they continue to grapple. They remind us that defendants have mothers who love them or children whose worlds revolve around them. They make us think about the fact that they may serve us coffee at Dunkin' Donuts or sweep the floors of our office building. Through public defenders, we can understand a more complete narrative.

Civil rights lawyer Bryan Stevenson argues that justice requires decision makers to get proximate to those whom their decisions impact. Understanding someone, and therefore being proximate to that person, requires that we learn who they are, that we understand their whole story. Public defenders are the vehicles through which everyone in the criminal justice system gets proximate to the accused. They have the power to challenge the assumptions of the one-dimensional story and to restore dignity by revealing the mosaic of the person's experience.

At the heart of American injustice is the reality that we simply do not value poor people. We seek to address every problem that plagues our most marginalized communities by criminalizing those impacted. In our most vulnerable communities, we criminalize those afflicted with mental illness, substance addiction, poverty, and illiteracy. The victims of these social ills fill our nation's jails and prisons. Their lives intersect in the criminal justice system. It is the last chance for their voices to be heard—their stories to be told—before they are condemned and effectively banished from society.[4]

My work over the last fifteen years has taught me that if we are truly to realize justice in America, we must embrace three axioms. First, meaningful criminal justice reform demands that we engineer a cultural transformation. We must move beyond policy fixes that tweak around the edges. Second, this effort requires that we amplify the voices of impacted communities. This will be the engine necessary to humanize the system and overcome prevailing assumptions and biases. Finally, an army of public defenders is the most effective vehicle to drive this change.

Public defenders are key to this effort. Yet they are universally ignored.

IN THE SPRING OF 2015, the Brennan Center for Justice published a collection of essays called *Solutions: American Leaders Speak Out on Criminal Justice Reform.*[5] It featured an impressive assortment of voices from across the ideological spectrum. Contributors included Hillary Clinton, Joe Biden, and Cory Booker representing the Democratic Party and Rand Paul, Ted Cruz, and Chris Christie as voices of the Republican Party. It even featured a foreword by former president Bill Clinton.

Bipartisan agreement that we had lost our way when it came to criminal justice was a recent development. The nation was finally embarking on a conversation about criminal justice reform. Policy priorities were being set as experts considered how best to guide us out of the wilderness. For someone who had dedicated his life to criminal justice, it was an exciting time. We finally had a consensus that this challenge needed to be addressed. I looked forward to reading the publication, which seemed to be evidence of a new, universal commitment to tackling the problem.

But as I read essay after essay, I grew increasingly dismayed. Twenty-three thought leaders voiced their ideas over a hundred and thirty pages of text. The words *public defenders* were painfully absent. Not a single contributor saw these advocates as important enough to mention as they envisioned a healthier criminal justice system.[6] I saw public defenders as essential to any comprehensive strategy to transform our justice system. How could so many thought leaders overlook this?

Later that year, President Obama hosted a panel discussion at the White House to discuss criminal justice reform. He invited a federal prosecutor from Colorado and a police chief from Los Angeles. No public defender was invited to the stage.[7] In fact, the words *public defender* were never uttered during that conversation.

Over the next two years, I listened to many panel discussions and read countless articles focused on criminal justice reform. One after another, reformers paraded out their favorite reforms. Virtually everyone ignored the role of public defenders and our national failure to live up to the promise of *Gideon*.

One of President Obama's last pronouncements about criminal justice came in the form of a comprehensive law review article about what we need to do to reform criminal justice. In the article's sixty-four pages, Obama never mentioned public defenders.[8]

Not surprisingly given the momentum, criminal justice reform featured heavily in the Democratic primary race. Both Hillary Clinton and Bernie Sanders featured a criminal justice platform on their websites.[9] Public defenders were not considered on either site.

Given the increased national scrutiny it was getting, funders began to invest more heavily in criminal justice reform. Yet, virtually none of that money was going to support public defense.

I thought back to when Illy and I first launched our organization. There were very few national foundations that invested in criminal justice. But our strongest support came from two that did. They continued to fund our work for several years. But strangely, as the cry for a bipartisan approach to reform grew louder, they ended their support, diverting that money to other projects.

The focus on criminal justice prompted additional foundations to invest in criminal justice. Certainly, a small group of funders have been supportive. For the most part, however, although they expressed their commitment to criminal justice reform most were unwilling to invest resources in public defense.

When Illy and I talked to program officers at these various foundations, we heard a common, and perplexing, refrain: "We are not funding public defense; we are focused on addressing mass incarceration."

"What the—?!" I thought in my head every time I heard this. "Public defenders are indispensable to addressing mass incarceration!" I wanted to scream. How could they not see this? To add to the frustration, several of these foundation representatives had backgrounds in public defense. As if to assure us that, although they would not invest in our work, they understood the value of it, they would often remind us that they were once public defenders.

I never doubted that these men and women appreciated public defenders. In fact, most of the advocates who were leading the criminal justice reform charge were allies to public defenders. They appreciated what a good public defender meant to an individual accused of a crime. They just did not see public defender reform as a critical component of the effort to challenge mass incarceration.

In fact, thanks to the groundbreaking work of Michelle Alexander and scholars who followed, addressing mass incarceration became the focus of many criminal justice reformers. Alexander's work helped us understand mass incarceration as the "new Jim Crow." The push to address the staggering number of Americans behind bars became so urgent that it was often conflated with criminal justice reform. Reformers and funders consequently looked to support policy fixes that had a direct impact on the number of people behind bars.

There was support for decriminalizing some of the most minor offenses, thereby reducing the number of people dumped into the system in the first place. Sentencing reform was widely hailed as a mechanism to reduce the amount of time those convicted of some crimes would spend in prison. And with roughly one in five of those locked up being held pretrial, the cry to reform pretrial detention practices grew louder.

Of course, this all made sense. If policymakers could engineer it so that fewer people were arrested on the front end and those who were arrested spent less time in prison, the number of people incarcerated would logically shrink. If we could reduce the number of people held in jail awaiting trial we could not only shrink the jail population; evidence suggested those men and women would be more likely to avoid prison sentences down the road.[10]

No one could quarrel that these reforms would lead to fewer bodies in prison. Anyone concerned about our addiction to caging human beings would support these efforts. But why weren't public defenders also seen as critical to a decarceration strategy?

My wife, Illy, watched her father get swept into a prison cell at Attica without an advocate to resist the process. She understood that good public defenders were needed to interrupt that process. In fact, her experience with a bad public defender led her to believe no one in the system cared about people like her. Her later introduction to some great public defenders helped her realize there are some who do.

Illy often used an analogy to describe the criminal justice system to friends who did not work in this space. She would liken it to a fast-paced conveyor belt that zipped poor people from freedom to incarceration in three stages. On the front end, poor people were loaded onto the conveyor belt as they were rounded up and charged with a seemingly endless menu of criminalized behavior. On the back end, they would be deposited into prison cells for ridiculous amounts of time thanks to draconian sentencing laws. And in the middle there was the well-oiled machinery that whisked the accused from arrest to sentencing. In her analogy, public defenders were meant to provide friction during this middle stage. Ideally, they would slow the apparatus down, at times plucking people from the belt before they could reach the end.

As public defenders became overwhelmed, under-resourced, and beaten down, they could no longer provide the necessary friction. Without a strong army of public defenders, a person who was arrested was almost guaranteed a conviction. The front- and back-end reforms might lead to a smaller system. But those who were left to navigate it still wouldn't stand a chance. Like her father, their lives would be throwaway lives, even if there were fewer of them.

Of course, Illy was right. By ignoring public defenders, reformers were missing an opportunity to rescue many of those who remained in the system. With no advocate to make sure the police did not cut corners, to test the strength of the state's evidence, and to make sure the prosecution played by the rules, those who entered the system would have no chance at justice. They may serve shorter sentences at the end, but we would never know if they ever deserved to reach that end.

Over the past few years, I watched the lobby to reduce our prison population grow, and like everyone committed to a less cruel system, I cheered for its success. But I continued to work with heroic public defenders who were stretched beyond the breaking point. They struggled to deal with the emotional toll of watching people fall through the cracks, people they could have helped if they just had the time and resources. I knew neglecting this army was a strategic mistake.

But my work addressing culture change leads me to believe that an even greater failing is defining the problem as mass incarceration in the first place. Of course, mass incarceration has to be addressed. But the challenge we face is much deeper than that. Our overflowing prisons are a symptom of a pervasive cultural phenomenon. Mass incarceration is just one manifestation of much broader disease. Our broken criminal justice system is, at its core, a cultural dilemma.

It presents an adaptive challenge. Police, prosecutors, and judges are conditioned to see targeted communities as dangerous. They are primed to act on these assumptions. The policy fixes we have championed are technical solutions. They are designed to alter the behavior of criminal justice actors. But without an adaptive solution, criminal justice professionals will continue to try to engineer the outcomes they value.

Take bail reform in Maryland as an example. In 2017, criminal justice reformers cheered a new rule that promised to end the practice of holding people pretrial on money bonds they could not afford.[11] Justice reform advocates envisioned a system with far fewer people locked away pending trial.

However, in some counties judges would not easily abandon their assumptions about who deserved to be locked away upon arrest. They looked for ways to maintain the status quo. They may have been forced to stop giving poor people money bonds that they could not afford. But rather than release them on a promise to return, judges started using "no-bail" holds to compensate. Rather than setting cash bonds they knew poor people could not afford, they simply ordered detention without bail. It appears that, despite the new rule, pretrial detention may have increased in places like Prince George's County and Baltimore.

Reformers in California have pointed out similar issues with bail reform there as legislators, conditioned to presume guilt and desire pretrial detention, replaced a system of money bail with a new system that allows judges to hold people without bond and threatens to increase the number of Californians detained pretrial.[12]

But even in places where fewer people are jailed pretrial, without an accompanying shift in the narrative about the dangerousness of those targeted by our legal system, people released pretrial will likely be overmonitored through other means. They will still be given overwhelmed public defenders. They will still be processed through a system that does not truly respect their constitutional rights. They will still risk exposure to excessive punishment in inhumane prisons. One system of control will replace another.

Of course we should decriminalize more behavior. Yes, we should reform sentencing laws to give judges more discretion. We absolutely should end wealth-based pretrial detention. But if these are done without transforming culture, the impact will not be transformative. Police who are conditioned to see some people as criminals will still find ways to monitor and arrest targeted populations. Judges who view the accused as dangerous will continue to find ways under the new regime to overuse pretrial detention and sentence harshly upon conviction.

Our criminal justice system suffers from a disease. It is a narrative of otherness. That we overincarcerate is a symptom. That we use the criminal justice system almost exclusively for the poor is a symptom. That the system disproportionately targets communities of color is a symptom. That criminal convictions render it virtually impossible to fully reintegrate into society is a symptom. Of course we need to find ways to address these symptoms. Doing so makes the system less cruel. But we cannot do that to the exclusion of addressing the disease. We must engage in the hard work of culture change.

When public defenders work hand in hand with the communities they represent, their power can extend well beyond the four walls of the courtroom. A movement of public defenders, spread across the nation, connected to oppressed people everywhere, has the potential to begin to rewrite the criminal justice narrative.

But to realize this potential, public defenders need to reimagine their role in this human rights struggle. This is a tall order. As a young public defender, I certainly did not appreciate this collective power. But I now see public defenders serving a dual role. Individually we speak for singular clients, one case at a time. Collectively, we can speak for targeted communities as we employ strategies to shift culture. If we are to break the cycle of trading one system of oppression for another, public defenders must see themselves as both protectors of individual rights as well as change agents.

Traditionally, public defenders have only been taught to see themselves as the former: the warrior who courageously battles the state when it comes for the accused. This role is noble and important. And it explains why reformers with public defender backgrounds can love public defenders but not understand them as a catalyst for systems change.

I recognize that this broader vision is ambitious, but realizing a country that actually embraces its democratic ideals and applies them to everyone equally is just as aspirational. In the meantime, we must work to reduce the number of people in cages. We must fight to eliminate barriers to reentry facing those with criminal records. Individual public defenders must prioritize the fight that immediately faces each client they represent. But we must also develop a strategy to transform the existing culture. When we understand the power of public defenders more broadly, it becomes clear how this army can be a catalyst of real justice reform.

In recent years, the nation has been shaken by the loud reality that equal justice is a myth. In the summer of 2014, Americans learned that a white Ferguson, Missouri, police officer named Darren Wilson shot and killed Michael Brown, an unarmed African American teenager. Divergent narratives about what happened quickly emerged. Wilson claimed he was left with no choice. He presented Brown as a superhuman presence, coming toward him in a threatening manner, seemingly unfazed by a volley of bullets. He had no choice but to shoot the young man multiple times.[13]

But for many across the country, this story made little sense. The public finally began to question whether this shooting provided a glimpse into a broader culture in which police reacted to communities of color much more aggressively than they did their white counterparts.

While many in the law enforcement community went on the defensive, denying the existence of any cultural problem, a seemingly endless stream of encounters in which police killed unarmed black men came to light. And, unlike Michael Brown's killing, many were captured on cell phone video recordings.

Protests in the wake of the Ferguson shooting were fueled by video footage of officer Daniel Pantaleo choking Eric Garner to death the same summer, as Garner lay on a New York City sidewalk restrained by a swarm of officers, repeatedly gasping, "I can't breathe."

In November 2014, the country saw Cleveland police officer Timothy Loehmann shoot twelve-year-old Tamir Rice to death within seconds of arriving at the park where Rice was playing with a toy gun. Loehmann and his partner left Rice defenseless and dying on the ground for several minutes before other officers arrived and attended to the boy.

Over the next two years, the nation watched video footage of police officers shooting a series of unarmed black men, including Walter Scott in North Charleston, South Carolina; Samuel DuBose in Cincinnati, Ohio; Alton Sterling in Baton Rouge, Louisiana; Philando Castile in Falcon Heights, Minnesota; Terence Crutcher in Tulsa, Oklahoma; and Keith Lamont Scott in Charlotte, North Carolina. The list continues to grow to this day.

These encounters are so shocking, and so violent, that they can easily be viewed as an outlying problem. The officers involved can understandably be considered a batch of "bad apples." But this view can cause us to focus on these most egregious examples of abusive policing to the exclusion of the more routine variety.

For every person killed by a police officer, tens of thousands are arrested, processed through the courts, and locked up in cells. Many of these encounters begin with behavior by police that belongs in the broad category of "abusive." Stopping groups of young men and lining them against a wall to be frisked is abusive. Pulling a citizen from their car based on a stereotype when other similarly situated citizens wouldn't be bothered is abusive. These forms of abuse are more routine. They are often normalized. They are met with far less outrage. But they are part of the broader criminal justice story. They are driven by a narrative that sees some populations as dangerous and subhuman.

This is the narrative behind highly publicized police killings. It is also behind violent police encounters that do not result in death. And it is behind the routinized policing, prosecuting, and punishing that fuels mass incarceration.

These problems cannot be addressed in isolation of one another. And challenging the assumptions behind this vicious narrative must be at the heart of any solution.

A focus on front-end policy fixes may keep some off the conveyor belt. Attending to back-end reforms may soften the landing a bit once those on the conveyor belt reach the end. But only through the guarantee of a robust right to counsel can we make sure that those who are on that conveyor belt through discriminatory policing and prosecution have a means to escape. Most people never have that chance. Our failure to provide lawyers for the poor is at the heart of a criminal justice system that discriminates based on class and race. This failure is an essential chapter in the story.

REFORMERS WHO FOCUS ON prosecutors frequently say that the prosecutor is the most powerful player in the system. This is understandable, since prosecutors have largely been responsible for fueling mass incarceration. As we have discussed, prosecutors have used the power to charge to flood the system with more cases than it can handle. They have used their power to seek pretrial detention and threaten harsh sentences to pressure defendants to plead guilty and abandon their constitutional rights. Their abuse of power has crippled individual lives, families, and communities. Undoubtedly, they have a tremendous amount of power. It is the power to destroy lives.

By rethinking how they use their power, prosecutors can make the system less cruel. They can make it less unjust. But they do not have the power to transform the system. They must work within the existing system. As described here, it is a system that has been engineered to punish marginalized populations. The prosecutor's job is to administer that system. While they have discretion over the degree of cruelty to exert, that discretion is limited.

They are limited in that they exert control almost exclusively over the most marginalized. As policing focuses on poor communities, this is the subset of the population that prosecutors largely exert power over. Prosecutors have little control over who the police choose to monitor and arrest.

Prosecutors also have no control over which behavior is criminalized. While prosecutors have discretion over what to charge from a menu of options, those options are made by the legislature.

If you disagree with the behavior we have decided to criminalize as a society or have little interest in disproportionately punishing the communities targeted by policing policies, becoming a prosecutor makes little sense. The prosecutor does not have much impact on those factors.

Where the prosecutor does have incredible influence is in deciding how harshly to treat the poor people whose files land on their desks. This reminds me of a story about a high school student named Christopher who desperately wanted to go to college. I learned about Christopher from a TED talk given by a former juvenile prosecutor named Adam Foss.[14] When Christopher realized that his minimum-wage job would not support his college dreams, he foolishly made what Adam calls "a series of bad decisions." He stole thirty laptops and sold them on the internet. Christopher was arrested and charged with thirty felonies.

Christopher's case was assigned to Adam, who had had his own legal troubles as a teenager and empathized with the young man. He realized Christopher's potential. He understood that a criminal conviction would hamper Christopher's chances of going to school, securing employment, and leading a productive life. He knew that charging Christopher could prove fatal to his dreams. He saw something in Christopher, so he decided to divert the case out of the criminal justice system. Without a criminal record, Christopher went to college. Adam's story ends with him running into Christopher several years later at a gathering of professional men of color. Christopher had become a successful bank manager. Christopher hugged Adam and thanked him.

Adam tells this story to illustrate the power of the prosecutor to make a more just system. It is meant as a rallying cry for prosecutors to lead this charge. But if one reads between the lines, it is really a story about the power of the public defender. To be sure, Adam never mentions Christopher's lawyer. He briefly mentions a couple other examples in which prosecutors gave breaks to sympathetic defendants. Their lawyers are not part of their stories either. But when one understands how these stories work their way into the system, the public defender becomes the hero.

Why? Because the only way prosecutors ever learn these stories is through defense counsel. Prosecutors are not allowed to communicate with defendants directly. We certainly should want more empathetic prosecutors who will be inclined to give breaks to defendants they deem deserving. But their ability to appreciate the circumstances of the accused's life depends on a defense lawyer committed to learning, and telling, that story. For every account of a prosecutor who treats a defendant humanely, there is a story of a defense lawyer who has helped them understand the whole person. And for every story in which a prosecutor never learns the full story of the accused, there is the potential that a good public defender could have persuaded them to work toward a more just outcome.

Even the most empathetic prosecutor cannot act on their enlightened instincts without a committed public defender to help them understand the stories of the people they judge.

Most prosecutors have their own version of a Christopher story. It is their experience with an exceptional and sympathetic defendant, who clearly made a mistake. A person with a story, who would certainly succeed if only given a break. Those stories are only known to the prosecutor through the lawyer. But for every Christopher there are hundreds of people processed through the system. Their stories are never considered. For every story a prosecutor can share about rescuing a worthy defendant from this unforgiving system, there are countless others about lives they selected to deposit into it. The prosecutors who see themselves as reform-minded never share these stories.

The fallacy of the "compassionate prosecutor as savior" narrative is that it assumes there is some subset of defendants who are worthy of being rescued. The compassionate prosecutor plucks these deserving few from the cruel system. But for everyone else, the system continues to churn. The compassionate prosecutor remains a critical cog in the machinery of that system. They do not reject the system itself. They simply believe there are some defendants who should be spared its wrath. The compassionate prosecutor does not, nor could they, transform the system to work for everyone. Undeserving defendants are left to suffer its harshness. And they suffer it at the hands of that same prosecutor.

This narrative assumes there are some who have stories worth hearing. It implicitly rejects the idea that all have stories. It also assumes the compassionate prosecutor can know who is worthy of mercy through intuition. It overlooks the critical role public defenders must play in bringing those stories to light. Without that piece the story is incomplete.

Adam was willing to listen to Christopher's story. Many prosecutors are not. We must transform the culture in prosecutor offices so that every prosecutor is open to hearing the stories of the people they accuse. We cannot just tell prosecutors who have been conditioned to see the people they prosecute as criminal to change their mind-set. We must engage in a process to develop empathetic prosecutors who understand that every person has a story they need to understand. But for that transformation to be impactful, we must also make sure every person has a defender with the skill and inclination to learn and amplify that story. That piece cannot be left out of the solution.

The idea that prosecutors are the key to criminal justice reform has helped fuel a nationwide campaign to elect reform-minded district attorneys. But the same faulty implications that struck me as I watched that TED talk—the idea that there is some subset of lives worth sparing, and that the prosecutor can engineer just outcomes without the advocates who are charged with giving voice to impacted people—are reflected in the larger movement.

First, even the best prosecutors have largely embraced a misguided notion that while there are some categories of impacted people who deserve mercy, for the most part those in the system are deserving of the treatment they receive. Second, these assumptions about the people deemed unworthy of mercy can most effectively be challenged through an army of public defenders. Collectively, these advocates have the power to give voice to 80 percent of the people in the system. Impacted families and communities depend on these defenders to ensure their stories are heard.

Reform-minded DAs believe they can unilaterally identify those worthy of being spared the wrath of the system. To prove their progressive credentials, they often talk about the groups that they agree are treated unfairly.

They generally agree that it is a waste of resources to prosecute some of the least offensive misbehavior. They usually appreciate the absurdity of pretrial detention of people for minor infractions simply because they are poor. They may show that they recognize the humanity of the most vulnerable by promising to hold police accountable when the most abusive conduct garners national attention. For this they have been hailed as "progressive." Yet, none of this is especially progressive. It is merely common sense. While I do not doubt that there are progressive people who become prosecutors for admirable reasons, the title "progressive prosecutor" is a misnomer. These are less punitive prosecutors. They can help forge a less cruel system. They do not have the power to transform it.

Those who "progressive" prosecutors would spare from the system's brutality tend to be lumped into relatively small categories. Without advocates to push these less punitive DAs to see the humanity of those they would otherwise overlook, their reform will be small.

I do not mean this as a criticism of any of these reform-minded prosecutors. I believe most are well intentioned. However, they are products of a culture that limits the imagination on what justice looks like. The benchmark is so low that what they view as progress still results in injustice.

Progressive prosecutors tend to champion reforms that the system is most likely to tolerate. They don't often push the outer boundaries, either because they understand the limits of the system or because they do not object to many of the existing practices. The prosecutor who feels good about 90 percent of the existing system and works to change 10 percent will be viewed as very progressive. But for most people impacted by the system, there will be little relief. Without a strategy to transform a culture that accepts the inhumane treatment of so many, reform will necessarily be small.

Over the last several years, reformers have become more aware of the crippling impact our tough-on-crime approach to criminal justice has had on our democracy. Frustrated with a lack of meaningful solutions, they have been drawn to a new crop of reform-minded prosecutors. There was a consensus growing around the belief that wayward prosecutors caused the damage, and a hope that a more thoughtful group of DAs could fix it.

But a look at the rise of some of these early "progressive" prosecutors illustrates the power of the cultural undertow of the waters in which they swim.

In spring 2015, Marilyn Mosby emerged as one of the earliest "progressive" prosecutors when she elected to prosecute Baltimore police officers in relation to the death of Freddie Gray. Her decision came at a time when there was growing frustration with prosecutors nationally who had been unwilling to hold rogue officers accountable. So praise for Mosby was understandable. But if you ask public defenders in Baltimore, her concern about black lives has not extended to those her office has charged.

Baltimore police have been accused of carrying BB guns to plant on suspects, stealing money during investigations, making false reports, and violating citizens' constitutional rights.[15] The tainted officers have been involved in many investigations still working their way through the system.

Despite Mosby's stated commitment to ferreting out abusive policing, her office has resisted public defenders' attempts to get information about these officers that might exonerate their clients. Public defenders would tell you that Mosby's office routinely uses oppressive pretrial detention practices and defends police who violate civil rights.[16] Mosby may have zealously pursued highly publicized police misconduct. But her office has unfortunately been tolerant of more routine and less-publicized police abuse.

A couple of New York City prosecutors were counted among the early wave of progressive DAs. Cy Vance, the former defense attorney turned Manhattan DA, self-identified as a race-conscious DA committed to reducing reliance on the criminal justice system to address the borough's woes.[17] But in an op-ed in the *New York Times*, reformer Josie Duffy Rice pointed out that Manhattan was significantly overrepresented among inmates at Rikers Island, the city's main jail complex, and that people of color were disproportionately represented among pretrial detainees and marijuana prosecutions.

Brooklyn's reform-minded DA, Eric Gonzalez, promised to refrain from requesting bail in most misdemeanor cases. But, in the months following this announcement, court watchers found his assistants doing the opposite.[18] Monitors identified so many exceptions to the new policy that line prosecutors found ways to continue to routinely request bail.[19] In one case, a Brooklyn ADA asked for $1,500 bail for someone accused of stealing four bars of soap.

In Boston, Rachael Rollins ran on a promise to end cash bail. She even released a list of fifteen offenses her office would no longer prosecute. One hundred days into her tenure, court watchers expressed disappointment. They found that Rollins's ADAs were still using cash bail to detain low-income defendants and prosecuting crimes on the "do not prosecute" list.[20] One example cited by court watchers involved a homeless man charged with larceny under $1,200. He was detained after the judge set bail at $200, an amount he could never afford. Rollins's ADA actually requested bail in the amount of $500.[21]

Among this early wave of reform-DAs, one who most fit the image of a change agent was Mark Gonzalez, elected as the head prosecutor in Corpus Christi, Texas. He was a career defense attorney with the words "Not Guilty" tattooed across his chest. Gonzalez immediately implemented a diversion program for people found in possession of small amounts of marijuana. While he rightfully received praise for his pretrial diversion program, critics have accused him of tolerating prosecutorial misconduct, and of keeping on staff senior prosecutors who embrace a "convict at any cost" mind-set.[22] We have become so accustomed to cruel prosecutors that we celebrate minor reforms while accepting an unjust status quo for everyone else.

In pointing out these stories, I do not mean to be especially critical of any particular DA. They have enough critics who prefer a return to an even more draconian norm. I believe they all sincerely view the status quo as unjust and are significant improvements over their predecessors. I assume they fully expected their policy pronouncements to be followed. I certainly do not mean to suggest that they directed, or even always knew of, the behavior of all the prosecutors in their offices. They all ran for office because they recognized problems with business as usual and, I presume, are sincere in their desire to address them. The problem that each of these anecdotes points out involves the power of culture. Each person operates within organizations that have limited their worldview of what real reform is and saddled them with assistant prosecutors who are incapable of deviating from the status quo.

They all rode into power with a menu of their favored policy prescriptions. But without a plan to transform an office culture that would ultimately drive the outcomes, progress can only be marginal. With line attorneys shaped by a tough-on-crime set of assumptions, it was inevitable that their reformist resumes would be littered with accusations that they overlooked abusive policing, wealth-based pretrial detention, racially discriminatory charging, and conviction-driven prosecutions.

But the internal culture of the DA's office is not the only thing that limits the transformative power of the reform-minded DA. They also face an external culture. Even when they can get their staff to embrace their vision, they operate within systems that are addicted to punishment. The DA who embraces truly bold change will run into powerful systemic resistance. Arguably, no one faced this reality more than Philadelphia's Larry Krasner.

In the wake of a Supreme Court ruling that required that juveniles previously sentenced to life without parole be resentenced, Krasner offered some of those affected plea deals that he believed were more just. However, some Philadelphia judges disagreed and refused to accept the deals.[23]

Concerned that Krasner might forgo prosecution of some gun cases, lawmakers in Pennsylvania passed legislation to give the state's attorney general authority to prosecute certain firearms offenses. Police who are concerned that the Philly DA will be too lenient can bypass him altogether. As if putting an exclamation point on the fact that this is directed at curtailing Krasner's reformist tendencies, the new law is set to expire when his term ends.[24]

The shortcoming of this progressive prosecutor movement is that it does not have a strategy to address either the cultural challenges within DA's offices or those that shape the broader system. As a result, most policy fixes are limited to those the existing culture can tolerate, and those that are too bold for the systems to accept are rendered impotent.

To be clear, I am not critical of incremental progress when it is part of a broader vision for truly transformative change. That is what our Close the Gap model is all about. But that requires a clearly stated transformative vision and a plan to achieve it. When decriminalizing marijuana is understood as part of a larger plan to achieve a real justice, that step is progressive. When a commitment to not locking up people who smoke weed *is* the reform plan, it is anything but. The latter can be easily accomplished with a policy prescription. The former requires culture change.

Getting the entire organization on board with a transformative vision first requires that leadership clearly articulate it. Next, leadership must clearly state the values at the heart of that vision. Then it must develop a strategy to get every member of the organization to internalize that value set. Firing resistant staff and hiring a new team that embraces the core values is an important first step. But it is not enough. The team must have a strategy to resist an external culture hostile to those values while always moving toward the aspirational ideal.

Just as we identified guiding values to drive our culture-change model in public defense, lead DAs must articulate a set of fundamental values prosecutors must embrace. Every prosecutor must respect the dignity of each person they charge. This means more than refraining from "stupid defendant jokes." They must do away with the commonly used labels steeped in degrading assumptions—labels like *defendant*, *offender*, and *criminal*, to name a few. They must respect constitutional protections and be committed to ferreting them out, rather than waiting to see if the defense brings them up. They must prioritize a just process over convictions. And they must respect the right to counsel and refuse to go forward when a person does not have the counsel they deserve. Every prosecutor must understand that it is better to forgo a prosecution than to engineer a conviction without ensuring all the protections consistent with justice are realized.

But hiring people who embrace these values is only a first step. Without doing more, the prosecutor will lose sight of these values after a short time in a system that is hostile to them. The office must have a training program that intentionally teaches prosecutors *how* to practice consistent with these values and gives them strategies to resist the pressure to abandon them. The leader must buttress this training with mentors who embrace these values, and who can help newer prosecutors confront practical challenges in ways consistent with them, and with a supportive community that shares the vision. This is the beginning of an effort to transform office culture.

But that is only a necessary first step for the prosecutor to help drive just outcomes. Once these prosecutors are conditioned to understand what real justice looks like and hear the voices of those impacted by their decisions, they need public defenders to share those stories. Without these advocates, they are left to make assumptions based solely on the offense charged. If line prosecutors do not hear the stories, they cannot mete out individualized justice in every case. If the elected district attorney and other leaders of the criminal justice system do not hear the collective voice of the communities impacted by their decisions, they cannot be entrusted to ensure justice is done for these communities. This is the most important contribution public defenders collectively make to the larger cause of transforming our justice system.

AS MARILYN MOSBY WAS preparing to charge the Baltimore police officers, members of neglected communities throughout Baltimore took to the streets to denounce their inhumane treatment at the hands of city officials. The reaction was severe. In the first week, nearly five hundred protesters were arrested. Many were illegally detained, swept up for simply being in the vicinity of protests, and thrown in jail cells.[25]

City officials were unconcerned about the constitutionality of their behavior or the inhumanity of the treatment visited upon the arrestees.

They left the protesters in cramped cells while they closed the courts and took the day off. This was routine injustice, the kind that goes unnoticed every day across America.

But it would not go unnoticed in Baltimore. If no one else felt a sense of urgency about the situation, the city's public defenders did. They immediately mobilized to challenge illegal detentions and to visit the terrified citizens who otherwise would have had no idea why they were being held or what to expect next. They worked heroically throughout the day to interview the detainees and fight to ensure their rights were protected. What these defenders found was jarring.

One public defender described the conditions under which the protesters were confined.[26] She described a section of the jail holding women, fifteen to a cell designed to hold only a few people for a few hours. There were no beds, pillows, or blankets. There was not enough room for all the women to lie down at the same time. The women were given four pieces of bread, a slice of American cheese, and a small bag of cookies three times a day. Rather than eat the bread, the women used it as pillows so they would not have to lay their heads on the filthy concrete floors. Each cell had one sink and one toilet. Water was scarce and the women were instructed that the water from the sink was not safe for drinking.

By the time the rest of the criminal justice system returned to work two days after the arrests, the public defenders had succeeded in demonstrating the illegality of many of the detentions and were able to get nearly half of the arrestees released without charges ever being filed.

But not only did these defenders vindicate the rights of the protesters, they shared their stories with the world. The public defenders took to social media, television, and blog posts to document the egregious treatment of those arrested. They made the nation aware of abusive behavior that usually goes unnoticed.

As I watched the story unfold, I could not hide my pride. I knew the young defenders who mobilized to tell these stories. They were part of the newly launched partnership between Gideon's Promise and the Maryland Public Defender. This was a new breed of public defender who embraced their power not only to fight for individuals in court but also to amplify the voices of the communities they serve more widely.

The power of public defenders to be the voice for populations that have been historically disregarded was on display that day. Just as it was on display when Michele Purvis-Harris issued a press release alerting the world to Judge Weill's attempts to bully her public defenders when they resisted injustice in Jackson, Mississippi. It was on display when Kelly Pretzer and a dozen public defenders got on buses and traversed Memphis to challenge the assumptions of the Mental Health Court judge about the people they represented. And it was on display when the public defenders in New Orleans mobilized the Second Line for Justice in partnership with the community to raise awareness of the unjust practices happening at the courthouse every day.

Transformative change requires that the voices of those impacted by the system be heard. Not just the voices of the least culpable few. All of them. When prosecutors and judges learn the stories of the people they judge they will understand them better. They will begin to get proximate. They will see them as human beings and treat them with greater dignity. In our criminal justice system, the public defender is the only vehicle through which 80 percent of those voices are heard. Collectively, public defenders are the channel through which these stories are infused into the system. That is more powerful than the power to punish. That carries with it the power to transform.

A POTENTIAL FUNDER ONCE asked Illy what Gideon's Promise does that is unique among criminal justice reformers. Her answer was short and to the point: "We are grooming a generation of lawyers who care."

The follow-up caught Illy off guard. "Why does that matter?" asked the potential funder.

When we first started our work with public defenders, we never considered the answer to this question. "Of course caring lawyers matter," we both thought. "Isn't that obvious?"

As I came to understand that the focus on criminal justice reform was largely seen through the lens of mass incarceration, the question made more sense. Funders wanted to know how our work led to fewer people behind bars and other quantifiable positive outcomes. Did our lawyers get shorter sentences? More dismissals? Lower bonds? What are the metrics? How could we quantify our work?

It certainly struck me that caring lawyers should map into these better outcomes. Caring motivates a lawyer to work harder, to invest more time, to be more creative, and to be less willing to settle for the status quo. So we began to look for funding to measure this success. Thanks to support from the Department of Justice and a partnership with a cutting-edge organization called Measures for Justice, we produced a report that suggests our lawyers got better outcomes.

Preliminary findings from this unpublished study showed that clients represented by Gideon's Promise lawyers were more likely to get pretrial diversion and less likely to plead guilty, and were incarcerated less often and had their cases resolved more quickly. But we still did not believe these outcomes were the best measure of the value we added to the criminal justice reform effort. There was something that caring lawyers brought to the fight for justice that was just not captured in this data.

We knew that there were times when our lawyers could not overcome an inevitable injustice, but that the relationship they built with the client had made a big difference.

I thought about the stories of accused men and women, sitting in jail for weeks without a single visit from a lawyer. Shuffled out of court after their initial appearance before a judge and deposited into a dirty jail cell. Not understanding what just happened, or when they would appear in court again. Worried about their job, their apartment, their family. The only thing they did understand was that they could not afford the cash bond that the judge set. They would sit in jail until their next court date.

I imagined two similarly situated defendants: Defendant 1 had a lawyer who did not have any information he believed was worth sharing with his client. He had not gotten anything about the case from the prosecutor. This lawyer saw a jail visit as a waste of time. Lawyer 1 did not visit Defendant 1. Defendant 2's lawyer visited the jail weekly. Although she had nothing more from the prosecution than Lawyer 1, she would take time to explain what was happening with the case. She provided a timeline that laid out when they could expect to get information from the state and when they might be back in court. She identified legal issues that she was exploring and shared the results of any early investigation. She promised to check in on family members for her client and always asked if there were any messages she could deliver for him.

It is obvious that this caring lawyer mattered. But metrics that measured the length of pretrial detention would suggest she added no value. If we only focus on case outcomes, treating the accused with dignity and respect become valueless. This cut against everything I believed about the problem with our justice system. It did not value the dignity of the accused.

I thought about the number of times I consoled a lawyer who had prepared so thoroughly and fought so hard at trial, only to have the client found guilty and given the maximum sentence. I knew that lawyer mattered to the client. I also knew that an army of lawyers insisting their clients be treated with dignity was critical to a longer-term culture shift. However, metrics that measured not-guilty verdicts or lengths of sentences would not capture that.

I thought about Elliott Johns thanking me after he was found guilty and sentenced to die in prison. I knew what it meant to his family that his lawyers treated their loved one with respect. I knew that many public defenders had similar stories of clients, and their loved ones, expressing deep gratitude for simply caring, even in the wake of what would be a devastating defeat by any measure.

We understood that transformative change required criminal justice professionals who genuinely cared about the dignity and humanity of every person. It was not enough to engineer a smaller prison population while leaving demeaning assumptions about marginalized populations in place.

An army of advocates for marginalized populations is the vehicle for challenging these assumptions and driving culture change. Therefore, the first step was to create a generation of public defenders who cared. The next step was to equip them to infuse the system with a new value set as they chiseled a more equitable narrative of justice.

Fifty years ago, Dr. King gave notice that the fight for justice demands that "we as a nation must undergo a radical revolution of values." He tried to get the nation to understand that equal justice required that we truly see the value in all human beings. Civil rights activists had long been challenging our collective assumptions about oppressed communities. They exposed the public to the abuse heaped on black, college-aged, lunch counter protesters. They showed the world African American teenagers forced to endure fire hoses and attack dogs. They understood that by exposing these stories to the American public, they could begin to shift attitudes.

I frequently ask myself how these activists would respond to today's funders. How would they quantify a national shift in values? I imagine a conversation in which activists meet with a funder to ask for support for their grassroots work. I imagine the funder asking for metrics and the activists responding with blank stares. And I imagine the funder offering a suggestion: "If you want us to fund your efforts to get white people to see black people as equals, you have to put a value on desegregation. Why don't we measure the cost savings of having to install half as many drinking fountains?"

Of course the economic benefit of not having to install twice as many water fountains did not get at the value of eradicating white supremacy in America. Segregation was a symptom of this disease. There was a clear moral imperative that we resist discrimination in America. That discrimination may have caused some economic inefficiencies was true. But if we measured progress in our ability to lessen these economic inefficiencies, we would risk doing so with policies that leave white supremacy intact. Measuring moral health is more challenging. But changing corrupted values, rather than only inefficient behavior, is critical to transformative change. Forcing people to come together through legislative change might be cause to celebrate. But it does not amount to a revolution of values. How does one measure the value of treating another person with dignity?

Interestingly, as I was thinking about how to measure the impact of caring lawyers, I found some promising ideas coming out of the medical field. There was a growing awareness in the medical profession that caring doctors mattered. Medical experts were finding that the ability to explain, listen, and empathize has a profound impact on patient well-being.[27] Researchers set out to demonstrate that patients treated by medical care providers who communicated with empathy experienced better patient outcomes.[28] There was a growing movement to teach medical professionals to practice empathetically.[29]

As I read about this movement in the medical profession, I was struck by how analogous it was to the work we were doing in the field of public defense. We had been trying to get criminal justice reformers to focus on the value of building more empathetic justice systems. The first step was showing that caring lawyers led to clients experiencing a better quality of justice, which, in turn, mapped into better client outcomes. Better outcomes meant much more than the length of a prison sentence. We had to capture the increased sense of dignity and self-worth impacted people experience when they interact with more just systems.

I learned that researchers in the medical field developed an empathy scale to gauge the degree to which medical providers embraced empathetic values.[30] They then developed an instrument to assess the extent to which empathetic caregiving resulted in better patient outcomes.[31]

This idea particularly resonated with me after being with my mother throughout her battle with cancer. After exhausting chemotherapy treatments and a double mastectomy, she thought the doctors were successful. Several months later, a lesion was found on her brain. We knew it was unlikely she would survive. My mother was devastated.

She was being treated at a hospital with the best cancer care in the region. However, at her initial appointment after getting the tragic news, the first person we met was a nurse. When she walked into the examination room, she was clearly preoccupied. Without any effort to make a connection with my mother, she immediately pulled out a clipboard and began rattling off questions. Questions that seemingly had nothing to do with my mother's illness. Have you ever had heart disease, gout, appendicitis? As she ran through the list, I could see the fear growing in my mother's face. Did this woman even know that my mother had cancer? I saw my mother turn white. She stopped listening.

We soon learned that my mother had less than six months to live. The best doctors in the world would not change that. But what would have made all the difference in the world was if that nurse had sat down with my mother, placed a gentle hand on her forearm, looked her in the eye, and said, "Ms. Rapping, let's talk about what you would like out of the next few months," and, "Let's work together to figure out how to make these next weeks all you want them to be."

I am sure medical professionals would agree that my mother received great medical care. But that was not all my mother needed at the time. What she really needed, that specialist was incapable of providing. My mother would have given her care provider a failing grade.

These studies that showed the value of empathetic medical care made me think of my mother. Of course, caring medical providers matter. Training medical professionals to practice empathetically would have a powerful impact on the profession.

As I read about this innovative work in the medical field, I grew excited. That evening I shared what I learned with Illy. She was equally intrigued. Could we develop a set of instruments to prove that caring lawyers matter to the clients who need them?

We soon partnered with a team of social-impact analytics experts at a UK-based firm called Get the Data. They were enthusiastic about the project, and we set out to develop the model. We developed a defender values spectrum scale to measure the extent to which our lawyers embrace the client-centered values at the heart of our theory of change, and a client expectations survey to gauge the degree to which clients associate the quality of justice with client-centered lawyers.

The exercise of developing an instrument to measure the correlation between caring lawyers and client experiences opened our eyes to more ambitious possibilities. We could use this approach to gauge the impact of client-centered public defender offices on the assumptions of judges and prosecutors. We could modify the tool to evaluate the degree to which these more empathetic judges and prosecutors mapped into client outcomes and how impacted communities perceived the justice system. And, ultimately, this methodology could be used to correlate how a system of empathetic justice administrators impacts public perceptions of justice and how poor people deserve to be treated. A system that can examine these qualitative measures along with quantifiable metrics will provide a much more accurate assessment of whether we are truly living up to our declared ideals. It can help reformers understand why the culture-change model we have developed in the public defense arena should be applied to every actor in the justice system.

ILLY IS ABSOLUTELY RIGHT about the criminal justice conveyor belt. Public defenders offer friction. They offer friction by ferreting out where police, prosecutors, and judges are cutting corners—shortcuts that would otherwise go unnoticed. Public defenders are needed to force system actors to follow the rules.

But they play another role—the role of pushing well-intentioned judges and prosecutors to see the human being before them and to treat them with dignity.

Without the public defender, judges will find new ways to detain people pretrial. We can give judges more discretion in sentencing, but without advocates they will fall back on the same practices.

We can cultivate a community of prosecutors who actually care about the people they prosecute (which requires a culture-change strategy), but we will still need public defenders to help them understand the people they judge.

Even with structural reform that allows judges and prosecutors to be less cruel, progressive judges and prosecutors cannot act on their progressive instincts without knowing the person before them. Only public defenders can offer these stories.

Experts in organizational culture call the visible manifestations of culture "artifacts." They are like the sores that appear on the skin from an undetectable virus. These sores help us understand the virus, but they are not the disease itself. A doctor may remove a sore or prescribe a palliative, but that does not cure the virus. New sores will reappear if the disease is not addressed.

The narrative about poor people at the heart of our consciousness is a disease that infects our democracy. The number of people in cages is a sore that results from this narrative. The ongoing consequences of a conviction that makes it impossible to reintegrate into society is a sore. The racial and economic disparities in the system are sores. Attempts to alleviate the suffering from these sores are welcome. But we must also attack the disease, lest new sores reappear. They may pop up in a different form. They may affect us differently. But until we kill the virus we will live with new sores.

Transforming culture—rewriting the narrative—is the criminal justice equivalent of killing the disease.

So what's next?

We can no longer afford a focus on policy fixes or look to progressive prosecutors to pursue less draconian practices against the same targeted communities, to the exclusion of developing a strategy to transform a narrative in which some lives are devalued. Equal justice requires that every person who has a hand in administering the system embrace the humanity of every life they touch and internalize a justice-centered set of values.

While we should develop ideas to help all Americans truly embrace justice-centered values, the first step, if we are to right the course of our misguided criminal justice ship, is to reshape the hearts and minds of criminal justice decision makers. Because most professionals who administer justice are lawyers, there is clearly a critical role for America's law schools to play in readying future lawyers to lead this charge. It starts with law schools actually teaching the values that are at the heart of our vision of justice and preparing them to live up to these values in systems hostile to them. This will require a new vision for legal academia, as law schools tend be fairly agnostic when it comes to teaching lawyering values.

But teaching law school graduates to understand the values that are at the heart of our democracy is not enough. Culture is powerful. Without ongoing support, these professionals will be quickly reshaped by systems that have abandoned these values. As law schools work on preparing lawyers to appreciate what justice requires of them, criminal justice professionals should adopt culture change plans similar to the model Gideon's Promise developed for public defenders. When public defenders, prosecutors, judges, and lawmakers all embrace a core set of values tied to our democratic ideal, we will see a shift in how we administer justice. Through values-based recruitment, training, and mentoring we can begin to mold these professionals to serve as criminal justice change agents.

Finally, we must build and support a strong army of public defenders to serve as the conscience of the system. It is only through public defenders that system actors remain proximate to impacted populations. This requires that we imagine a broader role for public defenders. They must be prepared to do more than be technically proficient at handling individual cases. They must embrace their role as partners with threatened communities. They must learn the stories of the people they serve and continually infuse the system with a more humane narrative. For it is only by being confronted with the humanity of the people accused of crimes that criminal justice actors can keep from slipping into the embrace of an otherizing worldview.

Each of these is an important step in fostering a humane justice system.

THE SYSTEM'S CONSCIENCE

PUBLIC DEFENDERS ARE the conscience of our criminal justice system. They are the force needed to remind us of the ideals at the heart of American democracy and to ensure we do not lose sight of the human beings the system is there to serve.

Without robust public defense, the most marginalized among us are rendered invisible. The criminal justice system has no conscience, no rudder. It can never be the system we aspire to have. My work over the past fifteen years has helped me understand how easily well-intentioned people can lose sight of the values they hold dearest in environments that have become hostile to them.

I was reminded of this on the most recent Father's Day, when my children gave me a screen print as a gift. The painting, by the artist Frank Wu, is simply titled "Indifference." It is an image that I frequently discuss when I am giving a talk about culture.

In the painting, several pairs of robotic legs walk past a homeless veteran, curled in a fetal position on a city sidewalk. The message is straightforward. We are all so inundated with misery, poverty, and suffering that it is human nature to become desensitized to it. We are helpless to fix it and focusing on it is too painful. So we learn to walk past it, as if we are robots. Without realizing it, we become indifferent.

Illy and I have always tried to raise our children to remain conscious of other people's struggles. We teach our children to treat every person with dignity. They have been raised to always do what they can to help others. For example, as a family, we take sandwiches or toiletries to the park to give to homeless men and women. The kids know never to walk past a person in need without looking them in the eye and acknowledging them. Illy and I try to instill that no person should ever be treated as though they are invisible. My children know that every person is worthy of respect.

I am proud of how they have responded to this life lesson. When my daughter Aaliyah was only six or seven years old, she would break open her piggy bank each morning and put change in a baggie to give to the homeless man we drove past on the way to school.

A few years ago, Lucas, at about the same age, asked me a question: "Dad, if you could be anyone in the world when you grow up"—I love that he is still waiting for that to happen—"other than me, Aaliyah, or Mommy, who would you be?"

I answered, "I don't know, Lucas. Who would you be?"

"I would either be Troy Polamalu," he said, referring to his favorite football player at the time, "or a homeless person."

"A homeless person?" I asked, a bit taken aback. "Why would you be a homeless person?"

"Because then I could know what it feels like and I could grow up to do something about it."

My children constantly remind me that the world has not yet stripped them of their sensitivity. Even someone like me, who spends a lot of time thinking about how we foster empathetic public defenders, needs reminding.

Not long ago, I was walking down the street with my daughter when a man asked if I could spare a dollar. I offered a faint smile and said, "I am sorry, sir, but I can't help you today." I kept walking, not giving the man a second thought. I then felt a tug on my sleeve. I looked down, and it was my daughter.

"Daddy?" she said.

"Yes, baby?"

"Daddy, doesn't that man need a dollar more than you?"

My first thought was, "Of course he does."

My next thought was, "Who did she learn that from?"

I knew the answer. She learned it from me and from Illy. It was a reminder that any one of us can lose sight of the values we hold dearest—the values we teach our own children—if we do not guard against indifference.

One of the greatest gifts my children have given me is that they frequently remind me when my actions may be inconsistent with the values I have taught them. They never let me stray too far from my ideals. They serve as my conscience. We all need that.

ACKNOWLEDGMENTS

AS I RAISE TWO AMAZING CHILDREN, I always strive to make sure they have both a good head and a good heart. I learned this from my parents. Each modeled this ideal. My father died when I was twenty-six years old. He never saw me go to law school. But for the first half of my life, he was the primary person who helped me develop my mind—the "head" part. He guided me through high school, college, and graduate school. My mother was my closest confidant as I worked my way through law school and into public defense. I primarily learned my social justice values through her— the "heart" part. My mother was my editor for every writing project before this book. She constantly urged me to write a book. She died the year before I began writing *Gideon's Promise*. Without my parents, there would be no book, no Gideon's Promise, no me. They deserve my greatest thanks.

Both my parents avoided having to deal with me through the book-writing process. My immediate family did not. My wife, Illy, and my children, Aaliyah and Lucas, were the inspiration that kept me focused when I felt like writing a book was just too much on top of being a full-time law professor and the president of an ever-growing nonprofit. Illy has been my partner in every aspect of my life—personal, professional, and parental. I am ever so grateful for you, Baby. My children remind me every day why I can't stop working to make a better world for those who will inherit what we leave. I love you, Lucas and LiLi.

Thanks to my sister, Alison Rapping, who has walked with me for fifty-three years as we honed our commitments to social justice. No one did more to help Illy and me get Gideon's Promise off the ground than you. "Pap," there would be no Gideon's Promise without you. You are a terrific best friend and social entrepreneurship partner.

As far as writing goes, only three people other than Illy read the manuscript before the book went to production. My sister and my closest friend, Andrew Jaffee, read the final version. They each know Gideon's Promise well but do not live it day-to-day—they are both close enough and far enough removed to help me appreciate whether I captured the essence of Gideon's Promise for my intended audience.

The third person is my amazing editor at Beacon, Rakia Clark. Rakia read the manuscript multiple times, and helped me get well over a hundred thousand words down to a powerful and manageable manuscript. I am grateful to Rakia, and to Beacon Press, for believing in this book, and for believing that public defenders deserve to be part of the broader criminal justice conversation. I am fortunate to have found a publisher that understands that vision.

Thanks to Marcus Rediker for your guidance and counsel along the journey.

Thanks to Atlanta's John Marshall Law School for supporting me as I took on this project and for the past thirteen years as I built Gideon's Promise while a member of its amazing faculty. I also must thank my two students who provided research assistance, Sharif Fulcher and Robert Leone.

As I was thinking about this acknowledgment, I initially focused on who helped me write the book. I mean literally, as in after I first put pen to paper. It was a short list. It then dawned on me that the list was short because I was narrowly focused on those who gave editorial input. In fact, this book was written before I developed a relationship with Beacon. It was written by countless people, all of whom deserve more thanks than I can give. It was written by the people who taught me to be a public defender, who gave me the opportunities I had to shape my criminal justice outlook, who supported Illy and me as we built Gideon's Promise, and who have continued to spread its philosophy nationwide.

I have to thank all of my family at the DC Public Defender Service for teaching me what it means to be a public defender, modeling client-centered representation, and providing me guidance and counseling as I developed into the lawyer I became. With respect to my early development as a public defender I owe special thanks to my mentor, Jonathan Stern, and my training director, Mary Kennedy. It was my PDS family who supported me in those early years, and who continue to be at the center of a growing community of Gideon's Promise supporters.

I have to thank Stephen Bright, who has been my greatest influence since I moved to the South to do this work. I also thank Sam Starks and Gary Parker for joining Steve in encouraging me to take a chance and move to Georgia.

Thanks to the Totenberg-Green family—particularly Aunt Amy, Uncle Ralph, and Clara for sharing your home with me, Illy, and three-month-old Aaliyah when we first moved to Atlanta, and for being our family ever since.

Thanks to the Southern Center for Human Rights, which housed the Southern Public Defender Training Center when we first started, and provided Illy and me office space as we evolved into an independent non-profit organization.

Thanks to our incredible staff, both past and present, who worked tirelessly to make the organization run because of a shared commitment to its vision. Special thanks to Erika Berrien, who has been with us since 2011. You were our first staff member and have always been one of the most important. We will not let you go.

Gary Kohlman deserves special recognition for being the catalyst behind development of our inaugural board. We could not ask for a greater champion. He, and inaugural cochair Mark Rochon, refused to let Gideon's Promise fail in the early days and continue to rally support to our cause. I'd be remiss to not recognize, in addition to Gary and Mark, members of the inaugural board: Mark Stephens and Claudia Saari—who were also leaders of two of our earliest partner offices, Blair Brown, Steve Bumbaugh, Cait Clarke, Ernie Lewis, and Michele Roberts. Thanks are also due to all of our board members since those early days. Our board has always taken ownership of Gideon's Promise and been completely invested in the success of our public defenders.

I also want to recognize Emmet Bondurant, another founding board member, who was the chair of the Georgia Public Defender Standards Council when I first came to Georgia and has been an ambassador for our work ever since.

Thanks to all of the public defender offices that have partnered with Gideon's Promise over the years. We now have a presence in more than half the states from coast to coast. Special thanks to our two original partners: Atlanta Fulton County Public Defender and Orleans Public Defenders were the first two offices to join us in 2007 and have been steadfast allies ever since. Recognition also is deserved by the Maryland Office of the Public Defender and its director, Paul DeWolfe, for working with us to establish our first statewide partnership in 2014.

We could not build this movement without an all-volunteer faculty of some of the most committed and talented public defenders from across the country. You give so much time, talent, and heart to our defenders and the communities they serve. There are dozens of defenders who are part of this story. I regretfully cannot name them all. But there are some who have been consistently involved and/or have continued to support our community. I feel compelled to mention some of them by name. Thanks to Brandi Harden, Heather Pinckney, David Singleton, Steve Singer, Tim Saviello, Joseph Ross, Russell Gabriel, Shawna Geiger, Samantha Buckingham, Chris Flood, Andre Vitale, and Jenny Andrews. You have each given so much of yourselves, from the early days of the Georgia Honors Program and SPDTC to the present.

There is an extra-special group of people who have not only invested in training and mentoring hundreds of our public defenders but have worked with me week after week, month after month, year after year, to develop training programs and curriculum. Cathy Bennett, Patrice Fulcher, Sean Maher, Mary Moriarty, and Jeff Sherr signed on to be part of this vision back in the early days of the Georgia Honors Program. Violeta Chapin, Lori James-Townes, William Montross, David Patton, and Dehlia Umunna joined in the early days of SPDTC. We simply could not have built this movement without this team. Extra gratitude to Sean and Patrice, who have been sounding boards since before the Georgia Honors Program launched, and have been two of my rocks ever since. I love all you guys!

I want to take some space to remember three of the best lawyers I have known, who gave so much of their time to support our community. Each left us way too soon but continue to inspire through the memory and lessons they left. Steve Greenberg, Tamar Meekins, and Mike Starr—thank you for what you left this world!

At Gideon's Promise we recognize that public defenders are ultimately responsible for amplifying the voices of impacted communities. We could not fulfill this obligation without working closely with the communities we serve. Thanks to the communities public defenders serve that are working with public defenders to resist injustice and fulfill our democratic promise. I am especially grateful to all of the amazing people who have had experience with the criminal justice system and take time to help our defenders do their jobs better. I am so appreciative of Daryl Atkinson, Susan Burton, Norris Henderson, Regina Kelly, Billy Neal Moore, Lane Nelson, Serena Nunn, Tyra Patterson, and John Thompson (rest in peace dear friend). Dr. Sharon Davis-Williams (you have been critical to our leadership team) and Tamara Cotman, thank you for bringing what you learned through your experience with the criminal legal system to our team at Gideon's Promise. Your selflessness has benefited tens of thousands of people served by our public defenders each year.

We are grateful for other nonprofits in the criminal justice space who recognize the critical role of public defenders and show them love and support. Special shout out to Raj Jayadev, Alec Karakatsanis, and Gina Clayton-Johnson for being invaluable partners in this struggle.

We are thankful for media outlets that have used their platform to lift up public defenders; special thanks to Rose Scott of Atlanta's WABE, who has always shown love to Gideon's Promise and to the movement we are building.

Thank you to all of our amazing institutional funders. We are particularly grateful to those of you who believed in us, and invested in us, in the early days: Kim Ball, Maya Harris, Kirsten Levingston, and Lenny Noisette. Thanks!

We owe a huge debt of gratitude to the MacArthur Foundation for recognizing, and lifting up, the vision that Gideon's Promise brings to the ongoing struggle for criminal justice transformation.

To all of our individual donors—you are our life's blood.

We have also been so fortunate to have developed a groundswell of community support. To all of our community supporters, and in particular Dr. Ben Williams, you are the best!

Thanks to the Cumberland School of Law at Samford University, and particularly then-dean John Carroll, for providing us a home for our first eight years. Thanks to the University of Mississippi School of Law, and especially Tucker Carrington and Cliff Johnson, for providing us a home when we outgrew space at Cumberland.

Thanks to Morehouse College, Spelman College, and the Atlanta Bar Association Summer Law Internship Program for always providing us exceptional interns. These students are the future!

To the twenty-four law schools from coast to coast that are part of our Law School Partnership Program, we appreciate you joining forces with us to build pipelines that bring some of the best future public defenders to the places where they are most needed.

Of course, we could not build this movement without the hundreds of public defenders who participate in Gideon's Promise. Endless love to the members of our Core Program, our incredible alumni, and the leaders and supervisors we work with in our partner offices. As our alumni increasingly become leaders in this community, our sense that transformation is coming grows!

Last, but not least, *thank you* to all of the public defenders working tirelessly to give voice to communities that have been deemed expendable in our modern approach to criminal justice. Included in this group of "public defenders" are all of the social workers, mitigation specialists, investigators, support staff, and other nonlegal professionals. Being a public defender is about more than having a law degree and standing next to a person without means. It is about a mind-set. I have met countless nonlegal professionals who embrace this mind-set and who are true "public defenders." To all of the public defenders out there—whether or not you have a law degree—thank you. Because of you, I am confident we will fulfill the promise of equal justice—Gideon's Promise.

NOTES

CHAPTER 1: VOICE FOR THE VOICELESS

1. The Awesomer, "Baseball, Hot Dogs, Apple Pie, and Chevrolet—2015 Edition," published July 15, 2015, YouTube video, 0:59, https://www.youtube.com/watch?v=21rUjwAn5GI.

2. National Research Council, *The Growth of Incarceration in the United States: Exploring Causes and Consequences* (Washington, DC: National Academies Press, 2014), 35, http://johnjay.jjay.cuny.edu/nrc/nas_report_on_incarceration.pdf; "Mass Incarceration," American Civil Liberties Union, https://www.aclu.org/issues/smart-justice/mass-incarceration, accessed September 6, 2019.

3. Alexi Jones, "Correctional Control 2018: Incarceration and Supervision by State," Prison Policy Initiative, December 2018, https://www.prisonpolicy.org/reports/correctionalcontrol2018.html.

4. Peter Wagner and Wendy Sawyer, *States of Incarceration: The Global Context 2018* (Northampton, MA: Prison Policy Initiative, June 2018), https://www.prisonpolicy.org/global/2018.html.

5. Adam Looney, "5 Facts about Prisoners and Work, before and after Incarceration," Brookings Institution, March 14, 2018, https://www.brookings.edu/blog/up-front/2018/03/14/5-facts-about-prisoners-and-work-before-and-after-incarceration.

6. Adam Looney and Nicholas Turner, "Work and Opportunity before and after Incarceration," Brookings, March 14, 2018, https://www.brookings.edu/research/work-and-opportunity-before-and-after-incarceration.

7. "Racial Disparity," Sentencing Project, https://www.sentencingproject.org/issues/racial-disparity, accessed November 10, 2019.

8. US Census Bureau, Quick Facts, Population Estimates, July 1, 2018, https://www.census.gov/quickfacts/fact/table/US/PST045218.

9. Peter Wagner, "Incarceration Is Not an Equal Opportunity Punishment," *Prison Policy Initiative*, August 28, 2012, http://www.prisonpolicy.org/articles/notequal.html.

10. Sentencing Project, "Racial Disparity."

11. "Half of Young Black Men in Nation's Capital in or Being Pursued by Criminal Justice System," National Drug Strategy Network, http://www.ndsn.org/sepoct97/blackmen.html, accessed May 15, 2013 (accounting also for those in prison or jail, on probation or parole, out on bond or being sought on an arrest warrant).

12. "Criminal Justice Facts," Sentencing Project, https://www.sentencingproject.org/criminal-justice-facts.

13. John Grisham, "Why the Innocent End Up in Prison," *Chicago Tribune*, March 14, 2018, https://www.chicagotribune.com/opinion/commentary/ct-perspec -innocent-prisoners-innocence-project-death-row-dna-testing-prosecutors-0315 -story.html. More conservative estimates put the figure at between 2 and 5 percent. Matt Ferner, "A Record Number Of People Were Exonerated in 2015 for Crimes They Didn't Commit," *Huffington Post*, February 3, 2016, https://www.huffpost .com/entry/exonerations-2015_n_56ac0374e4b00b033aaf3da9.

14. Alan Berlow, "Requiem for a Public Defender," *American Prospect*, December 19, 2001, https://prospect.org/article/requiem-public-defender.

15. Berlow, "Requiem for a Public Defender."

16. Berlow, "Requiem for a Public Defender."

17. Berlow, "Requiem for a Public Defender."

18. Stephen Bright, "Counsel for the Poor: The Death Sentence Not for the Worst Crime but for the Worst Lawyer," *Yale Law Journal* 103 (1994): 1836.

19. Bright, "Counsel for the Poor," 1838.

20. Bright, "Counsel for the Poor," 1838.

21. Henry Weinstein, "Georgia Fails Its Poor Defendants, Report Says," *Los Angeles Times*, December 13, 2002, http://articles.latimes.com/2002/dec/13/nation /na-indigent13.

22. Weinstein, "Georgia Fails Its Poor Defendants."

23. Amy Bach, *Ordinary Injustice: How America Holds Court* (New York: Holt, 2009), 17.

24. Bach, *Ordinary Injustice*, 17.

25. Berlow, "Requiem for a Public Defender."

26. Berlow, "Requiem for a Public Defender."

27. Berlow, "Requiem for a Public Defender."

28. Max Rivlin-Nadler, "Our Right to an Attorney Is in Jeopardy," *Vice*, October 5, 2015, https://www.vice.com/en_us/article/nn94ad/the-right-to-an-attorney -is-in-jeopardy-456.

29. Jaeah Lee, Hannah Levintova, and Brett Brownell, "Charts: Why You're in Deep Trouble If You Can't Afford a Lawyer," *Mother Jones*, May 6, 2013, https:// www.motherjones.com/politics/2013/05/public-defenders-gideon-supreme-court -charts.

30. Bach, *Ordinary Injustice*, 17.

31. David Von Drehle, "If Your Lawyer Wants You Executed," *Time*, June 2, 2008, http://content.time.com/time/nation/article/0,8599,1811174-1,00.html.

32. Bach, *Ordinary Injustice*, 15.

33. Bach, *Ordinary Injustice*, 15.

34. Bach, *Ordinary Injustice*, 17.

35. Bach, *Ordinary Injustice*, 13.

36. Alexandra Natapoff, "Why Misdemeanors Aren't So Minor," *Slate*, April 27, 2012, http://www.slate.com/articles/news_and_politics/jurisprudence/2012/04 /misdemeanors_can_have_major_consequences_for_the_people_charged.html.

CHAPTER 2: THE EVOLVING NARRATIVE OF JUSTICE

1. William Blackstone, *Commentaries on the Laws of England* (William Carey edition, 1916), 2596.

2. Duncan v. Louisiana, 391 U.S. 145, 152 (1968). As the court articulated in *Duncan*: among the resolutions adopted by the first Congress of the American

colonies (the Stamp Act Congress) on October 19, 1765—resolutions deemed by their authors to state "the most essential rights and liberties of the colonists"—was the declaration: "Trial by jury is the inherent and invaluable right of every British subject in the colonies."

3. Nancy J. King, "Duncan v. Louisiana: How Bigotry in the Bayou Led to the Federal Regulation of State Juries," in *Criminal Procedure Stories*, ed. Carol S. Steiker (New York: Foundation Press, 2006), 261.

4. *Duncan*, 391 U.S. at 156.

5. Ira Glasser, V*isions of Liberty: The Bill of Rights for All Americans* (New York: Random House, 1995), 41.

6. Powell v. Alabama, 287 U.S. 45, 68–69 (1932). The court discussed the importance of counsel as follows:

> The right to be heard would be, in many cases, of little avail if it did not comprehend the right to be heard by counsel. Even the intelligent and educated layman has small and sometimes no skill in the science of law. If charged with a crime, he is incapable, generally, of determining for himself whether the indictment is good or bad. He is unfamiliar with the rules of evidence. Left without the aid of counsel he may be put on trial without a proper charge, and convicted upon incompetent evidence, or evidence irrelevant to the issue or otherwise inadmissible. He lacks both the skill and knowledge adequately to prepare his defense, even though he have a perfect one. He requires the guiding hand of counsel at every step in the proceedings against him. Without it, though he be not guilty, he faces the danger of conviction because he does not know how to establish his innocence. If that be true of men of intelligence, how much more true is it of the ignorant and illiterate, or those of feeble intellect.

7. Gina Kolata, "Simpson Trial Shows Need for Proper Use of Forensic Science, Experts Say," *New York Times*, October 11, 1995, http://www.nytimes.com/1995/10/11/us/simpson-trial-shows-need-for-proper-use-of-forensic-science-experts-say.html?pagewanted=all.

8. "The O. J. Simpson Murder Trial, by the Numbers," *Los Angeles Times*, April 5, 2016, http://www.latimes.com/entertainment/la-et-archives-oj-simpson-trial-by-the-numbers-20160405-snap-htmlstory.html.

9. Bill Wallace, "Ng Case Cost Taxpayers Nearly $10 Million," *SFGATE*, February 25, 1999, http://www.sfgate.com/news/article/Ng-Case-Cost-Taxpayers-Nearly-10-Million-2945106.php; "O. J. Simpson Civil Trial: The O. J. Simpson Murder Trial, by the Numbers," *USA Today*, October 18, 1996, https://usatoday30.usatoday.com/news/index/nns062.htm.

10. Jane Wells, "20 Years Later, Winning OJ Civil Suit Was Never a 'Pot of Gold,'" CNBC, June 12, 2004, https://www.cnbc.com/2014/06/10/oj-simpson-murder-money-trial.html.

11. Jason Guerrasio, "How O. J. Simpson Paid for the 'Dream Team' of Lawyers on His Murder Trial," *Business Insider*, June 19, 2016, http://www.businessinsider.com/how-oj-simpson-paid-for-the-dream-team-2016-6.

12. Gina Kolata, "Simpson Trial."

13. "The O. J. Verdict," *Frontline*, PBS, October 4, 2005.

14. "The O. J. Verdict."

15. "The O. J. Verdict."

16. "Lynching in America: Confronting the Legacy of Racial Terror," Equal Justice Initiative, https://eji.org/reports/lynching-in-america, accessed June 29, 2018.

17. Anne Emanuel, *Elbert Parr Tuttle: Chief Justice of the Civil Rights Revolution* (Athens: University of Georgia Press, 2011), 1–4.

18. Bill Broadway, "Relentless Advocate of Mercy," *Washington Post*, February 6, 1999, https://www.washingtonpost.com/archive/local/1999/02/06/relentless -advocate-of-mercy/f7728141-c915-4207-9f57-85d5090ac43e.

19. "Mrs. Clinton Campaign Speech," C-SPAN, January 25, 1996, https:// www.c-span.org/video/?c4582473/user-clip-hillary-clinton-superpredators-1996.

20. Mike Royko, "Jesse Jackson's Message Is Too Advanced for Most," *Baltimore Sun*, December 3, 1993, https://www.baltimoresun.com/news/bs-xpm-1993 -12-03-1993337169-story.html.

21. "The O. J. Verdict."

CHAPTER 3: ROUTINE INJUSTICE

1. Marc Bookman, "This Man Sat in Jail for 110 Days—After He Already Did His Time," *Mother Jones*, August 6, 2015, https://www.motherjones.com/politics /2015/08/public-defender-cordele-georgia-eric-wyatt.

2. Richard Fausset, "Murder Trial Cost Puts the Heat on Georgia Judge," *Los Angeles Times*, October 26, 2007, http://articles.latimes.com/2007/oct/26/nation/na -nichols26.

3. Rhonda Cook, "Nichols' Defense Costs 3.2 Million," *Atlanta Journal-Constitution*, July 22, 2009, http://www.ajc.com/news/local/nichols-defense-costs -million/xazeVQwMAyFKe4joU8ZRGJ.

4. Fausset, "Murder Trial Cost Puts the Heat on Georgia Judge."

5. Fausset, "Murder Trial Cost Puts the Heat on Georgia Judge."

6. Marie Pierre-Py, "Public Defender System Fails Georgians and Their Lawyers," *Atlanta Journal-Constitution*, March 30, 2009, on file with author.

7. State v. Peart, 621 So. 2nd 780 (1993).

8. *State v. Peart*, 790.

9. *State v. Peart*, 791–92.

10. Catherine L. Schaefer and Robert L. Spangenberg, *The Orleans Indigent Defender Program: An Overview* (February 1997), 11, prepared for Orleans Indigent Defender Program, on file with author.

11. Independence is the first of the ABA's ten principles of a public-defense delivery system. American Bar Association, "Ten Principles of a Public Defense System," February 2002, https://www.americanbar.org/content/dam/aba/administrative/legal _aid_indigent_defendants/ls_sclaid_def_tenprinciplesbooklet.authcheckdam.pdf.

12. Louisiana Rev. Statute Ann. §§ 15:144, 145, 145.1 & 151.2. This legislation was repealed. See Louisiana Rev. Statute Ann. §§ 15:141–43, 149.2, and 152–84 (2007).

13. James Gill, "Fight Looms for Control of Indigent Defense," *Times-Picayune*, April 25, 2007. "State law gives the judges the power to appoint indigent board members from candidates recommended by local bar associations. But long before Katrina, the judges of New Orleans quit asking for nominations and made appointments off their own bat. The statutes impose no term limits, and appointees remained in place as long as they wished. State law requires the judges to 'adopt rules and regulations to establish policy regarding the appointment of

members to the indigent defender board,' but they haven't done so." Available in Jonathan Rapping, "Directing the Winds of Change: Using Organizational Culture to Reform Indigent Defense," *Loyola Journal of Public Interest Law* 9 (2009): 187n36.

14. See National Legal Aid & Defender Association, *A Strategic Plan to Ensure Accountability & Protect Fairness in Louisiana's Criminal Courts: A Report to the Louisiana State Bar Association and the Louisiana Bar Foundation* (September 22, 2006), 66n11, http://www.nlada.net/sites/default/files/la_strategicplantoensure accountabilityjserio9-2006_report.pdf.

15. Nicholas Chiarkis, D. Alan Henry, and Randolph N. Stone, *An Assessment of the Intermediate and Longer-Term Needs of the New Orleans Public Defender System* (Washington, DC: BJA National Training and Technical Assistance Initiative Project, American University, April 10, 2006), 8, http://lpdb.la.gov/Serving%20The% 20Public/Reports/txtfiles/pdf/An%20Assessment%20of%20the%20Immediate %20and%20Longer%20Term%20Needs%20of%20the%20Orleans%20Public% 20Defense%20System.pdf.

16. Chiarkis, Henry, and Stone, *An Assessment of the Intermediate and Longer-Term Needs of the New Orleans Public Defender System*, 7.

17. Chiarkis, Henry, and Stone, *An Assessment of the Intermediate and Longer-Term Needs of the New Orleans Public Defender System*, 7.

18. Chiarkis, Henry, and Stone, *An Assessment of the Intermediate and Longer-Term Needs of the New Orleans Public Defender System*, 8.

19. Southern Center for Human Rights (SCHR), *A Report on Pre- and Post-Katrina Indigent Defense in New Orleans* (March 2006), 9–10, https://www.schr.org /files/post/katrina%20report.pdf.

20. SCHR, *A Report on Pre- and Post- Katrina Indigent Defense in New Orleans*.

21. Schaefer and Spangenberg, *The Orleans Indigent Defender Program*, 21.

22. National Legal Aid & Defender Association, *A Strategic Plan to Ensure Accountability & Protect Fairness in Louisiana's Criminal Courts*, 65n10.

CHAPTER 4: A MIGHTY STREAM

1. Abir Hassan, "Strategy or Culture: Which Is More Important?," LinkedIn, August 10, 2016, https://www.linkedin.com/pulse/drucker-said-culture-eats -strategy-breakfast-abir-hassan.

2. Barbara Allen Babcock, "Defending the Guilty," *Cleveland State Law Review* 32 (1983): 175.

CHAPTER 5: THE FIRST STEP IS RESISTANCE

1. Available in Jonathan Rapping, "Directing the Winds of Change: Using Organizational Culture to Reform Indigent Defense," *Loyola Journal of Public Interest Law* 9 (2009): 196–97.

2. Gwen Filosa, "Charges Dropped against City Investigator in Child Rape Case," *Times-Picayune*, January 10, 2010, http://www.nola.com/crime/index.ssf /2010/01/charges_dropped_against_city_i.html.

3. Stephen B. Bright to Michael J. Bowers and other members of the Judicial Nomination Commission, June 16, 2010, available at http://d3gcj4nzojrapq.cloud front.net/wp-content/uploads/2010/08/Mack-Crawford-letters.pdf.

4. This model builds on the work of scholars including Charles Ogletree and Abbe Smith, who have explored public defender motivators. Charles Ogletree, "Beyond Justifications: Seeking Motivations to Sustain Public Defenders," *Harvard*

Law Review 106 (1993): 1239; Abbe Smith, "Too Much Heart and Not Enough Heat: The Short Life and Fractured Ego of the Empathetic, Heroic Public Defender," *U.C. Davis Law Review* 37 (2004): 1203.

5. While we use "social worker" as one of the three motivators, it has been pointed out to us by some social workers that this might suggest social workers are not also warriors and movement builders. This critique is valid, and resonates with me very much. Social workers, investigators, and non-legal staff in public defender offices each play all three roles at different times. The label is meant to highlight the special aptitude social workers tend to have in connecting with the people we serve. It is not meant to be limiting to professionals who serve as social workers in public defender offices. In recognition of this concern, Jeff has used other labels like "counselor" or "helper" when discussing this motivator.

6. Stephen B. Bright and Sia M. Sanneh, "Fifty Years of Defiance and Resistance after Gideon v. Wainwright," *Yale Law Journal* 122, no. 70 (2013): 2150–65.

7. Jan Skutch, "Savannah's Christopher Middleton Lends Voice, Skills to 'Little People,'" *Savannah Morning News*, July 25, 2011, http://www.savannahnow .com/accent/2011–07–25/savannahs-christopher-middleton-lends-voice-skills -little-people.

CHAPTER 6: DAVID'S SLINGSHOT

1. Budget Hearings before the House Commission on Finance, Ways and Means, 108th Leg., 1st Session (2013), http://tnga.granicus.com/MediaPlayer.php ?view_id=217&clip_id=6951.

2. "Guy Thomas Wilkinson," Avvo.com, https://www.avvo.com/attorneys /38320-tn-guy-wilkinson-1710601.html. According to AVVO, Guy Wilkinson was barred in Tennessee in 1977.

3. Ronald A. Heifetz and Marty Linsky, *Leadership on the Line: Staying Alive through the Dangers of Leading* (Boston: Harvard Business Review Press, 2002). The most common cause of failure of leadership is produced by treating adaptive challenges as if they were technical problems.

4. Fielding Pringle, e-mail message to author, April 5, 2017.

5. Pringle, e-mail.

6. Dawn Deaner, chief public defender, Nashville Metro Public Defender's Office, interview with author, March 15, 2018.

7. "Tremé," NewOrleansOnline.com, http://www.neworleansonline.com/tools /neighborhoodguide/treme.html, accessed July 19, 2018.

8. Mark Hertsgaard, "Shortchanged: New Orleans Public Defender Turns Away Felony Cases," *Daily Beast*, November 25, 2016, https://www.thedailybeast .com/new-orleans-public-defender-turns-away-felony-cases.

9. Hertsgaard, "Shortchanged."

10. Hertsgaard, "Shortchanged."

11. Derwyn Bunton, "Public Defender Reform Shows Both the Challenge and the Possibility of Post-Katrina New Orleans," *Huffington Post*, August 26, 2016, https://www.huffingtonpost.com/derwyn-bunton/new-orleans-public-defenders _b_8039698.html.

12. Nicole Lewis and Maurice Chammah, "Seven Years Behind Bars for Two Joints—and Now He's Free," Marshall Project, April 12, 2018, https://www.the marshallproject.org/2018/04/12/seven-years-behind-bars-for-two-joints-and-now -he-s-free.

13. "Orleans Parish Public Defenders, Clients Protest against Injustices," WDSU.com, December 16, 2014, YouTube video, 1:35, https://www.youtube.com /watch?v=9Ljj6dYhq1s.

14. Derwyn Bunton, "When the Public Defender Says, 'I Can't Help,'" *New York Times*, February 19, 2016, https://www.nytimes.com/2016/02/19/opinion /when-the-public-defender-says-i-cant-help.html; Tina Peng, "I'm a Public Defender. It's Impossible for Me to Do a Good Job Representing My Clients," *Washington Post*, September 3, 2015, https://www.washingtonpost.com/opinions/our -public-defender-system-isnt-just-broken—its-unconstitutional/2015/09/03/aadf 2b6c-519b-11e5-9812-92d5948a4of8_story.html?utm_term=.bf7712efb351; "Defenseless," *60 Minutes*, CBS, April 16, 2017, https://www.cbs.com/shows/60 _minutes/video/fSRo_PmwJZFxUXGaZ_VvoewXS6rWxyOA/defenseless; John Oliver, "Public Defenders," *Last Week Tonight with John Oliver*, September 13, 2015, YouTube video, 14:59, https://www.youtube.com/watch?v=USkEzLuzmZ4.

15. Lorelei Laird, "Starved of Money for Too Long, Public Defender Offices Are Suing—and Starting to Win," *ABA Journal* (January 1, 2017), http://www .abajournal.com/magazine/article/the_gideon_revolution.

16. Zach Despart, "Harris County Public Defender Keeps Job amid Questions from Commissioners Court," *Houston Chronicle*, June 12, 2018, https://www.chron .com/news/politics/houston/article/Commissioners-Court-grills-Harris-County-s -12988278.php.

17. Emily Lane, "Prosecution of Orleans Public Defender's Investigator 'Destroyed My Life,' She Says: Report," *Times-Picayune*, May 2, 2017, https://www .nola.com/crime/index.ssf/2017/05/prosecution_of_orleans_public.html.

18. Steven Hale, "Metro Public Defender's Office Creates 'Client Advisory Board,'" *Nashville Scene*, July 7, 2017, https://www.nashvillescene.com/news/pith -in-the-wind/article/20866885/metro-public-defenders-office-creates-client -advisory-board.

19. "Nashville PDO Forms Client Advisory Board," Nashville Public Defender, http://publicdefender.nashville.gov/about-us/client-community-advisory-board.

20. "The Defend Nashville Initiative," Nashville Public Defender, http:// publicdefender.nashville.gov/defend-nashville-initiative/introduction.

21. Dawn Deaner, "Introducing the Defend Nashville Initiative," https://www .courtinnovation.org/sites/default/files/media/document/2018/Introducing%20 the%20Defend%20Nashville%20Initiative.pdf.

22. Rahim Buford, "Empowering the Unheard," *Medium*, October 31, 2016, https://medium.com/@TheCFSY/empowering-the-unheard-voices-9af12e363c3.

23. Rahim Buford, interview with author, February 13, 2018.

24. Steven Hale, "Buried under Workload, Public Defender's Office Pushes Back," *Nashville Scene*, February 2, 2017, https://www.nashvillescene.com/news /cover-story/article/20850716/facing-an-unmanageable-workload-the-public -defenders-office-is-now-limiting-the-cases-it-takes.

25. Hale, "Buried under Workload, Public Defender's Office Pushes Back."

26. Raj Jayadev, "Gideon's Army Deserves Back Up," *Silicon Valley De-Bug*, September 15, 2013, http://archives.siliconvalleydebug.org/articles/2013/09/15 /gideons-army-deserves-back.

27. David Waters, "Attorneys Ride Bus in Clients' Shoes," *Commercial Appeal*, May 1, 2017, https://www.commercialappeal.com/story/news/columnists/david -waters/2017/05/01/david-waters-attorneys-ride-bus-clients-shoes/100936874.

28. "Public Defenders Walk (Bus) in Clients' Shoes," Shelby County Public Defender, May 24, 2017, http://defendshelbyco.org/public-defenders-walk-bus-in -their-clients-shoes.

29. "Shelby County Public Defender on Dismantling the School-to-Prison Pipeline in Tennessee," Shelby County Public Defender, http://defendshelbyco.org /category/public-defenders-office, accessed January 5, 2018.

CHAPTER 7: CLOSING THE GAP

1. Simon G. Talbot and Wendy Dean, "Physicians Aren't 'Burning Out.' They're Suffering From Moral Injury," *STAT*, July 26, 2018, https://www.statnews .com/2018/07/26/physicians-not-burning-out-they-are-suffering-moral-injury.

2. Petula Dvorak, "Metro Snack Patrol Puts Girl in Cuffs," *Washington Post*, November 16, 2000, https://www.washingtonpost.com/archive/politics/2000/11/16 /metro-snack-patrol-puts-girl-in-cuffs/4115f324-1783-45d4-b71a-3f76ca83e4fb /?noredirect=on.

3. Khadijah Z. Ali-Coleman, "Mom Jailed for Enrolling Kids in School Tells Her Story in New Book, Film," *Ebony*, March 20, 2014, https://www.ebony.com /news-views/mom-jailed-for-enrolling-kids-in-school-tells-her-story-in-new-book -film-405.

4. Jessica Reaves, "Feel Confined by Your Seat Belt? How about Handcuffs?," *Time*, April 24, 2001, http://content.time.com/time/nation/article/0,8599,107548,00 .html.

5. Thaddeus Miller, "Merced Cyclist, Whose Arrest Was Caught on Video, Has Been Charged," *Merced Sun Star*, June 15, 2016, https://www.mercedsunstar .com/news/local/crime/article83835077.html.

6. Miller, "Merced Cyclist, Whose Arrest Was Caught on Video, Has Been Charged."

7. Arguing that "[f]or most of our history . . . the government officials who administer the justice system, along with the voters who elect them, have behaved as though criminal punishment were sometimes necessary but always dangerous, something to be done sparingly and avoided when there is a plausible excuse for doing so," but that over the past few decades we have reimagined "a healthy criminal justice system [as one that] should punish all the criminals it can." William J. Stuntz, *The Collapse of American Criminal Justice* (Cambridge MA: Harvard University Press, 2011), 55–56.

8. "The Overcriminalization Phenomenon," *American University Law Review* 54 (2005): 703n66.

9. "Kemba Smith," Sentencing Project, http://www.sentencingproject.org /detail/feature.cfm?feature_id=1, accessed February 19, 2012.

10. After spending six and half years in prison, Smith was granted clemency by President Clinton. "Kemba Smith," Sentencing Project. For other stories of offenders receiving unjustly harsh sentences under mandatory minimum sentencing law, see "Families Against Mandatory Minimums," https://famm.org.

11. Rummel v. Estelle, 445 U.S. 263 (1980).

12. "Texan Fights His Life Sentence for Nonviolent, $230 Offenses," *New York Times*, November 13, 1977, https://www.nytimes.com/1977/11/13/archives/texan -fights-his-life-sentence-for-nonviolent-230-offenses.html.

13. Michael Vitiello, "Reforming Three Strikes' Excesses," *Washington University Law Quarterly* 82 (2004): 1–2.

14. Vitiello, "Reforming Three Strikes' Excesses."

15. Ewing v. California, 538 U.S. 11 (2003).

16. Lockyer v. Andrade, 538 U.S. 63 (2003).

17. Ramon Antonio Vargas, "Fourth Marijuana Conviction Gets Slidell Man Life in Prison," *Times-Picayune*, May 6, 2011, http://www.nola.com/crime/index.ssf/2011/05/fourth_marijuana_conviction_ge.html.

18. Laura Sullivan, "Inmates Who Can't Make Bail Face Stark Options," *NPR News*, January 22, 2010, http://www.npr.org/templates/story/story.php?storyId=122725819.

19. Sullivan, "Inmates Who Can't Make Bail Face Stark Options."

20. Peter Wagner and Wendy Sawyer, *Mass Incarceration: The Whole Pie 2018* (Northampton, MA: Prison Policy Initiative, March 14, 2018), https://www.prisonpolicy.org/reports/pie2018.html.

21. Jeremy Travis, Bruce Western, and Steve Redburn, eds., *The Growth of Incarceration in the United States: Exploring Causes and Consequences* (Washington, DC: National Academies Press, 2014), 35.

22. United States v. Bayless, 913 F.Supp. 232 (S.D.N.Y. 1996).

23. "New York Federal Judge Reverses Decision in Controversial Drug Case; Clinton, Dole Had Threatened to Ask for Resignation, Impeachment," National Drug Strategy Network, April 1996, http://www.ndsn.org/april96/bayless.html.

24. David McCullough, *John Adams* (New York: Simon & Schuster, 2001), 68.

25. "Prosecutor or Politician?," *Economist*, January 13, 2010, https://www.economist.com/democracy-in-america/2010/01/13/prosecutor-or-politician; Heather Haddon, "Ex-Prosecutor Use Links to Forge a Path to Politics," *Wall Street Journal*, December 26, 2012, https://www.wsj.com/articles/SB10001424127887323300404578203881614820230; Jed Shugerman, "'The Rise of the Prosecutor Politicians': Database of Prosecutorial Experience for Justices, Circuit Judges, Governors, AGs, and Senators, 1880–2017," Shugerblog.com, July 7, 2017, https://shugerblog.com/2017/07/07/the-rise-of-the-prosecutor-politicians-database-of-prosecutorial-experience-for-justices-circuit-judges-governors-ags-and-senators-1880–2017; Wendy Sawyer and Alex Clark, "New Data: The Rise of the 'Prosecutor Politician,'" Prison Policy Initiative, July 13, 2017, https://www.prisonpolicy.org/blog/2017/07/13/prosecutors.

26. Tom Brokaw, "Sen. Kerry: Nation 'Is Polarized,'" NBCNews.com, November 1, 2004, http://www.nbcnews.com/id/6354942/ns/nbc_nightly_news_with_brian_williams/t/sen-kerry-nation-polarized/#.XWlNHihKg2w.

27. Ruth Marcus, "Blocking the Nomination of Debo Adegbile Is a 'Travesty' in the Senate," *Washington Post*, March 7, 2014, https://www.washingtonpost.com/opinions/ruth-marcus-blocking-the-nomination-of-debo-adegbile-is-a-travesty-in-the-senate/2014/03/07/ae718948-a632-11e3-8466-d34c451760b9_story.html?utm_term=.7fd53ff4f9b1.

28. All Political Ads, "Powerful GOP Attack Ad on Tim Kaine: America Deserves Better—GOP Web Ad," October 4, 2016, YouTube video, 1:24, https://www.youtube.com/watch?v=TIKz216YDPw.

29. Aaron Rupar, "Republicans Attack Tim Kaine for Defending the Constitution," *ThinkProgress*, October 4, 2016, https://thinkprogress.org/rnc-tim-kaine-defense-attorney-capital-cases-c3baf8752ac7.

30. Melinda Henneberger, "Conservatives are Making Hay Out of Hillary Clinton's Defense of an Accused Rapist," *Washington Post*, June 16, 2014, http://

www.washingtonpost.com/politics/conservatives-are-making-hay-out-of-hillary
-clintons-defense-of-an-accused-rapist/2014/06/16/7d087efa-f576-11e3-a606
-946fd632f9f1_story.html.

31. Amy Chozick, "Clinton Defends Her Handling of a Rape Case in 1975," *New York Times*, July 7, 2014, http://mobile.nytimes.com/2014/07/08/us/08clinton.html?partner=rss&emc=rss&_r=3&referrer.

32. Oliver Laughland, "The Human Toll of America's Public Defender Crisis," *Guardian*, September 7, 2016, https://www.theguardian.com/us-news/2016/sep/07/public-defender-us-criminal-justice-system; Teresa Wiltz, "Public Defenders Fight Back Against Budget Cuts, Growing Caseloads," Pew Charitable Trusts, November 21, 2017, https://www.pewtrusts.org/en/research-and-analysis/blogs/stateline/2017/11/21/public-defenders-fight-back-against-budget-cuts-growing-caseloads.

33. Paul Butler, *Let's Get Free: A Hip-Hop Theory of Justice* (New York: New Press, 2009), 101–16.

34. Butler, *Let's Get Free*, 105.

35. Butler, *Let's Get Free*, 104.

36. Butler, *Let's Get Free*, 116.

37. Jonathan A. Rapping, "Who's Guarding the Henhouse? How the American Prosecutor Came to Devour Those He Is Sworn to Protect," *Washburn Law Journal* 51 (2013): 513, 519–23.

38. Berger v. United States, 295 US 78, 88 (1935), making clear that "[the prosecutors'] interest . . . in a criminal prosecution is not that it shall win a case, but that justice shall be done." See, also, American Bar Association Rules of Professional Conduct 3.8, Comment 1, "A prosecutor has the responsibility of a minister of justice and not simply that of an advocate."

39. Adam M. Gershowitz and Laura R. Killinger, "The State (Never) Rests: How Excessive Prosecutorial Caseloads Harm Criminal Defendants," *Northwestern University Law Review* 105 (2011): 261, 287.

40. Bordenkircher v. Hayes, 434 U.S. 357 (1978).

41. Sullivan, "Inmates Who Can't Make Bail Face Stark Options."

42. Jed S. Rakoff, "Why Innocent People Plead Guilty," *New York Review of Books*, November 20, 2014, http://www.nybooks.com/articles/2014/11/20/why-innocent-people-plead-guilty/; Emily Yoffe, "Innocence Is Irrelevant," *Atlantic*, September 2017, https://www.theatlantic.com/magazine/archive/2017/09/innocence-is-irrelevant/534171.

43. Rakoff, "Why Innocent People Plead Guilty."

44. Yoffe, "Innocence Is Irrelevant."

45. "The Trial Penalty: The Sixth Amendment Right to Trial on the Verge of Extinction and How to Save It," National Association of Criminal Defense Lawyers, https://www.nacdl.org/getattachment/95b7f0f5-90df-4f9f-9115-520b3f58036a/the-trial-penalty-the-sixth-amendment-right-to-trial-on-the-verge-of-extinction-and-how-to-save-it-report-final.pdf, accessed September 10, 2019.

46. John Simerman, "Public Defender Layoffs Could Gum Up the Works at New Orleans Criminal Court," *Times-Picayune*, February 3, 2012, http://www.nola.com/crime/index.ssf/2012/02/public_defender_layoffs_could.html.

47. Laura Maggi, "N.O. Public Defenders Office Says It Will Refuse New Murder and Rape Cases Due to Council Budget Cuts," *Times-Picayune*, December 3, 2009, http://www.nola.com/crime/index.ssf/2009/12/orleans_parish_public_defender.html.

48. "Public Defenders Back Off of New Cases," WDSU News, March 5, 2010, http://www.wdsu.com/news/22757902/detail.html. According to the report, due to budget shortfalls, public defenders in Orleans Parish were handling an average of three hundred felonies per year, twice the national and state standard. Available in Rapping, "Who's Guarding the Henhouse?," 553n224.

49. Brendan McCarthy, "New Orleans Public Defenders Office Warns of Lay-offs," *Time-Picayune*, January 19, 2012, http://www.nola.com/crime/index.ssf/2012/01/new_orleans_public_defenders_o.html.

50. Simerman, "Public Defender Layoffs Could Gum Up the Works at New Orleans Criminal Court."

51. Simerman, "Public Defender Layoffs Could Gum Up the Works at New Orleans Criminal Court."

52. John Simerman, "Judge Taps New Orleans Noteworthies to Handle Criminal Cases," *Times-Picayune*, February 15, 2012, http://www.nola.com/crime/index.ssf/2012/02/judge_taps_new_orleans_notewor.html.

53. Simerman, "Judge Taps New Orleans Noteworthies to Handle Criminal Cases." For example, in Judge Arthur Hunter's courtroom, which is the focus of the story, nine of the thirty-two defendants left lawyerless are detained.

54. "Dade Defender Rejects Some Cases Due to Workload," *Miami Herald*, June 25, 2008, MiamiHerald.com.

55. David Ovalle, "Miami-Dade Public Defender Caseload Dispute in Court's Hands," *Miami Herald*, March 31, 2009, in Jonathan Rapping, "National Crisis, National Neglect: Realizing Justice through Transformative Change," *University of Pennsylvania Journal of Law and Social Change* 13 (2009–10): 344n98.

56. "Dade Defender Rejects Some Cases Due to Workload," *Miami Herald*, June 25, 2008.

57. Bennett H. Brummer, "The Banality of Excessive Defense Workload: Managing the Systemic Obstruction of Justice," *St. Thomas Law Review* 22 (2009): 104, 151.

58. Amicus brief submitted to the Florida Supreme Court by the Florida Prosecuting Attorneys Association, on file with author.

59. Letter from State Attorney, 11th Judicial Circuit of Florida, to American Bar Association dated July 22, 2010, on file with author.

60. Maria Altman, "Public Defenders Can Now Refuse Cases—But Seek Long-Term Solution," St. Louis Public Radio, September 26, 2012, http://news.stlpublicradio.org/post/public-defenders-can-now-refuse-cases-seek-long-term-solution#stream/0.

61. "Statement of MAPA President Bob McCulloch in Response to Supreme Court of Missouri Opinion in Public Defender Case," Missouri Association of Prosecuting Attorneys, August 3, 2012, http://sixthamendment.org/wp-content/uploads/2012/08/MAPA-Response-to-Public-Defender-Caseload-Decision.pdf.

62. "National Advisory Commission on Criminal Justice Standards and Goals, The Defense (Black Letter)," National Legal Aid and Defender Association, http://www.nlada.org/defender-standards/national-advisory-commission/black-letter.

63. Maggie Shepard, "Public Defenders Plead for Relief, Claim Continuing Caseload Crisis," *Albuquerque Journal*, January 19, 2018, https://www.abqjournal.com/1121713/public-defenders-plead-for-relief-claim-continuing-caseload-crisis.html.

64. Maggie Shepard, "Key DAs Oppose Public Defender Proposal," *Albuquerque Journal*, May 21, 2018, https://www.abqjournal.com/1175019/public-defender-proposal-draws-opposition-from-key-das.html.

65. Andy Cunningham, "Orleans Public Defender's Office Fundraising Campaign Garners National Attention," *WDSU News*, September 16, 2015, http://www.wdsu.com/article/orleans-public-defender-s-office-fundraising-campaign-garners-national-attention/3379871.

66. Tim Young, "The Dark Side?," National Association for Public Defense, September 10, 2014, https://www.publicdefenders.us/blog_home.asp?display=406.

67. Andrew A. Mickle, "Is the Process Choking the PD System?," *Daily Report* (Atlanta), April 11, 2008.

68. Dan Winn, "Sharing the Load," *Daily Report*, February 16, 2010.

69. Casey Tolan, "Inside the New Orleans Public Defenders Office, Where Attorneys Are So Overworked They're Turning Down New Clients," *Splinter*, April 6, 2016, https://splinternews.com/inside-the-new-orleans-public-defenders-office-where-a-1793856019.

70. Tolan, "Inside the New Orleans Public Defenders Office."

71. Phaedra Haywood, "Judge Finds Cash-Strapped Chief Public Defender in Contempt," *Santa Fe New Mexican*, November 29, 2016, http://www.santafenewmexican.com/news/local_news/judge-finds-cash-strapped-chief-public-defender-in-contempt/article_1384bdd6-397d-5e90-9962-9bc1399b12d1.html.

72. State v. Jones, 2008-Ohio-6994 (Ohio Ct. App. 2008), available at http://www.sconet.state.oh.us/rod/docs/pdf/11/2008/2008-ohio-6994.pdf.

73. The court of appeals reversed the contempt conviction, noting that the judge "improperly placed an administrative objective of controlling the court's docket above its supervisory imperative of facilitating effective, prepared representation and a fair trial." *State v. Jones* at 10.

74. Andrew Cohen, "How Much Does a Public Defender Need to Know about a Client?," *Atlantic*, October 23, 2013, https://www.theatlantic.com/national/archive/2013/10/how-much-does-a-public-defender-need-to-know-about-a-client/280761.

75. State v. Miller, Supreme Court of New Jersey (2013), available at https://caselaw.findlaw.com/nj-supreme-court/1645886.html#footnote_3.

76. Brian Rogers, "Defense Attorneys Protest Houston Judge's Procedures," *Houston Chronicle*, June 27, 2014, http://www.houstonchronicle.com/news/houston-texas/houston/article/Defense-attorneys-protest-Houston-judge-s-5584669.php#/0.

77. Jason Sosa, interview with author, August 5, 2014.

78. Alisa Smith et al., "Rush to Judgement: How South Carolina's Summary Courts Fail to Protect Constitutional Rights," National Association of Criminal Defense Lawyers, 2017, https://www.nacdl.org/getattachment/ab9d6b03-2b45-4235-890e-235461a9bb2d/rush-to-judgment-how-south-carolina-s-summary-courts-fail-to-protect-constitutional-rights.pdf; see, also, David Carroll, *Why Our Misdemeanor Courts Are Filled with Counselled Defendants*, Sixth Amendment Center (May 12, 2015), http://sixthamendment.org/why-our-misdemeanor-courts-are-filled-with-uncounselled-defendants, a report on why so many people remain uncounseled in misdemeanor courts.

79. Sean Lavin, "Lawyer: Taxpayer Money Wasted on Undeserving Defendants," *ClickOrlando*, November 12, 2014, https://www.clickorlando.com/news/lawyer-taxpayer-money-wasted-on-undeserving-defendants_20151107085154379.

80. Jimmie E. Gates, "Judge Weill Orders Public Defender Jailed for Contempt," *Clarion-Ledger*, April 14, 2016, https://www.clarionledger.com/story/news/2016/04/14/hinds-county-circuit-judge-jeff-weill-and-public-defenders-office-odds-once-again/83042736.

81. "Incarceration of Assistant Public Defender," press release, Hinds County, MS, Public Defender's Office, April 14, 2015, on file with author.

82. Email to the author, April 14, 2016.

83. Shelley C. Chapman, "I'm a Judge and I Think Criminal Court Is Horrifying," Marshall Project, August 11, 2016, https://www.themarshallproject.org/2016/08/11/i-m-a-judge-and-i-think-criminal-court-is-horrifying.

84. Chapman, "I'm a Judge and I Think Criminal Court Is Horrifying."

85. Andrew Wolfson, "Judge's Remarks Show She Often Assumes Guilt," *Courier Journal*, September 5, 2014, http://www.courier-journal.com/story/news/local/2014/09/05/judge-admits-making-inappropriate-comments/15121213.

86. Wolfson, "Judge's Remarks Show She Often Assumes Guilt."

CHAPTER 8: UNTIL THE LION LEARNS TO WRITE

1. Illinois v. Wardlow, 528 U.S. 119 (2000).

2. Jonathan A. Rapping, "Implicitly Unjust: How Defenders Can Affect Systemic Racist Assumptions," *New York University Journal of Legislation and Public Policy* 16 (2013): 99, 1011.

3. When crack cocaine laws were enacted in the 1980s, the penalty for an offense involving possession of crack carried a sentence a hundred times as great as the sentence for possession of the same quantity of powder cocaine. The law was revised in 2010 to reduce the disparity from 100 to 1, to 18 to 1. Despite this reform, the penalty for possession of crack, a crime for which blacks are disproportionately more likely to be arrested, remains significantly more severe than for powder cocaine. See Lucia Graves, "Crack-Powder Sentencing Disparities: Whites Get Probation, Blacks Get Decade Behind Bars," *Huffington Post*, August 3, 2010, https://www.huffingtonpost.com/2010/08/02/crack-powder-sentencing-d_n_667317.html; https://www.prisonpolicy.org/scans/sp/1003.pdf; "Crack Cocaine Sentencing Policy: Unjustified and Unreasonable," Sentencing Project, https://www.prisonpolicy.org/scans/sp/1003.pdf; Danielle Kurtzleben, "Data Shows Racial Disparity in Crack Sentencing," *U.S. News and World Report*, August 3, 2010, https://www.usnews.com/news/articles/2010/08/03/data-show-racial-disparity-in-crack-sentencing.

4. See Michelle Alexander, *The New Jim Crow: Mass Incarceration in the Age of Colorblindness* (New York: New Press, 2010), for a discussion of how our criminal justice system perpetuates a caste system in America.

5. Inimai M. Chettiar, Michael Waldman, Nicole Fortier, and Abigail Finkelman, *Solutions: American Leaders Speak Out on Criminal Justice* (New York: Brennan Center for Justice, New York University, 2015), https://www.brennancenter.org/publication/solutions-american-leaders-speak-out-criminal-justice.

6. The words "public defender" were mentioned once. In his piece on community policing, Joe Biden wrote, "I served these communities as a public defender and for 36 years as Delaware senator." It was a throwaway line that had nothing to do with reform. See Michael Waldman et al., *Solutions: American Leaders Speak Out on Criminal Justice* (New York: Brennan Center, New York University Law, April 27, 2015), https://www.brennancenter.org/our-work/policy-solutions/solutions-american-leaders-speak-out-criminal-justice, 4.

7. Maurice Chammah, "Obama Defends Black Lives Matter in Conversation on Criminal Justice," Marshall Project, October 22, 2015, https://www.themarshall project.org/2015/10/22/watch-president-obama-and-the-marshall-project-in-a -conversation-today-about-criminal-justice#.OFRLzBDKt.

8. Barack Obama, "The President's Role in Advancing Criminal Justice Reform," *Harvard Law Review* 130 (2017): 881.

9. See "Criminal Justice Reform," Office of Hillary Rodham Clinton, https://www.hillaryclinton.com/issues/criminal-justice-reform, accessed February 25, 2017; "Racial Justice," Bernie Sanders, https://berniesanders.com/issues/racial-justice, accessed February 25, 2017.

10. Christopher T. Lowenkamp et al., *Investigating the Impact of Pretrial Detention on Sentencing Outcomes* (Houston: Arnold Foundation, 2013), https://www.arnoldfoundation.org/wp-content/uploads/2014/02/LJAF_Report_state-sentencing _FNL.pdf.

11. Lynh Bui, "Reforms Intended to End Excessive Cash Bail in Md. Are Keeping More in Jail Longer, Report Says," *Washington Post*, July 2, 2018, https://www.washingtonpost.com/local/public-safety/reforms-intended-to-end-excessive -cash-bail-in-md-are-keeping-more-in-jail-longer-report-says/2018/07/02/bb97 b306-731d-11e8-b4b7-308400242c2e_story.html?utm_term=.dcd87a07e2ea.

12. Erwin Chemerinsky, "This Is Not the Way to Reform California's Bail System," *Sacramento Bee*, August 22, 2018, https://www.sacbee.com/opinion/op-ed /article217018990.html; Raj Jayadev, "The Future of Pretrial Justice Is Not Money Bail or System Supervision—It's Freedom and Community," *Silicon Valley De-Bug*, April 4, 2019, https://www.siliconvalleydebug.org/stories/the-future-of-pretrial -justice-is-not-money-bail-or-system-supervision-it-s-freedom-and-community.

13. Amy Davidson Sorkin, "Darren Wilson's Demon," *New Yorker*, November 26, 2014, https://www.newyorker.com/news/amy-davidson/demon-ferguson-darren -wilson-fear-black-man.

14. Adam Foss, "A Prosecutor's Vision for a Better Justice System," TED, 2016, https://www.ted.com/talks/adam_foss_a_prosecutor_s_vision_for_a_better_justice _system#t-747926.

15. Chris Baynes, "Baltimore Police Officers 'Carried BB Guns to Plant on Unarmed Suspects They Shot,' Court Hears," *Independent*, February 1, 2018, https://www.independent.co.uk/news/world/americas/baltimore-police-carried -bb-guns-plant-unarmed-suspects-shooting-victims-corruption-maurice-ward -a8189731.html.

16. Daniel Denvir, "Debacle in Baltimore: Prosecutors, Part of the Problem, Struggle with Solution," *Salon*, July 24, 2016, https://www.salon.com/2016/07/24 /debacle_in_baltimore_prosecutors_part_of_the_problem_struggle_with_solutions.

17. Josie Duffy Rice, "Cyrus Vance and the Myth of the Progressive Prosecutor," *New York Times*, October 16, 2017, https://www.nytimes.com/2017/10/16 /opinion/cy-vance-progressive-prosecutor.html.

18. Zoe Azulay, "Court Watchers Hold 'Progressive' DAs Accountable," WNYC News, July 24, 2018, https://www.wnyc.org/story/court-watchers-hold -progressive-das-accountable.

19. Azulay, "Court Watchers Hold 'Progressive' DAs Accountable."

20. Catherine Elton, "The Law According to Rachael Rollins," *Boston Magazine*, August, 6, 2019, https://www.bostonmagazine.com/news/2019/08/06/rachael -rollins; see, also, Walter Wuthmann, "Rachael Rollins, 100 Days In: What Has

Changed, and What Hasn't, under the Reformer DA," *WBUR News*, August 12, 2019, https://www.wbur.org/news/2019/04/12/rachael-rollins-first-100-days.

21. Wuthmann, "Rachael Rollins, 100 Days In."

22. Carimah Townes, "Is Mark Gonzalez the Reformer He Promised to Be?," *Appeal*, November 21, 2017, https://theappeal.org/is-mark-gonzalez-the-reformer-he-promised-to-be-462f199a6oc.

23. Samantha Melamed, "Philly Judges Block DA Krasner's Deals for Juvenile Lifers," *Philadelphia Inquirer*, April 6, 2018, http://www.philly.com/philly/news/crime/krasner-juvenile-lifer-judge-rejecting-deals-20180406.html.

24. Akela Lacy and Ryan Grim, "Pennsylvania Lawmakers Move to Strip Reformist Prosecutor Larry Krasner of Authority," *Intercept*, July 8, 2019, https://theintercept.com/2019/07/08/da-larry-krasner-pennsylvania-attorney-general.

25. Karen Houppert, "44 Hours in a Baltimore Jail for Filming the Police," *Nation*, May 6, 2015, http://www.thenation.com/article/206481/44-hours-baltimore-jail-filming-police.

26. Joanna Rothkopf, "Baltimore Public Defenders Speak Out against Brutal Holding Cell Conditions: 'Using Bread as Pillows,'" *Salon*, April 30, 2015, http://www.salon.com/2015/04/30/baltimore_public_defender_speaks_out_against_brutal_holding_cell_conditions_using_bread_as_pillows.

27. Nirmal Joshi, "Doctor, Shut Up and Listen," *New York Times*, January 4, 2015, https://www.nytimes.com/2015/01/05/opinion/doctor-shut-up-and-listen.html.

28. See "Why Empathy?," Empathetics, http://empathetics.com/why-empathy; see, also, Sandra G. Boodman, "How to Teach Doctors Empathy," *Atlantic*, March 15, 2015, https://www.theatlantic.com/health/archive/2015/03/how-to-teach-doctors-empathy/387784.

29. Miriam Knoll, "Oncotalk: Helping Physicians Practice the Art of Medicine," *ASCO Connection*, September 3, 2015, https://connection.asco.org/blogs/oncotalk-helping-physicians-practice-art-medicine.

30. Mohammadreza Hojat et al., "The Jeerson Scale of Empathy: A Nationwide Study of Measurement Properties, Underlying Components, Latent Variable Structure, and National Norms in Medical Students," *Advances in Health Sciences Education* 23 (6A) (2018), DOI: 10.1007/s10459-018-9839-9.

31. Karen M. Glaser et al., "Relationships Between Scores on the Jefferson Scale of Physician Empathy, Patient Perceptions of Physician Empathy, and Humanistic Approaches to Patient Care: A Validity Study," *Medical Science Monitor* 13, no. 7 (2007), https://www.medscimonit.com/download/index/idArt/487348.

INDEX

ABOUT THE AUTHOR

JONATHAN RAPPING IS A NATIONALLY RENOWNED criminal justice innovator who is the founder and president of Gideon's Promise, a nonprofit organization whose mission is to transform the criminal justice system by building a movement of public defenders who provide equal justice for marginalized communities. Gideon's Promise provides training, leadership development and mentorship to improve the quality of legal representation for the clients and communities they serve. In addition to Rapping's leadership of Gideon's Promise, he is a professor of law and the director of the Criminal Justice Certificate Program at Atlanta's John Marshall Law School and a visiting professor of law at Harvard University Law School.

Rapping is a recipient of the prestigious MacArthur Foundation "Genius" Grant, the Harvard Law School Wasserstein Public Interest Fellowship, the Cardozo Law School Inspire Award, and the George Soros Open Society Fellowship, along with many other honors and recognitions. He has written extensively on issues related to criminal justice reform and has been published in numerous scholarly and professional journals.

He is a frequent contributor to the national conversation on criminal justice reform and has been featured by numerous media outlets that include the *New York Times*, *Washington Post*, *Huffington Post*, *Atlanta Journal-Constitution*, *Mother Jones*, *Essence*, and NPR stations across the country. Rapping and his work with public defenders was the inspiration for the award-winning HBO documentary *Gideon's Army*. He lives in Atlanta with his wife and partner at Gideon's Promise, Ilham Askia, and their two children.